FREEDOM AND GROWTH
AND OTHER ESSAYS

E. G. A. Holmes

FREEDOM
&
GROWTH
AND OTHER
ESSAYS

BY

EDMOND HOLMES

Essay Index Reprint Series

 BOOKS FOR LIBRARIES PRESS
FREEPORT, NEW YORK

First Published 1923
Reprinted 1968

LIBRARY OF CONGRESS CATALOG CARD NUMBER:

68-57320

MANUFACTURED BY
HALLMARK LITHOGRAPHERS, INC.
IN THE U.S.A.

INTRODUCTION

FOR nearly thirty-six years I inspected Elementary Schools for " My Lords " and their successors at Whitehall. I retired from official life in 1910, just as I was beginning to take a more or less intelligent interest in some of the larger and deeper problems of education. All the essays in this volume have been written since I retired. I have arranged them in the order in which they appeared. As it happens, half of them deal with education and half with " things in general." But my views on education are now closely interwoven with my views on " things in general "; and the book has therefore a certain unity of conviction and purpose which makes the chronological arrangement of the essays preferable to their division into two groups.

In the essay which gives its title to the book—the seventh in the series—I have dealt with a problem which belongs, under one of its aspects, to that criticism of " things in general " which we call philosophy, and, under another, to the theory and practice of education. The question, Is man a free agent?—if answered, with whatever reservations, in the affirmative, at once gives rise to another: Is man free, in any respect and in any measure, to direct the process of his own mental and spiritual growth? If he is, if the idea of growth, with its fatalistic associations—for what is growth but movement towards a mainly predetermined form?—admits of being harmonised with the idea of freedom, the problem of giving the growing child freedom for self-development becomes one of paramount interest to the teacher. And perhaps it is in the sphere of practical education that the most elusive of all metaphysical riddles will find its

v

appropriate solution. It is impossible to think logically about freedom, for one cannot begin to think about it without introducing an incalculable element into the very heart of one's calculations. But the experimental treatment of the problem may deliver one from this *impasse*. One who has seen how the mind and heart of the average child can expand and blossom in response to the stimulus of freedom knows that on the higher levels of man's nature freedom, far from being incompatible with growth, is the only thing that makes growth possible. And he who knows this knows more than this. He knows that the freedom of the human spirit is the very counterpart of its infinitude, and that therefore it is not so much a possession as a possibility—an ideal to be realised, a prize to be won.

My best thanks are due to the Editor of the *Nineteenth Century and After* for permission to publish the third, fourth, sixth, eighth, thirteenth, and sixteenth of the essays; to the Hibbert Trust and the Editor of the *Hibbert Journal* for permission to publish the fifth, seventh, eleventh, and fifteenth; and to the Editor of *The Quest* for permission to publish the second, tenth, and twelfth.

Some of the essays have been incorporated, with sundry additions, omissions and other changes, in books which I have published. My excuse for republishing these in their original form is that there are many persons who find it easier to follow an argument through the pages of an essay than through the chapters of a book.

EDMOND HOLMES.

CONTENTS

FREEDOM AND GROWTH AND OTHER ESSAYS

SOCIALISM AND EDUCATION

A PAPER READ IN FEBRUARY 1912 AT A MEETING OF THE
CAMBRIDGE UNIVERSITY FABIAN SOCIETY

LAST autumn your Secretary did me the honour of asking me to read a paper to your Society. In a moment of rashness I accepted the invitation. And in a moment of still greater rashness I suggested as the subject of my paper, " Socialism and Education." When I had time to reflect on what I had done, I began to realise that though I knew a little—a very little—about Education, I knew nothing or next to nothing about Socialism, and that until I had taken steps to remedy this defect in my mental training my paper would perforce remain unwritten. Early in December I got into correspondence with the Secretary to the Fabian Society in London,— the parent Society, as I suppose I may call it; and I told him that I wanted to know what Socialism really was and really aimed at. In reply, he sent me some Fabian tracts to study, and told me that " Socialism was a complex and elusive entity like Christianity, Liberalism or Democracy."

" Like Christianity "—these words set me thinking. What would happen to a Hindoo of an inquiring mind who set to work to study Christianity with the firm resolve to ascertain what it really taught? By the time

I

that he had read the Gospels and Epistles, and sat at the feet (1) of a Jesuit Father, (2) of a Roman Catholic Modernist, (3) of a Neo-Anglican Divine, (4) of a Methodist Preacher, (5) of a Unitarian Pastor, (6) of a Rationalist critic of Christianity, of the Joseph McCabe type, and (7) of two or three *Hibbert Journal* controversialists,—his mind would, I believe, be in a state bordering on chaos, and he would probably agree with the Secretary to the Fabian Society that Christianity was a " complex and elusive entity," with a special emphasis on the word *elusive.*

My fate, as an inquirer into the esoteric mysteries of Socialism, has been somewhat similar to that of the hypothetical Hindoo. Socialism, as expounded by William Morris in *News from Nowhere*, promises us a new heaven and a new earth, or rather a new heaven— a somewhat tiresome heaven, as it seems to me,—on a new earth. Socialism, as expounded by the writer of the Red Peril articles in the *Standard*, promises us a veritable hell. For William Morris and those who think with him, peace and goodwill among men, with all tears wiped away, are of the essence of Socialism. According to the writer in the *Standard*, secularism, atheism, materialism and other terrible " isms " are of the essence of Socialism. Indeed, that writer, who is perhaps a trifle too hysterical, seems to regard " socialistic " and " anti-Christian " as interchangeable terms. A Socialistic bagman tells me that the periodical re-distribution of property is of the essence of Socialism. But other Socialists tell me that the entire abolition of private property is of its essence. And it is difficult to reconcile these two statements; for one cannot well distribute or re-distribute what has ceased to exist. Mr. Stewart Headlam says that the socialisation of land values by confiscatory taxation is the very Alpha and Omega of

Socialism; and he lectures the Fabians for having to some extent lost sight of this fundamental truth. But Mr. Stewart Headlam is an avowed follower of Henry George; and I am therefore disconcerted to find that Mr. Hyndman, another ardent Socialist, has a very poor opinion of George's knowledge of political economy, and that the great Marx tossed *Progress and Poverty* aside with open contempt. Mr. Robert Blatchford dreams of a Socialist Utopia in which all factories will be closed and the inhabitants of these islands will live off the produce of their own land, which will yield fruit in abundance in response to their intensive culture of it. But Mr. Blatchford's prophetic dream seems to be all his own; for *Merrie England* does not appear to belong to the Canonical Scriptures of any Socialistic Church.

Are there any such Scriptures? I have read some eight or ten Fabian tracts, with real interest and no small measure of sympathy. But how far am I to regard those tracts as an authoritative exposition of Socialistic doctrine? In Christendom each church and sect claims to be *the* one correct exponent of the truths of Christianity. Is there anything like this in Socialism? Or is there any Socialistic body which claims to be the one *Ecclesia docens* and regards all other bodies as heretical or schismatic? One hears that the Socialists have captured the Trades Unions. Is this true? And if it is, in what sense and to what extent is it true? Does it mean that there is a central Socialist organisation which has captured the whole Trades Union machinery? Or does it merely mean that Socialistic ideas are in the ascendant in the councils of the Trades Union leaders? Is there such a thing as a central Socialist organisation? And if so, where are its headquarters? These are points on which I seek enlightenment.

Meanwhile, having read many Fabian tracts and sundry

other Socialistic works, I have ventured to form certain conclusions of my own about Socialism. I see, to begin with, that it is a movement rather than a system— a vast, spontaneous, largely subconscious, many-sided movement—a broad-bosomed stream of tendency which many lesser rills of experience, and feeling, and thought, coming from various quarters, have helped to form and are still helping to swell. I see that, however closely and deeply we may study the Socialistic movement, we are not yet in a position to map out its course and forecast its goal,—or, in the language of mathematics, to determine the equation to its curve. I see in it, first and foremost, an instinctive protest against the chaos, the wastefulness, the ugliness, the injustice, and the cruelty of the existing social system, and an instinctive desire to give labour a larger share than it has hitherto enjoyed of the wealth which it has helped to produce and the power which goes with wealth, and to make the struggle for existence less of a scramble and less of a gamble than it has hitherto been. I see, in a general way, that Socialism is diametrically opposed to social individualism, that it proposes to limit the rights and powers and privileges of individuals in the interest of Society as a whole, and that it wishes to redress the wrongs which the unequal distribution of possessions and of the opportunities for acquiring possessions has inflicted on Society, in all its grades, and is tending to inflict on it in ever-increasing measure. And I see that it proposes to achieve these ends by substituting co-operation for selfish competition, corporate for individual action, and strong centralised administration for *laissez faire*. Descending further into the concrete, I am disposed to accept as a fair statement of the aims of modern Socialism the following paragraph from Mr. Sydney Webb's interesting tract on *The*

Difficulties of Individualism: " Modern Socialism is not a faith in an artificial Utopia, but a rapidly-spreading conviction, as yet only partly conscious of itself, that social health and consequently human happiness is something apart from and above the separate interests of individuals, requiring to be consciously pursued as an end in itself; that the lesson of evolution in social development is the substitution of consciously regulated co-ordination among the units of each organism for their internecine competition; that the production and distribution of wealth, like any other public function, cannot safely be entrusted to the unfettered freedom of individuals, but needs to be organised and controlled for the benefit of the whole community; that this can be imperfectly done by means of legislative restriction and taxation, but is eventually more advantageously accomplished through the collective enterprise of the appropriate unit in each case." And as a corollary to the last of these propositions I accept as authoritative Mr. Edward Pease's statement that " the chief purpose of all Socialists is to transfer the capital (including the land) of each nation from the hands of private owners to the community organised as the State."

My Socialistic friend, Mr. Sydney Ball, in his tract on *The Moral Aspect of Socialism*, distinguishes between the " Socialism of the chair " and the " Socialism of the street "; and it is possible that the kind of Socialism which I am disposed to regard as the real article belongs to the " chair " rather than to the " street." In the Socialistic, as in every other great, movement, there is no doubt a right wing, a centre, and a left wing; and I can well believe that on its left wing Socialism tends to shade off into Anarchism, to which it is in reality directly opposed, and that the extremists of the left wing are capable of anything, capable even of justifying some of the hysterical statements of the writer of the Red Peril articles in the *Standard*. I can well believe, to change my metaphor, that as the advance-guard of the " Socialism of the chair " has its poets and prophets, its idealists and dreamers, so the advance-guard of the " Socialism of the street " has its rioters and ' peaceful " picketers in this country, and its " saboteurs " and bomb-throwers abroad.

But behind the teachings of the various schools of Socialism, behind the aims and efforts of its various sections and factions, behind the theories of its armchair economists, behind the speculations of its armchair idealists, behind the very excesses and outrages of its left-wing extremists, I seem to feel the subtle, all-pervading influence of one beautiful and inspiring ideal,— the ideal of broad-based unity, of organised comradeship, of " Each for All, and All for Each." If devotion to that ideal is of the essence of Socialism, then I for one am a whole-hearted Socialist.

But the difficulties in the way of realising this ideal, the difficulties in the way of carrying out the programme of even the most temperate and reasonable section of the Socialist body, are enormous. The first and greatest difficulty is the obvious fact that individualism—individualism of character and temperament—is in full possession of almost the entire field of social life. For this there are many reasons. The externalism of the West (by which I mean its whole-hearted and unhesitating acceptance of an outward standard of values, and its consequent tendency to regard material possessions and comforts as " the good things of life "); the tradition of centuries; the existing organisation of society; the influence of religion and literature, both of which have accepted the existing organisation of society as of quasi-divine institution; the materialistic trend of scientific thought; the materialistic outlook of popular thought; the rapidity with which the resources of physical nature have been developed in recent years, and the consequent rapidity with which wealth has been acquired,—have all combined to minister to the self-seeking, self-aggrandising instincts of ordinary, undeveloped, unemancipated human nature. But the chief cause of the rampant individualism of the present day is, in my opinion, our misdirected education. During the years when human nature is most pliable, an individualistic bent is given to it from which it never recovers. For our schools of all grades are hotbeds of individualism and training-grounds in vanity and competitive selfishness. This is a point on which I shall have more to say.

The resistance which the individualistic or egoistic instincts of ordinary men offer to Socialism takes many forms. In the first place, to nearly all men, including thousands and even millions who call themselves Socialists, the prospect of having their freedom abridged, their lives closely supervised, and their action subjected to what they regard as vexatious interference, is most distasteful. I once heard a man who was half drunk formulate his ideal of life in a sentence which, after the manner of those who are " concerned in liquor," he repeated again and again: " What I wants is to be let alone." *In vino veritas.* This is what most people want, especially in this country of ours, where every man's home, however humble, is his castle, and where bureaucratic despotism and inquisitorial officiousness have always been strongly resented. It is this instinctive feeling which has been responsible for much of the opposition to Mr. Lloyd George's National Insurance Bill, and in particular for the violent and quite genuine opposition to the proposals for the insurance of domestic servants, proposals which have arrayed against them a serried phalanx of mistresses and an almost equally serried phalanx of maids.

In the next place, the " Haves," the propertied classes, with some honourable exceptions, will bitterly oppose measures for the transference of land and capital from private ownership to the ownership of the State. Both the Haves and the Have-nots are well content that the functions of both National and Local Government should be extended almost indefinitely in the direction of ministering to their creature comforts, *e.g.* by providing them with water, light, facilities for travelling, facilities for inter-communication by post, telegraph and telephone, and so on. They are well content that the whole telephone system of the country should be taken over by the State, though that is a distinctly Socialistic measure, because they think that it will give them increased facilities for " 'phoning," and eventually cheaper rates. But the moment the State threatens to lay its hands on their property, whether directly, as by high income taxes, super-taxes, or heavy succession duties, or indirectly, as by increasing the burden on the liquor trade, the propertied classes begin to make a noisy outcry; and when the State proposed, in recent years, to take to itself part of the unearned increment on land, the outcry raised was so violent that it shook the British Constitution to its very base, if it did not (as some people think) shatter it beyond the possibility of repair.

In order to overcome the opposition which the Haves are prepared to offer to its programme, Socialism finds itself compelled to make an alliance with the Have-nots, by promising them higher wages, shorter hours of work, healthier conditions of life, and other things which they naturally desire, but which it is easier to promise than to give. The alliance between the Socialists and the

Labour Party is natural and probably unavoidable; but it is, I think, unfortunate from the Socialists' own point of view. For, in the first place, Socialism, which is concerned with the welfare of society as a whole, ought not to identify itself closely with any one party. In the second place, in allying itself with the Labour Party, and offering, as a first instalment, to better the social state of the working-classes within the limits which an individualistic society prescribes, Socialism runs the risk of abandoning its own true programme, and descending from the level of its own ideal. And in the third place, the Labour Party, who, as individuals, are nearly all individualistic at heart, will gladly accept from Socialism whatever it can get for them in the way of higher wages, shorter hours of work, increased comforts, etc., but it will not accept their authentic programme. For the Have-nots cling to such possessions as they have as fondly as the Haves cling to their wealth; and they are not in the least willing that the State should nationalise the cottages that they own, the capital that they have saved, or (as in Ireland) the farms that they are gradually acquiring.

If you have any doubt as to the real attitude of the working-classes towards the Socialist programme, look at Australia. There the Labour Party controls the Government; but it has no real sympathy with Socialism. It has, I believe, come near to realising its exalted ideal of eight hours' work, eight hours' play, eight hours' sleep and eight shillings a day; but with this, or perhaps with some further development along these lines, it would fain rest content. Its outlook on life is in its essence anti-social. Its selfishness is colossal. Being accidentally in possession of a whole continent, which, in its desire to keep up its standard of quasi-bourgeois comfort, it will not take the trouble to people, it yet wishes to exclude from its immense undeveloped territories all the rest of mankind. Until quite recently it sought to exclude white labour. It still excludes all coloured labour. Had it not suddenly realised that it needed men to guard its undefended ramparts, its policy of excluding white labour would not have been reversed.

Or take the case of Ireland. I am an Irishman, and last year I paid two visits to my native land. I found that a marvellous change had come over the country. A wide and strong wave of prosperity was sweeping over even the poorest and most remote parts of it. And why? Chiefly because the magic of private property was at work, and had been at work for some years. The small farmers, who constitute the bulk of the population, had become or were in process of becoming the owners of their own farms.

The truth is that the masses, as we call them, are not Socialistic at heart. They will accept the help of Socialism so long as they find it convenient to do so. For example, they will allow Socialism to organise their forces for them in their battle against Capital. But when they have got what they want, they will show Socialism the door. At any rate they will try to do so. It is possible that they will not succeed. It is said that Socialism has captured the Trades Unions. If this is so, an interesting duel has begun, the end of which no one can foresee. Will the Labour Party use Socialism to achieve its ends? Or will Socialism use the Labour Party to achieve its ends? Whatever may happen elsewhere, I am by no means sure that in this country the final victory will not rest with Socialism. The Horse in the fable overcame his enemy the Stag, with the help of the Man; but when the fight was over the Man remained seated on the Horse's back.

One result of the diffusion of Socialistic ideas through a Society which has a false standard of values, and is therefore saturated with all that is poisonous in individualism,—with its spirit of acquisitiveness, of self-indulgence, of self-aggrandisement, of selfish competition —one result of this premature diffusion of Socialistic ideas, is that we are being brought to the verge of civil war. Compelled to rely on the doubtful help of Labour in order to bear down the fierce resistance of Capital, Socialism must needs add fuel to a fire which is already alight. The Battle of Armageddon between Capital and Labour may not actually have begun, but both sides are arraying their forces for the conflict; and already there have been many partial engagements on a considerable scale, not to speak of innumerable outpost skirmishes. In view of the statement that Socialism has recently captured the whole Trades Union organisation, it is a significant fact that last year the strikes in this country were more numerous, more violent, and on a larger scale than they had ever been before. It is true that both parties are showing a remarkable capacity for combination and organisation; and this may be regarded by Socialism as a hopeful sign. But at present they are combining and organising their respective forces for purely selfish purposes. The threatened war is a war between classes, to be waged for class interests only. The employers want to maintain and, if possible, increase their profits. The workers want higher wages and shorter hours of work. Other interests than these are at stake, but all other interests are subordinate to these.

But let us suppose that the Battle of Armageddon is over, and its smoke cleared away. And let us suppose that somehow or other neither Capital nor Labour but Socialism has been left in possession of the field. Let us suppose that Society, organised as the State, has nationalised and socialised all the land of the country, and acquired full control of its capital, or of so much of it as is concerned with the means of production. And let us further suppose that the existing false standard of values is still in the ascendant, and that the individual members of the community are still individualistic at heart, still eager to surpass one another in various outward ways, still dazzled by the glamour of wealth, still anxious to possess as much as possible of what are vulgarly regarded as the "good things of life." What then?

In the first place it is clear that the State will have become an immense trading society. On this point there can be but little doubt. In taking over and socialising the land and the capital of all private owners and public companies, the State will become, *ipso facto*, a trading society on a colossal scale. Even the thoughtful, temperate, and cautious Rodbertus looked forward to this as the economic goal of Socialistic reform. But in acquiring control of all the means of production, the State will enter into competition with the capitalists of all other countries. For in this country, which surpasses all others in the extent and variety of its manufactures, the productive output of capital is not limited by the needs and demands of the inhabitants of the land. The internal consumption of what is produced is probably less than the external. In many trades it is considerably less. Lancashire makes cotton, and Yorkshire woollen goods, not for the inhabitants of these islands only, but for people in all parts of the civilised and uncivilised worlds. Vickers and Armstrong build ships of war for foreign Powers as well as for our own Navy. The Tyne, the Wear, the Clyde and Belfast build trading and passenger ships for many countries besides their own. And so on, and so on. More than any other country in the world, we are dependent on our export trade for the bare means of subsistence. What would happen to our export trade during the period of transition, I cannot say. If it got through that period without serious loss, the State would have to take it up and push it with vigour. And if it suffered severely during the civil strife, the State would have to devote much of its energy and administrative ability to building it up again. For one thing at least is clear. The State could not possibly discriminate between the capital which produces for the Home markets and the capital which produces for Foreign markets. In nationalising the one it would find itself compelled to nationalise the other. Then, again, more than half the carrying trade of the world is at present in the hands of English capitalists. And this too would have to be taken over by the State, which could not, if it would, discriminate between the shipping interests which carry goods to and from the shores of these islands, and those which carry the commerce of other countries.

The State, then, would become, *inter alia*, a manufacturing and carrying company on an inconceivably vast scale. And the force of public opinion would always be at work, urging it with irresistible pressure to develop its manufacturing industries and to push its trade, by every possible means and in every possible direction. For the more it produced and exported, the greater would be its imports, and the higher—so men would argue— would be the standard of comfort in every household in the land. Its attempt to push its trade would take many forms. Competition with other exporting countries in neutral markets would be one. The opening-up of new markets would be another. The exploitation of undeveloped countries would be a third. The State would send its financial agents, its commercial travellers, its mining experts, its concession-hunters all over the world. And wherever it sent them, they would meet the financial agents, the commercial travellers, the mining experts, the concession-hunters of Germany, of France, of the United States, of Belgium, of Japan, and the rest.

They would meet them in friendly rivalry, let us hope. But would this rivalry always remain friendly? I doubt it. Whether the other countries of the world had by this time been socialistically organised or not, would matter little. If they had been so organised they would be ready to take up any weapons, in order to meet the competition of this country and of one another. If they had not, their rulers would not be the less amenable to the ever-growing pressure of commercial interests. Even as it is, commercial interests carry so much weight in the councils of the various nations, that their sinister influence must be held responsible, largely, if not wholly, for all the wars that have been waged or nearly waged in recent years. The war between the United States and Spain in Cuba is habitually spoken of as the *Sugar* war. The war in South Africa will, I suppose, be known to posterity as the *Gold* war. The war between Japan and Russia was, in a sense, predestined ; but its exciting cause was undoubtedly the rapacity of certain Russian Grand Dukes who had been given valuable timber concessions in Korea. And not many months have passed since the desire of Germany to take a hand in the exploitation of Morocco brought us to the very edge of a Titanic war.

When Dr. Obnubile, in Anatole France's *Penguin Island*, paid a visit to the industrial republic of New Atlantis, he felt sure that he had at last come to a land where the people were too much occupied with trade and industry to think of making war. But a visit to the Parliament House of Gigantopolis, the capital of the Republic, soon undeceived him. For accounts for recent wars were being passed by the Assembly with much *sangfroid*, and as a mere matter of business. " Have I heard aright? " asked Doctor Obnubile. " What! you an industrial people, and engaged in all these wars! " " Certainly," answered the interpreter, " these are industrial wars.   Peoples who have neither commerce nor industry are not obliged to make war, but a business people is forced to adopt a policy of conquest.   The number of wars necessarily increases with our productive activity.   As soon as one of our industries fails to find a market for its products a war is necessary to open new outlets.   It is in this way we have had a coal war, a copper war, and a cotton war.   In Third Zealand we have killed two-thirds of the inhabitants in order to compel the remainder to buy our umbrellas and braces."   There is something, as it seems to me, of prophetic insight, as well as of legitimate satire, in this bitter gibe.

If even under existing conditions financial interests are so powerful as to be responsible, largely if not wholly, for most of our wars and rumours of war, what may we not look forward to in the way of alarums and excursions when the State, with its full control of the naval, military and financial resources of the country, has become a vast trading company, having no rivalry to dread but that of other countries, and being ready to meet that rivalry, in response to the demand of its own rapacious shareholders, with all the energy, resourcefulness and unscrupulousness with which in the days of individualism one business firm met the competition of others!   For when the State had been organised on a Socialistic basis, it would be as easy as it now is difficult to persuade the rank and file of the nation that a proposed war would be to their own material advantage.   Only the Sugar interests stood to benefit by the Cuban.   Only the Gold and Diamond interests stood to benefit by the South African war.   But the rulers of the Socialistic State which had got to loggerheads with one of its neighbours over some trade dispute, would find no difficulty in persuading the people that the proposed war would be to the advantage, not of this or that gang or clique or faction, but of every member of the community. Indeed, it might well have happened that the pressure to wage the war had come in the first instance from the rank and file of the nation. For there is no reason to suppose that what I may call national egoism would be weakened by the triumph of social democracy. Jingoism is a malady which affects the " Masses " not less, or perhaps even more, than the " Classes." It was the mob of Paris which shouted " à Berlin " in 1870; and it was the mob of London whose rowdy rejoicings in 1900 over a military success enriched the English language with the verb " to maffick."

There is an old and faithful saying that one should not prophesy till one knows. But it is impossible to think about the past and the present without taking an occasional dip into the future; and when I dip into the future, under the inspiration of Socialistic literature, I see, to my dismay, as a lurid possibility, a long sequence of fierce commercial wars,—a sequence which will not end until stern experience, using another Norman Angell as its mouthpiece, shall have convinced the nations that war is a bad investment, and that there are better and cheaper ways of settling their commercial rivalries than that of drawing the sword. Then the war clouds will roll away, the sky will clear, and perhaps we shall have a league of peace.

But it will be a league of white nations only. If there was any one motive which could induce the white nations to leave off wrangling over tariffs and fighting about markets, it would be the fear of the industrial competition of the brown and yellow races. You have all read the *Great Illusion*, and you have no doubt found it, as I did, a most interesting and stimulating book. Up to a certain point it is, I think, a convincing book. But there are three grave omissions in it. It says nothing, as far as I can remember, as to the wisdom or unwisdom of fighting for the possession of undeveloped territories, such as Korea and Manchuria. It says nothing as to the impending war between Labour and Capital. And it says nothing as to the war between the White and the Yellow races—a war which may be said to have already begun. By seeking to exclude the Yellow races from all the vast undeveloped territories of Australia and North America, and so to shut up the overflowing populations of China and Japan within their own national limits, the White races have to all intents and purposes declared war against the Yellow; and to that declaration of war the Far East, with its tenacious memory and its inexhaustible patience, will, in the fullness of time, give an appropriate reply. For why do the White races seek to exclude the Yellow from the undeveloped territories which they—the White races—have been able—more by good luck than good management—to peg out and pre-empt? Not because of the vices of the Yellow races, but because of their virtues; because the Yellow workers are hardier, thriftier, more industrious and more easily contented than the White; and because, therefore, their competition imperils or seems to imperil the high scale of wages, combined with short hours of work, which an artificial scarcity of labour—only possible in countries which are still in the making—has enabled the white workers in Australia and the West of North America to command.

When the White nations have succeeded in establishing the league of peace to which I look forward, the first step to be taken by them in their Amphictyonic Council will be to fence themselves round against the industrial competition of China and Japan (not to speak of India, from which by that time we shall probably have recalled our legions). This they will do by shutting out the products of Yellow industries with prohibitive tariffs, and by excluding Yellow workers from all the lands under their control. To this policy of exclusion the

Yellow races will reply, if they have not already begun to do so, with the sword; and so will be begun the most colossal of all wars,—a war waged in the interests and at the bidding of the rank and file of the White people, with the object of enabling them to maintain a standard of comfort which they had come to regard as their natural right. I will not attempt to forecast the issue of this struggle. History tells us that, other things being approximately equal, the poorer and hardier peoples have usually vanquished the richer and more luxurious. How far other things would be equal at the beginning of the struggle, I cannot pretend to guess. So far as my prophecies are concerned, the curtain that guards the future from Man's prying imagination may now come down. And it is well that it should do so. For I have seen more than enough for my peace of mind. Looking down the vista that Socialism seems to open to me, I have seen first a bitter and destructive war between Labour and Capital; then a series of bloody wars between those great trading communities which will take the place of the nations as we now know them; then a colossal war between the White and the Yellow races, the former fighting for the right to be comfortable, the latter for the right to exist and expand.

Let us now consider the internal economy of the Socialistic State. I have hitherto assumed that the standard of values in the Western World is to remain at its present sordidly low level. I have assumed that the citizens of our ideal state will long continue to be the selfish, self-seeking, materialistic individualists which most of them are (through no fault of their own) at the present day. In dealing with the internal economy of the State, I will make the same assumption. My reason for making it is that until you would-be reformers of Society begin to do what you have never yet done—to take education seriously—the standard of values will remain where it is.

But will not increased comfort raise the moral and spiritual level of the masses? Not necessarily, I think. It does not seem to have done so in the case of the world's millionaires, who have comforts, not to say luxuries, enough and to spare, but who are, with few exceptions, materialists to the inmost core. It would no doubt raise the masses above that level of barbarity and savagery to which they seem to have sunk, if one may judge from what happened in the late Liverpool riots, in the slums of our great towns. But I am by no means sure that, as regards their general outlook on life, the poor savages of the slums are on a lower level than the comparatively prosperous artisans of the manufacturing towns, the comparatively well-paid miners on our coalfields, or the comparatively well-to-do workers of Australia, whose ideal of life is—to make a general statement—to have plenty to eat and drink, plenty of cheap amusement, and — above all — plenty of leisure for attending the modern equivalents of the ancient gladiatorial games. I am told that the carpenters of New Zealand recently struck for a Saturday whole holiday. If they got that, they would probably strike for a Monday half-holiday. And so on. Wherever a false standard of values prevails, the attempt to satisfy the demands of the "working-classes" may well become as futile, when the working-classes are masters of the political situation, as the attempt to fill up a bottomless pit.

The question for us Englishmen to consider is this: When Socialism has won the day, will the working-classes of this country be able to organise themselves so effectively as to secure that control of the Government to which their mere numbers would entitle them? Mr. Hyndman, in his recently-published *Record of an*

Adventurous Life, tells us that M. Clemenceau once re-marked to him: " La classe ouvrière en Angleterre est une classe bourgeoise," and " so far," adds Mr. Hyndman, " I am compelled to admit, with the deepest regret, that this caustic appreciation of my toiling countrymen is in the main correct." Were the working-classes, with their bourgeois ideals, to capture the machinery of the State, it would be an evil day for Socialism. In the first place the economic solvency of the State would be gravely imperilled, for its ability to compete as a trading com-munity with other countries would be seriously handi-capped by the ceaseless and ever-growing demands for higher wages and shorter hours of work. In the second place—and this is even more to the point—the moment the State began to legislate or to administer in the interest of a class or a stratum instead of in the interest of Society as a whole, it would cease to be Socialistic. You will tell me that in the Socialistic State there will be no classes and no strata. To this I answer that so long as bourgeois ideals are in the ascendant there will be both. This means perhaps that so long as " la classe ouvrière en Angleterre " remains " une classe bourgeoise," the triumph of Socialism will be indefinitely delayed. If it does not mean this, it means that Socialism will have missed its destiny in the very hour of its triumph.

But however this may be, one thing is clear. If the vast and complicated machinery of the Socialistic State is to work properly, it must be oiled, in all its parts and bearings, by honest and disinterested service. The majority of the workers of the country will be Civil Servants. A corrupt Civil Service will speedily bring the State to ruin. At the present day our Civil Service, though by no means free from idleness and malingering, is singularly free from corruption. This is, I think, mainly due to the fact that the higher grades of it are recruited from social levels in which a high standard of honour—which is quite compatible, let me say in passing, with many moral defects—has long prevailed, and staffed by men whose education, whatever else it may have done or failed to do for them, has at least fostered the sense of honour which they brought with them from their homes. But the Civil Service of the future will be ten or twenty times as numerous as the Civil Service of to-day. And it will be mainly recruited from classes—whether lower or lower middle—where bourgeois ideals and standards prevail, and staffed by men whose education —if education remains unreformed—will have either failed to foster their sense of honour or been actively inimical to its growth. Indeed, in the first instance it will be recruited from the *personnel* of those commercial and industrial interests which owe their very existence to the stimulus of the desire for gain, and which have made municipal government a by-word for jobbery. It is not the sense of honour, then, that will keep the self-seeking instincts of the servant of the State in check. And the influence of Religion, which, at its best, has done but little to restrain men from breaking the Eighth and Tenth Commandments, is not likely to be stronger then than it is now.

But you will tell me that when the State has been socialised there will be few, if any, temptations to its servants to feather their own nests at the expense of the community. I think, on the contrary, that there will be more temptations than there are now. For one thing, party politics, which will be more contentious than they are to-day, because there will be larger prizes at stake, will be an unfailing source of jobbery and corruption. When I say this, I am arguing from the present to the future. One of the recent Prime Ministers of New Zealand is said " to have kept himself in power by teaching the

people in every part of the Colony to keep in with the
Government if they wished to be remembered in the
distribution of the ' loaves and fishes.' " Political patronage does not make for efficiency in the Government
services. The Inter-Colonial Railway in Canada, which
is State-owned and State-managed, is a hotbed of political
jobbery and also a by-word for inefficient administration.
One of its general superintendents, on being taken to
task for undue expenditure, asked what he or any other
man in his place could do when the politicians were
imposing incompetent subordinates on him, and even
championing them when they were convicted of stealing.
And another manager, of great ability and experience,
wrote, at the end of his term of service, that " it was
utterly impossible for any Government in Canada to
conduct the railway as it ought to be conducted, for no
matter how great the power the head of the road may
have he cannot escape the malign influences of party,
which permeate every branch and render his best efforts
of no avail." If scandals such as these are of common
occurrence in the State organised as it is now, how much
more frequent will they be in the State of the future in
which the number of loaves and fishes at the disposal of the
Government will be many times as large as it is to-day,
while party strife will be proportionately keener and bitterer!

Moreover, the desire to feather one's own nest will
probably be as strong then as it is now. Private property
will still be permitted. For I understand that the individual ownership of furniture, books, pictures, clothes
and the like, is not to be prohibited. Nor will the rapacious
citizen of the future limit his cupidity to the accumulation
of domestic goods and chattels. Salaries will, I believe,
be paid by the State; and the economically-minded
Civil Servant will be able to save a part of what he earns.
This he will invest either in the Government funds of

his own country, or in the securities—public or private
—of other countries. And in this, and in other ways, he
will gradually build up what will be regarded as a fortune.
For though Socialism may abolish millionaires, it will
not abolish human cupidity; and experience has proved
that the competition for wealth can be just as keen when
£10,000 is regarded as a fortune, as it is to-day when a
Rockefeller is the unhappy possessor of £50,000,000.
If, then, our standard of values remains unchanged, if
self-interest (as we now understand the word) continues
to dominate our lives, we may look forward to much
dishonesty and corruption in that immense Civil Service
on whose honesty and integrity the well-being and even
the safety of the whole community will depend. And each
dishonest Civil Servant, whether his dishonesty take the
form of peculation, of jobbery, of nepotism, of favour-
itism, of neglect of duty, or of malingering (the last-
named being even now of common occurrence in the
Postal and some other branches of the Public Service),
will be a grit in the machinery of the State,—machinery
which will be brought to a standstill when there is a
sufficient accumulation of grits.

If I am taking a gloomy view of the future, the reason
is that my primary postulate compels me to do so. It is
the ingrained individualism—the selfishness, the self-
seeking, the self-assertion, the malignant egoism—of
undeveloped or ill-developed human nature, which
stands in the way of Socialism as of every movement
towards a higher type of social unity. This tendency,
if not restrained—and Socialism does not provide for
its being restrained, except by external forces which it
will itself render ineffective—this tendency, acting on
every social level and in a hundred different ways, will
hinder the advance, and postpone to the Greek Kalends
the triumph, of Socialism. Or, if it allows it to achieve

its end, it will make it abortive in the very hour of its triumph. Or, if it allows it to consolidate its authority, it will make its triumph a calamity to the human race.

If, then, Socialism is to achieve a real and a lasting triumph, Man must change, or at any rate begin to change, his whole outlook on life. His competitive selfishness, which is profoundly anti-social, is the outcome of an entirely false standard of values, and an entirely false criterion of reality. This criterion and this standard must somehow or other be altered. How is this to be done?

You may preach unselfishness and communal devotion to the adult men and women of your generation as widely and as eloquently as you please; but only those who happen to be unselfish and to have a capacity for communal devotion will respond to your appeal. So far as the rest of your audience are concerned, your eloquence will be so much waste of breath. Their education— their training, whether at home or in school or elsewhere —will have given a bias to their natures which you will not be able to alter. A wave of emotion may carry them away for a while; but the bent of their natures will reassert itself, and their short-lived enthusiasm will probably be followed by a reaction. If you want to proselytise the men and women of England, appeal to them as children and appeal to them from their very earliest years. It is your only hope.

Nothing surprises me so much as the way in which you Socialists neglect education. You profess to be deeply interested in it, and you promise to do great things for it when your day comes round. But it is the machinery of education in which you are interested. With education itself—the real thing, the life, the soul, the inwardness of it—you do not concern yourselves in the slightest degree. Yet you Fabians have your education group; and the said group has recently produced a tract called *What an Education Committee can do.* The Secretary to the Fabian Society sent me a copy of this tract, which I have duly read; and all I can say about it is that it is worthy of its own blue colour, and would do credit to the great Office in Whitehall in which the whole machinery of the nation's education is elaborated and controlled.   It is quite right that there should be such an office, for educational machinery is a hateful necessity; but I do not see why the Fabian Society should issue Blue-books in competition with it.   Some of you seem to think that if the machinery of education is complete, and if it works smoothly, all must be well. Let me assure you that the machinery of education may be complete to its last detail, and may work with perfect smoothness, and yet all may be wrong, as wrong as wrong can be.

There is a passage in the *Laws* of Plato which bears so directly and so forcibly on what I regard as the most vital of all our problems, that it might almost have been written yesterday, though I do not know which of us could have written it, for its point of view is not ours. Its author is speaking of the appointment of the Chief Director of the education of boys and girls (the President of the Board of Education, as we should call him, or perhaps the Secretary to the Board); and he says: "Both the man appointed, and those who appoint him— [our Prime Ministers would do well to lay this to heart] —must realise that this office is far the most important among the chief offices of the State.   Because, whatever the creature—be it plant or animal, tame or wild—if its earliest growth makes a good start, that is the chief step towards the happy consummation of the excellences of which its nature is capable.   Now we should call Man a tame animal; and while, with correct training, and a happy disposition, he will turn into the most divine and the gentlest of creatures, if reared carelessly or ill, he will be the savagest creature upon earth."

What is education doing to the children of this country? This is the great question which we should be for ever asking ourselves. Is it turning them into divine and gentle creatures—unselfish, self-forgetful, considerate of others, filled with the spirit of comradeship, capable of devotion to the common cause—creatures whose motto is " Each for All," with, as an afterthought, " All for Each" ? Or is it turning them into potential savages—selfish, self-assertive, rapacious, fiercely competitive, eager to outdo one another, ready to trample one another down,—potential savages, whose motto is " Each for himself, and the devil take the hindmost "? It is in the school, if anywhere, that the communal instinct, without which Socialism is an impracticable dream, must be gradually evolved. The instinct is there in each of our children, waiting to be evolved. The question is: " Will education foster or retard its growth? " It is in the school, if anywhere, that our criterion of reality, our standard of values, must be transformed. Yet not transformed so much as discovered. For the true criterion and the true standard are there, in each of our children, waiting to reveal themselves. Will education help them to reveal themselves, or will it allow them to be overshadowed by the false criterion and the false standard which dominate our social life, and in the deadly shade of which they will assuredly wither and die?

My answer to this question is that education, as at present conducted, is hostile to the growth of the communal instinct, and hostile to the emergence of the true criterion of reality and the true standard of values. The reason of this is that education, in all its grades and types, is completely dominated by our Western externalism,—our tendency to assume, as a self-evident truth, that nothing is real except what can be seen and handled, weighed and measured; and to infer from this that outward and visible results are the only prizes worthy of a man's ambition, that material possessions, material pleasures, material comforts are the only " good things of life," and that we must therefore look outside ourselves for success and happiness. Under the influence of this assumption the child is taught from his earliest years to make the production of outward and visible results the central aim of his life. And as the ends which are thus set before him do not as a rule appeal to him, he is driven towards them by stimuli of various kinds. He is threatened with punishment. He is bribed with the promise of reward. Prizes are offered to him which, instead of being attached to a certain level of attainment, are thrown open to public competition. He is thus taught to regard his class-mates as rivals and competitors, and even as potential enemies. His natural impulse to help them in difficulties is repressed as criminal. He is urged to outstrip them and to pride himself on doing so. His selfishness is exploited. His vanity is deliberately appealed to. " Each for himself, and the devil take the hindmost " is the conception of social life under which he is compelled to live.

And this anti-social influence of Western education is reinforced from another quarter. The motives which are brought to bear upon the child imply complete distrust of his nature. It is taken for granted that the ends which are set before him will not be congenial to him, and that in striving to attain them he will be working against the grain of his true self. The course of education which is dominated by this assumption must needs tend to devitalise the child, to repress his spontaneous energies, to arrest the whole process of his growth. Now growth, just because it is growth, because it is the expansion of life from within, is the most emancipative of all influences. For, in proportion as it is healthy and harmonious, it tends of inner necessity to widen the child's outlook, to enlarge the sphere of his sympathies and activities, to take him away from his petty, narrow, superficial, self-satisfied self. The education that arrests growth, and in doing so imprisons the child in his lower self, does a twofold wrong to him as a social being, from the effect of which he never wholly recovers. In the first place, it de-socialises his life, by externalising his aims and so plunging him, indirectly as well as of set purpose, into a vortex of selfish competition. It is because we are shut up in our petty, ordinary selves, that we cannot find happiness in ourselves, and are therefore driven, in rivalry with others, to look for it—or for that fraudulent imitation of it which we call *success*—outside ourselves. In the second place, it de-socialises the child's life, by damming back his expansive sympathies and energies, and preventing them from overflowing — as growth, if vigorous and unimpeded, would make them do — into the lives of others. For these, and for other reasons which I must not turn aside to consider, the atmosphere of the ordinary school is one in which the communal instinct necessarily dwindles and individualism grows apace.

There is a remedy for these evils. Let the teacher cease to think about " results," and begin to think about what is inward and vital, about the growth of the child's nature. Let him abandon his dogmatic attitude towards the child, with the formal and mechanical methods which it necessitates; and let him be content to stand aside and efface himself, allowing the child's nature to unfold itself, and merely giving him some measure of guidance and stimulus, and such materials as he may happen to need. Above all, let him cease to appeal to motives which are unworthy of the child's better nature—the fear of external punishment, the hope of external reward, the desire to surpass others and exalt himself at their expense. But let him allow the education that he gives to make its own appeal to the child's higher instincts and impulses—quickening those instincts and impulses into healthy activity, and so making it better able to respond to the progressive appeal that it makes to them.

The results (in the true sense of the word) of this course of education will surprise the teacher. One result, which is indeed the Alpha and Omega of all results, will be the happy, vigorous and harmonious growth of the child's whole inner being; and the proof that the growth made is happy, vigorous and harmonious, and therefore emancipative, will be the outgrowth in the child of what I have called the communal instinct—the sense of comradeship, of brotherhood, of oneness with others, with the cognate capacity of devotion to a common cause. When this instinct has been fully developed, when the "divine" and "gentle creature" has finally triumphed over the "savage," the cause of Socialism will have been potentially won.

And the mental results of the education which fosters growth will be scarcely less striking, and scarcely less significant from the point of view of Socialism, than the moral and spiritual results. When I speak of the growth of the child's nature, I am thinking of his nature as a whole, I am thinking of it on all its levels,—physical, mental, moral, social, spiritual. The formal, mechanical, dogmatic type of teaching which at present holds the field, represses mental growth quite as effectually as it represses all other kinds of growth. Wherever it has been abandoned, and a freer, more sympathetic, more imaginative type of education been substituted for it, the development of mental ability, or, to use a more comprehensive phrase, of all-round capacity, which has taken place, has exceeded the limits of what an experienced educationist might have regarded as possible. A wave of M. Bergson's "*élan vital*" has swept through the school; and the intelligence of the children has grown, *pari passu*, with their resourcefulness and initiative. We shall never know what immense reserves of latent capacity the average child possesses until we cease to repress his spontaneous activities, and try, for a change, the bold yet simple experiment of giving him free space in which to live and grow.

Now the State of the future, the State of which Socialists dream, will need intelligence and initiative in its servants quite as much as it will need unselfishness and devotion. At present there is not enough ability in the land—developed ability, I mean, as distinguished from the raw material—for a socialised state to be effectively administered. There is not enough developed ability for the existing services—the Civil, the Naval, and the Military—to be conducted with real efficiency, neither intelligence nor initiative being available in sufficient quantity. And the demands of the socialised State, with its immense, elaborate, and intricate machinery of administration, will be far greater than the demands of the State of to-day. On all the higher levels the demand for mental ability, for sheer brain power, will be enormous. In taking over the different industries which flourish in the country the State will no doubt take into its service much specialised ability. But it will need something more than specialised ability if the correlation of the different industries, the regulation of their respective outputs, the determination of their relations to one another and to the general interests of the State, is to be carried out with due effect. Its very specialists will —many of them—have to be men " of large discourse," capable of " looking before and after," and indeed all round the horizon. And, after all, the successful working of its various industries will be only one aspect of the administrative and executive work of the State. The task of running its enormous machinery without let or hindrance, of finding for each citizen the work which he will do best, of providing for the promotion of those who best deserve to be promoted, of allotting to each worker the due reward of his labour, of diffusing comfort widely while discouraging extravagance and luxury, of shielding even the poorest from hunger and want, of educating the youth of the nation on such lines as I am now advocating, of giving the adult citizen opportunities for self-education and self-culture, of encouraging literature, science, music, and art,—the task of doing these things, and a score of other things which anyone who pleases can set down for himself, will be truly Herculean, and will make a demand for mental ability which, if it were made now, we could not even begin to meet.

And if the need for mental ability will be great, the need for the other aspect of capacity—for initiative, for enterprise, for self-reliance—will be greater still. A friend of mine, who is a close observer and an acute critic, objects to any extension of the sphere of State action on the ground that public servants are tending more and more to play for safety rather than for efficiency,—to shirk responsibility and to take no risks. His criticism is, I think, justified. In these days, when the searchlight of public opinion, as organised by a free and sensation-mongering Press, is brought to bear on the action of every public department, when politicians are ready to make political capital out of any mistake made by a Government official, when the Ministers of the Crown, in their terror of public opinion, are ready to throw to the wolves any official on whom they can fix, or even pretend to fix, the responsibility for a mistake which has become public property,—it is but natural that the servants of the State should deliberately play for safety, should refrain in their minutes and memoranda from honest and outspoken criticism, and should make it their business to find out which way the official wind is blowing and to trim their sails accordingly. And in playing this safe but ignoble game, they will be true to the traditions of their School life. For the education given in our schools of all kinds and grades, with its demands for mechanical obedience and spurious accuracy, and its readiness to brand as criminal even the mistakes which strew the path of every honest beginner, is ever tending to discourage spontaneity and self-reliance, and to foster inertness and timidity in its victims. And the boy whose spirit of initiative and enterprise is damped, when at school, by the haunting fear of making mistakes, will take no risks when he becomes a servant of the State; and his ultra-caution will necessarily make for inefficiency in the public service, for one of the laws which govern human progress is that where no risks are taken nothing effective can be done.

In our industrial and commercial enterprises, the privacy which still enshrouds their doings and happenings makes it possible for risks to be taken and ventures to be made. But when the industry and the trade of the country have been nationalised and have therefore begun to be regarded as counters in the game of rival political parties, the veil of secrecy by which they are now guarded from the prying eyes of the Press will gradually be withdrawn, and the spirit of timidity and ultra-caution which tends even now to paralyse the activities of the great public services will gradually invade the new departments of the State.

Should this invasion be as successful as we may reasonably expect it to be, the day will surely come when the star of our industrial and commercial greatness will have set, and the impoverishment of the whole community—to be followed in due course by its political downfall —will have begun.

From every point of view, then, the need for a reform in education—for such a reform as I have recently sketched—is seen to be imperative and urgent. That the type of education which I advocate can be given, and that when given it can and will do all that I claim for it, I know for certain; for I have seen it at work, and I have been able to study its processes and judge of its results. In a book called *What Is and What Might Be* I have told the story of a school in which the teacher, by turning her back upon " results " (in the conventional sense of the word) and thinking only of life and of growth, produced results (in the deeper sense of the word) which were so wonderful that my plain unvarnished account of them has been received by some of my critics as a romance. My critics are mistaken. I do not possess the imagination with which they credit me. I wish I did. I am not capable of writing a romance. I may have under-coloured my picture—a man of letters who visited the school reproached me for having done less than justice to it —but I certainly did not over-colour it. You may believe me, then, when I tell you that in the free and happy atmosphere of that school all the faculties of the children —their moral and spiritual as well as their mental faculties, their character as well as their capacity—made vigorous, healthy and harmonious growth; and that, with the gradual growth of their faculties, the little society to which they belonged was gradually transformed into an ideal social community,—each living for all, and all for each,—such a community as the State itself might become if the education given in that school became the rule instead of being, as now, the almost isolated exception.

I have sometimes heard people say that we must change human nature before the dream of the Socialist can come true, and that human nature cannot possibly be changed. Both these propositions are false. Human nature can be changed; and we must cease to change it if we wish the dream of the Socialist to come true. Human nature can be changed. It is we educationists who change it—and change it for the worse—by training it badly during the period when its training is decisive of its destiny. The hooligan, the loafer, the wastrel, the youthful criminal, the savages of our civilised society, are all, or nearly all, manufactured articles, the artificial products of a system of education which changes human nature beyond recognition, changes it in the wrong direction by either arresting or perverting its growth. If you wish Socialism to triumph do not try to change human nature; but try to change our educational policy, —to change it in the direction of giving human nature a chance, of allowing it to evolve itself and to show us what it really is. Is not this the end that you Socialists have in mind when you propound your various social remedies? Do you not wish to make the conditions of life as favourable as possible to the growth of the gregarious animal which we call man? Do you not wish to give him every opportunity for developing himself freely and happily on all the planes of his being? Are you not at war with the existing social order because it is unfavourable to human growth? Well, then, begin your reform of society in that world of social life in which all the expansive forces of nature will be working on your side,—in the world of child-life,—in the school.

What interests and attracts me in Socialism is its instinctive recoil from separatism and its unswerving trend towards unity. For the sake of this trend, which I regard as the mid-stream movement of Socialism,— for the sake of your far-off divine ideal,—I say again to you Socialists: Educate, Educate, Educate. Proselytise the adult if you will. You will, I fear, make but little impression on him unless you appeal to motives which are unworthy of him and of you. Teach " civics " and " economics," if you will, to the adolescent in the continuation schools into which you propose to drive him. You will find, I fear, that you are tilling an unproductive soil. But in any case, and above all, educate the child. Educate him, not by making him learn Socialistic catechisms,—" that way madness lies,"—but by helping him to grow, by helping his communal instinct (which, if only you and he knew it, is stronger than all his individualistic instincts put together) to affirm itself, to come to the birth. With the child on your side, you will be irresistible; and your battle will have been won almost before you have begun to fight it.

For it is conceivable, to say the least, that when the standard of values has been changed and the communal instinct has been fully evolved, social service will come to be regarded as the first of moral duties, and the highest of outward activities, and men will begin to carry out, voluntarily and spontaneously and without any radical re-organisation of society, all that is vital in the programme of Socialism. It is conceivable, in other words, that a new generation will arise which will make Socialism as an organised movement unnecessary, in the very act of realising its deepest dream.

That its deepest dream, that your deepest dream, will somehow, somewhere, some day be realised, I have no doubt. If you are fighting, disinterestedly and wholeheartedly, under the banner of unity, the stars in their courses are on your side, and sooner or later victory will come to you as surely as to-morrow will dawn out of to-night. But though I say this with unwavering assurance, I must end, as I began, in an agnostic mood. The stars in their courses are fighting for Socialism; but until it finally triumphs we shall not know what it really is.

PROFESSOR EUCKEN AND THE PHILOSOPHY OF SELF-REALISATION

A FRIEND of mine recently announced his intention of giving a course of lectures on the " History of Civilisation," and he sent me his programme. I found to my surprise (though perhaps I ought not to have been surprised) that he meant by " Civilisation " the civilisation of the Western world, and of it only. The great and ancient and still living civilisations of Eastern Asia —not to speak of other parts of the world—he entirely ignored. I am reminded of this course of lectures by Professor Eucken's work on *Main Currents of Modern Thought*. The title of the book is slightly misleading. " Main Currents of *Western* Thought " would give a more accurate indication of its scope and purpose. For in the first place it is a survey of the movements of thought from the time of Plato and Aristotle down to the present day. And in the second place the thought with which it deals is almost exclusively Western. That, outside the limits of what is now called Christendom, man is and always has been incapable of thinking (in the deeper sense of the word) seems to be taken for granted. In the four hundred and seventy-eight pages of the book there are exactly four allusions—all very brief—to the philosophy of India; and in each of these the critical attitude adopted involves a radical misunderstanding of the Indian point of view.

What makes this uncompromising Occidentalism the more surprising is that Professor Eucken himself has formulated an idealistic scheme of life which has much in common with the teaching of the Upanishads, and only

36

falls below the level of that teaching because its author has not always the full courage of his convictions. Professor Eucken is, I believe, regarded as one of our greatest thinkers; and he is certainly—within the limits which he has imposed on himself—one of our greatest interpreters of the history of speculative thought. One feels that his scheme of life is not the work of a mere systemmonger, but has been distilled, so to speak, from a sympathetic and impartial study of the main movements of thought in many ages and many lands. All the more significant is the fact that his researches and reflections have led him—a whole-hearted Occidentalist—to conclusions which India had elaborated into philosophy and transfigured into poetry and religion, in an age so remote that it probably preceded the dawn of thought in Ancient Greece.

"How can man," asks Professor Eucken, "who at first appears to be an infinitesimal point, participate in a self-contained world, in a world as a whole, such as the spiritual life now represents?" "It is certain," he replies, "that he can only do so *if the spiritual life has existed within his being as a possibility, from the commencement,*[1] if it is in some way directly connected with him. It would not do for spiritual life to be communicated to him through the medium of his special nature (thus becoming alienated from itself); *it must in some fashion be presented to him as a whole in all its infinity; it must hence, working from within, open up to him (if at first only as a possibility) a cosmic life and a cosmic being, thus enlarging his nature.*[1] In the absence of such an indwelling spirituality humanity can have no hope of making any progress. *If, in laying hold of spiritual life, he did not discover his own true self, the former could never be a power to him.*"[1]

[1] The italics are mine.

This is the philosophy of the Upanishads; and if Professor Eucken could remain at this level he would stand where the sages of India stood 2500 years ago. But the prejudices of popular thought in the West are too strong for him; and again and again he relapses into a crude dualism which makes his scheme of life unworkable, and involves him in many contradictions and in much confusion of thought. For, having told us, not once but many times, that the spiritual life is the real life of man, that it is the " core of reality " and the " core of man's own being," that it is " rooted in the essential nature of things," and so forth, he must needs oppose it, not once but many times, to nature in general and to human nature in particular.

That he regards the spiritual life as the real life of man, and also as the " soul of all life," is made clear by a hundred passages. Here are some of them. " Spiritual life " is " true self-life " and " cosmic life." It is " the unfolding of the depths which reality contains within itself." To participate in it is " to participate in a world-life." It " must from the very beginning have been operative in the whole, directing it towards itself." It " appertains to man's innermost being . . . and is at once natural and ideal." The ascent to it " is a specifically human achievement." It is man's " specific nature " and " true being " and " genuine self." It is " the core of man's own being." In realising it man " rises to a life of his own." It is " a spiritual necessity ruling within humanity." It is " rooted in the essential nature of things." It is " the development of our own soul." It is " the coming to itself of the world-process." It is " a cosmic force operative in man from the very outset." It " elevates man's essential being." It is " the dominating fundamental life - force," — " the dominating soul of all life."

Reading these and similar passages, one naturally concludes that the spiritual life is at the heart of nature, both cosmic and human. But no. The spiritual life is "a new stage of reality against that of nature." It is "a new stage of life" and not "a mere prolongation of nature." It is not "a continuation of nature." It is not "derived from mere nature." It is opposed to "mere humanity." It is "separated from and elevated above what is merely human." It is opposed to "the mere life of the soul." It is "superior to all merely human existence." It "reverses the current of man's life." It is "independent and sharply separated from human life." It is opposed to "the mere man," to "merely human life - conduct," to "merely human culture," to "human life," to "our human existence."

From these passages and from scores of others which have the same general purport, one gathers that the popular belief in the supernatural, with its implicit depreciation of nature, has so far influenced Professor Eucken as to make him oppose the spiritual life, first to the life of nature, and then to the life of man. But as he has already told us that the spiritual life is "cosmic life" and "true self-life," that it is "a cosmic force operative in man from the very outset," and so on, he is open to the charge of having contradicted himself on a matter of vital importance; and in order to forestall this obvious criticism, he prefixes to the words "man" and "human" (and sometimes, though more rarely, to the words "nature" and "natural") the most elusive and delusive of all adjectives and adverbs,—*mere* and *merely*. "Mere humanity," "the mere man," "merely human," "mere life of the soul," "mere existence," are phrases which constantly occur in his writings. Now and again he speaks of "mere nature" and the "merely natural"; but as a rule he is content to assume (in company with the average man) that the " natural " is opposed to the " spiritual " as what is lower to what is higher, what is phenomenal to what is real.

Let us consider the phrase " merely human." What does it mean? The word " mere " means, in the first instance, *undiluted, unmixed, pure;* and so it comes to mean *that and that only, that and nothing more.*[1] Thus " mere folly " means *undiluted folly, folly and nothing but folly.* " A mere boy " is *a boy and nothing more than a boy, a boy who could not possibly be mistaken for an adult man.* " A mere joke " is *a joke and nothing more, a joke with no admixture of seriousness or malice.* " Mere " and " merely," then, are words which limit, or seem to limit, but which do so by exclusion rather than by restriction. This distinction is all-important. In more than one passage Professor Eucken uses the phrase " pettily human," as if it were equivalent to " merely human." That the two adverbs are not really equivalent, that they have little or nothing in common, I need not take pains to prove. It is true that both words seem to limit and disparage; but it will, I think, be found, if the matter be carefully considered, that *pettily* limits without really disparaging, whereas *merely* disparages without really limiting. The " pettily human " is the lower, more trivial, less worthy side of human nature. The " merely human " is that which is human and nothing more. " Pettily," when prefixed to " human," limits the idea of humanity, by restricting it for the moment to a particular level or aspect of human life. But it does not disparage human nature. On the contrary, it suggests to us that there is such a thing as the " grandly human," and in any case it leaves the intrinsic range and value of human nature unimpaired. " Merely," on

[1] I take it that this is the meaning of the German word, probably *bloss,* which Dr. Meyrick Booth has translated as *mere* (or *merely*).

the other hand, when prefixed to "human," excludes from the idea of humanity whatever is extraneous and accidental; and therefore, instead of limiting the idea, it suggests that there are limits to it and that these must be carefully observed. Hence its tendency to disparage. When I talk of the "merely human" I disparage human nature by suggesting that it has certain recognised limits which it can never transcend, and by leaving it to be inferred that the intrinsic range and value of human nature do not, after all, amount to very much.

It is clear, then, that if the word *mere* (or *merely*) is to be fairly and honestly used, we must give the noun (or adjective) to which it is prefixed its full range and depth of meaning, and we must not only know that the corresponding thing (or idea) has limits, but also know in a general way what those limits are. Do we know what are the limits of the human? Are we quite sure that it has limits? Professor Eucken tells us that man's "true life" is a "cosmic life." Would there be any meaning in the phrase "merely cosmic?" The plain truth is that, instead of giving the word "human" its full range and depth of meaning before he prefixes to it the disparaging adverb "merely," Professor Eucken deliberately empties the idea of humanity of all that is vital and essential in it. For on the one hand he expressly opposes the "merely human" to that "spiritual life" which "appertains to man's innermost being," which is "man's specific nature," and "true being" and "genuine self"; and on the other hand he expressly identifies the "merely human" with the "pettily human," with the "average dead level," with what is "temporal and accidental," with what is "inadequate and base," with "immediate sense-existence," with "narrowness," "pettiness," and "unreality." In other words he expressly marks off what a plain unsophisticated man would call the lower side of human nature, and then opposes this to what a plain unsophisticated man would call the higher side, as the " merely human " to the " specifically human" or the " genuinely human," as " mere humanity " to " humanity," as " human life " or " the mere life of the soul " to the " true self-life " of man.

To abstract from human nature what, *on his own showing,* is of the very essence of human nature, and then to label the residue as " human " (with or without the addition of " merely ") and oppose it to the " genuinely human," is a strange proceeding on the part of a responsible thinker; and one may well doubt the soundness of the philosophical structure which needs to be buttressed by such a wanton misuse of language and such grotesque confusion of thought. Nor will the need for such extraneous support surprise us when we remember that the misuse of language and confusion of thought in which Professor Eucken has involved himself are the direct outcome of his deliberate attempt to find a dualistic basis for an intrinsically pantheistic [1] philosophy.

What is the explanation of Dr. Eucken's leaning towards dualism? Why does he revel in " contrasts," " oppositions," " reversals," " sharp separations," and the like? The explanation is, I think (as I have already suggested), that, unconsciously or subconsciously, he is under the influence of one of the cardinal assumptions —or shall I say *the* cardinal assumption?—of popular thought. Behind human nature is nature as such; and the philosophy which recognised the essential unity and all-inclusiveness of human nature, would find itself compelled to predicate the same attributes of nature as such. But if nature as such were one and all-inclusive, what would become of that fundamental opposition of

[1] I am using the word *pantheistic* in its Indian, not its Western sense.

nature to the supernatural on which the whole system of popular thought is hinged? If this cardinal assumption is to be respected, provision must somehow or other be made for the division of the macrocosm into two dissevered worlds.[1] And if this division is to hold good, the microcosm (in which the macrocosm, as seen by us, reflects and bears witness to itself) must be similarly riven asunder.

The real reason, then, why Professor Eucken disparages " human nature " and opposes it to the true being of man, is that he may be free to disparage " nature " and oppose it to some higher order of things. And this he does with wearisome iteration. It is at the expense of nature, even more than of human nature, that the spiritual life is exalted. Nature is opposed to the " soul," opposed to the " spiritual life," opposed to the " spiritual world," opposed to man's " life of his own." " The life which develops in man " is " not a continuation of nature." " Man " and " humanity " " should rise above mere nature." " The development of spiritual life " has " raised man far above nature." Personality is developed by a " reversal of natural being." And so on.

What does Professor Eucken mean by *nature*? He tells us that " the natural world, with its thorough-going causal connexion " . . . " keeps man bound down to the mere ego "; that " the natural world " is " blindly indifferent " " to the aims of spiritual life "; that nature " threatens to oppress and overwhelm humanity "; that " naturalism " ignores " the right of the subject " and

---

[1] Now and again a philosophy arises in the West which suppresses one of the two worlds, and then labels itself as Monism, and boasts its superiority to Dualism. But the division into the two worlds must be made before either world can be suppressed; and this secret dualism is at the heart of almost *every* Western system of thought. A monism, whether materialistic or idealistic, is nothing but a dualism with one of its antithetical concepts reduced to zero.

" the life of the spirit." He identifies " nature " with
" the pettily human," and the " world of nature " with
" the sphere of visible existence." He speaks of " nature
as seen from the mechanical point of view," of " mere
natural self-preservation," of being " enslaved to nature."
In other words, when he uses the word " nature " in
a depreciatory sense, he is evidently thinking of the
" nature " of the " naturalist "; of physical nature, as it is
sometimes called; of the material plane of existence,
and the animal side of human life.

But he does not always use " nature " in a depreciatory sense. The intrinsic force of the word is too
strong for him. He speaks of " man's spiritual nature,"
and opposes this to " mere humanity." He says that
" nature and the inner world meet within a single reality ";
that " the spiritual life has a nature of its own "; that
it has its own " inner nature "; that it is at once " natural
and ideal "; that " spiritual culture " is " rooted in the
essential nature of things "; that " spiritual work separates what is genuine in nature from what is not "; that
nature " has behind it a deeper reality " (and so generates
spiritual life); that the " unity and inwardness of life "
are " the most valuable element in man's nature "; that
" man's specific nature " is " his own true being," " his
genuine selfhood "; that " nature (in an inward sense)
remains secret and aloof " and " withdraws its fundamental verities further and further from our gaze the
more science penetrates into its territory."

How are we to account for these extraordinary contradictions and inconsistencies? To oppose " spiritual
nature " to " nature " is as fatuous as to oppose the
" specifically human " to the " purely human," or
" humanity " to " human nature." One cannot get
on terms with the thinker who uses language so loosely
as this. Professor Eucken has well said that " words are

not to be treated lightly. Their misuse may contribute to the obscuration of genuine problems." And it is certain that his own misuse of the words " human " and " nature " has effectually obscured the " genuine problems " which he has undertaken to solve. Like many another thinker he seems to have forgotten that such a word as *nature* or *human* has an intrinsic meaning of its own (determined by centuries of usage), the range of which cannot be arbitrarily curtailed. He tries to limit the range of " nature " to the lower levels of existence; but the concept refuses to be kept down to those levels, and its inherent buoyancy is such that he himself has no choice but to use the word when he is dealing with the highest level of all.

What then is nature? That it is not a mere stratum or plane of being, that on the contrary it belongs to every plane and every stratum, Professor Eucken himself has made abundantly clear. Everything that exists has a nature of its own. Every section of the world, every level of existence, every mode of being, every form of life has a nature of its own. As there is outward nature, so there is inward nature. As there is physical nature, so there is spiritual nature. As there is specific nature, so there is generic nature. As there is individual nature, so there is cosmic nature. The attempt to divide the Universe into Nature and the Supernatural is eternally stultified by the patent fact that even the Supernatural has a nature of its own. Taking the widest possible view of nature we may perhaps define it as *the way of the universe*, the central way which controls and determines, and is itself the resultant of a billion lesser ways. This is nature in its totality. And when we speak of the nature of this or that particular thing we mean again *the way of that thing*, the central, the typical tendencies of its being.

It is of course true that within the illimitable limits of nature such distinctions as those between high and low, great and petty, spiritual and material, essential and accidental, hold good. But these opposites are ever interpenetrating one another, and it is impossible to say where one ends and the other begins. The contrasts and oppositions in which dualism revels belong to another order of thought. The thinker who divides the Universe into Nature and the Supernatural, or into the material and the spiritual worlds, must needs draw a hard and fast line between his " mighty opposites "; and this line of demarcation speedily opens out into a " great gulf " like that which is " fixed " between Heaven and Hell. And the Nemesis of dualism in this, as in every other case, is that the gulf of separation drains into itself the reality of both the worlds which it separates,—drains away from " Nature " its inwardness, its spirituality, its beauty, its glory, its vitalising purpose, till at last it becomes a mere body of death; drains away from " the Supernatural " its actuality, its substance, its knowableness, its significance, its nearness to human life, till at last it becomes the mere shadow of a shade.

When shall we learn that the remedy for dualism is not monism; that the opposition of dualism is itself dualistic; that a monism is at heart a dualism,—a dualism which maintains the fundamental antithesis that it began by postulating, but which allows the impetus of its preference to carry it so far in one direction that it ends by denying content to the opposing and competing term? Thousands of years ago the higher thought of India freed itself from bondage to " the opposites "; and the time has surely come for the higher thought of the West to take the same decisive step. Under the influence of the idea of evolution—with or without the consent of our " thinkers "—all great gulfs are being gradually filled up, and all hard and fast lines are being gradually effaced. Has not the time come for us to recognise the essential unity of the Universe, to realise that the All of Being is one living whole? If we could do this, if we could abolish the archetypal dualism of Nature and the Supernatural, all other dualisms (and monisms) would spontaneously disappear.

Not (I repeat) that oppositions and contrasts would disappear with them. Unity affirms itself in and through diversity, and self-identity is made possible by self-contradiction. Wherever there is development there is the opposition of *potential* and *actual*; and this primary opposition postulates a multitude of others. Language abounds in antithetical terms, such as *good* and *bad*, *true* and *false*, *high* and *low*, *swift* and *slow*, *strong* and *weak*. And in each of these antitheses the inferior term is, as it were, the " promise and potency " of the higher. Evil has been defined as " good in the making "; and it might perhaps be more accurately defined as " undeveloped good." Error has often proved to have been truth in the making. The low is on the way to becoming high. The slow is on the way to becoming swift. The weak is on the way to becoming strong.[1] There is no gulf fixed between opposites in any of these antitheses. On the contrary, each of the antithetical ideas interpenetrates the other, and even follows it in its progress towards its own ideal pole. The second highest mountain in the world is lower than Mount Everest. *High* as it is, it is also *low*. And so with the other antitheses. And each term owes its meaning to its contrast with the other, so that if either term

[1] If I were looking towards the negative pole of the antithesis, I should, of course, have to invert each of these statements. My reason for looking towards the positive pole is that the process of human development, for which I am trying to find analogies, is in its essence a movement towards the positive pole of existence.

were cancelled the other would share its fate. Take away evil, and what do we know of good? Take away error, and what do we know of truth? From dualism to monism is one step. From monism to nihilism is the next. To think away either of two opposing worlds or tendencies is to make the other null and void.

It is to the exigencies of everyday speech that we owe the dualism of popular thought. But though there is much dualism at the surface of language there is none at its heart. When one goes deeper into the usage of words, one sees that a never-ending effort is being made to correct the fallacies which arise from our careless handling of a very imperfect instrument. We assume off-hand that antithetical terms stand for mutually exclusive entities; and we think and act accordingly. But when we give ourselves time to reflect on the corresponding ideas we find that the relation between them is one of identity even more than of opposition; the antithesis, however complete it may seem to be, falling always within the limits of an essential unity. In the fundamental antithesis of the *potential* and the *actual*, the primary relation between the two ideas is obviously one of identity; for the actual is present in embryo in the potential, and the potential is what it is because the actual—real, but as yet unrealised—is at the heart of it. It is not by "reversing" the process of development that we pass from the potential to the actual. It is not by reversing his steps that the climber passes from a lower to a higher altitude. It is not by reversing its engines that a slow-moving locomotive quickens its pace. It is not by reversing the process of his physical growth that the weak child becomes the strong man. In each of these cases, and in every similar case, the change from the lower to the higher term in the antithesis is made by going forward, not by going back.

Is it not the same in that supreme antithesis which plays so prominent a part in Professor Eucken's system of thought? He calls the lower term in the antithesis *nature* (or *human nature*) and the higher term *the spiritual life*. He regards these as two separate worlds, and he holds that progress in the spiritual world is not to be achieved except by a " reversal " of the order of the natural world. If this were so, what hope would there be for humanity? Man, according to Professor Eucken, is the meeting-place of two worlds. If he is to live in the higher world he must reverse the whole course of the lower. Can he do this? Is it to be done? Will the mighty forces of nature suffer themselves to be reversed? If man is to wait for a reversal of the course of nature before he can begin to live in the spiritual world, will he not have to wait for ever; will not the spiritual life remain an unrealisable dream?

All analogy and all experience are against Professor Eucken. In every other antithesis the relation of opposition between the antithetical ideas is subordinate to and dependent on the more fundamental relation of identity. Let us assume, as we are surely entitled to do, that it is the same in the supreme antithesis. Let us assume that the relation between " nature " and " spirit " or " supernature " is one of fundamental identity; that the natural world is potentially spiritual; that the spiritual world is the self-realisation of the natural; that our choice lies, not between alternative worlds, but between the lower and the higher life of the same world; that our business is, not to " reverse " the order of nature, but to co-operate with the natural forces which are struggling to spiritualise life. Let us assume this much, and we shall be able to give its full content of meaning to Professor Eucken's pregnant saying that " the spiritual life is the coming to itself of the world-process," and to

a score of other passages in which the philosophy of his
intuition breaks away from the philosophy of his reason;
and we shall be able to provide for the due accomplish-
ment of the mighty *rôle* which he assigns to humanity.

" The spiritual life," according to Professor Eucken,
" has existed within man's being as a possibility from
the commencement." " It is (and has ever been) present
to him as a whole in all its infinity," and " working from
within it opens up to him a cosmic life and a cosmic
being," in realising which " he discovers his own true
self." How ill this philosophy harmonises with the
crude dualism which opposes " spirit " to " nature " in
a truceless and unending war! And how well it harmonises with the higher naturalism which sees in the
duality of " becoming " the very counterpart of the
unity of being, and which therefore infers the self-
identity of Nature from the opposition of her higher to
her lower self! The realisation of the spiritual life is
the first and last duty of man. " Have we not to face
great truths within ourselves," asks Professor Eucken,
" in the development of our own souls? " What place
is there, in such a life, for " reversals " of, and " sharp
separations " from, the course of nature? If there is
any place for them, it is the exact opposite of that which
Professor Eucken, in his dualistic moods, assigns to them.
Man, as a self-conscious being, is able either to further
or hinder the evolution of spiritual life in his own soul;
and in the choice between these two ways of living lies
the whole drama of human life. As the spiritual life is
the true life of the cosmos as well as the true life of
man, it stands to reason that it does not so much " reverse " the course of nature as crown and complete it.
It is the egoistic, self-centred life—the very antipole
to the spiritual—which tries to " reverse " the central
current of nature, and only fails because so far as it

succeeds it "sharply separates" itself from the life which is in its essence cosmic or universal, with the result that it is at last flung aside by the great stream of tendency with which it refuses to swim.

That what we call spiritual life is the real life of the cosmos and the real life of man, that in realising the potencies of spiritual life man both finds his own true self and attains to vital unity with—(a totally different thing from "dreaming absorption" into)—the self or soul of the cosmos,—is the idea which dawned upon the "deepest heart" of India in the far-off days of the Upanishads, and with which, through all the vicissitudes of the intervening centuries, she has never lost touch. On the vital identity of this idea with that which has inspired Professor Eucken I need not insist. It is in his interpretation of the idea that the Western idealist of to-day differs from his precursors in that far-off age and that far-off land.[1] The former thinks to glorify the spiritual life by disparaging its presumed opposite— "nature." The latter saw that from the glorification of the spiritual life to the deification of nature there was but a single step. To take that step, without hesitation or reserve, was (and is) India's supreme contribution

---

[1] There is a passage in one of the Upanishads in which the teacher explains to his disciple that just as the banyan-tree, "as a whole in all its" greatness, is present, "as a possibility," in each of the speck-like seeds of the banyan-fruit, so the World Soul, "the Self of all that is"—(the "spiritual life" or "cosmic life" of Professor Eucken)—is present, "as a possibility," in the heart of each one of us. It follows from this simile, the aptness of which Professor Eucken would, I think, admit, that self-realisation is an entirely natural process. And it was undoubtedly so regarded by the idealistic thinkers of Ancient India. But for Professor Eucken, in his dualistic moods, the process is unnatural, anti-natural, super-natural, anything, in fine, but natural. And we are thus led by him to the paradoxical conclusion that by reversing the course of human nature man finds his true self. Might it not be said, with equal propriety, that by reversing the course of banyan-nature the banyan-seed becomes the banyan-tree?

to the religious thought of the world. The cosmic life, which for India (as for Professor Eucken) is the reward of self-realisation, is the Divine Life; and the cosmic soul, with which the human soul, in the plenitude of its spiritual life, becomes one, is the Soul of God.

For teaching this, India has been accused of pantheism, a word which has no terrors for her, but which the Western mind, with its dualistic prejudices, uses as a term of bitter reproach. For in the popular thought of the West the supreme dualism is that of Nature and the Supernatural; and as the supernaturalist deliberately empties nature of its divine indwelling life, and as the anti-supernaturalist accepts and retains his rival's de-spiritualisation of nature, one cannot wonder that pantheism is regarded in the West as equivalent to materialistic denial of God. But to call the pantheism of India atheistic is to beg the whole question which is in dispute between the West and the Far East. If the sages of the Upanishads had regarded nature as soulless and godless they would not have deified it. The fact that they did deify it, shows that on the one hand they regarded it as all in all, and on the other hand that they conceived of its " essential being " as purely spiritual— that (in Professor Eucken's well-chosen words) they regarded spiritual life as the " core of reality," as " rooted in the essential nature of things," as " the unfolding of the depths which reality contains within its own being," as " at once natural and ideal," as " the dominating soul of all life."

We are confronted by a practical paradox. A Western thinker of the twentieth century, who proposes to base his scheme of life on the fundamental opposition of " nature " to " spirit," is constrained by subtle influences which seem to emanate from the very ideas that he handles, to emphasise in telling phrases the central doctrine of Indian " pantheism,"—the doctrine of the naturalness of spiritual life, and (by implication) of the spirituality of nature. In the presence of this paradox one begins to ask oneself whether the saying " East is East and West is West " is really the final argument in the controversy between the pantheism of the older world and the supernaturalism of the younger; and one begins to wonder what the future may not have in store for us in the way of bringing those antithetical tendencies under the control of a higher unity and blending their respective gospels into a higher creed. In any case, the broad fact remains that what seems to be the latest word of Western idealism was spoken 2500 years ago in India; and that, if the utterance of that word in the West is faltering and indistinct, the reason is that the speaker, deferring unduly to the prejudices of the " average man " (who makes and unmakes our systems and our creeds), cannot bring himself to accept in full the far-reaching consequences of the grand ideas which are at the heart of his faith.

April 1914.

IDEALS OF LIFE AND EDUCATION—GERMAN AND ENGLISH

A PAPER READ AT THE NEW IDEALS IN EDUCATION CONFERENCE AT STRATFORD-ON-AVON, IN AUGUST 1915

THE present war is a crisis in the life of the human race. I am using the word *crisis* in its true and literal sense. The war is passing judgment on us men and our ideals and standards. Its verdict has yet to be given; but we shall do well to prepare ourselves for it, and even try to anticipate it.

Foremost among our ideals are those which dominate our schemes of education. What verdict will the war pronounce on these? Will it find that they coincide with our ideals of life? That they ought to do so, that our schemes of education ought to be dominated by our ideals of life, will, I think, be generally admitted. To those who hold that the function of education is to foster growth the truth of the proposition is self-evident. For they see that education has to do with the unfolding of life, and that as a man is going to live his life when he is his own master so he ought to unfold it, or begin to live it, when he is under the control of others. They see more than this. They see that to live life is to unfold life, the potencies of life being inexhaustible, and that education is therefore a lifelong process which ought from first to last to be regulated by one paramount ideal. Even those who assign a different task to education, who deny that it should concern itself with growth, who contend that the sole function

54

of the teacher is to instruct and discipline the young,
will admit that a sudden dislocation of life on the threshold of manhood may have serious consequences. They
will admit, for example, that to keep a youth under
strict discipline and rigorous supervision till he reaches
the age of eighteen or twenty, and then to give him
complete freedom and leave him to his own devices, is
to run a grave risk of sending him to the devil.

As it is with the individual, so it is with a nation.
A nation's scheme of education ought to be in keeping
with its scheme of life. And both schemes ought to be
regulated by the same dominant ideal. But how seldom
does this happen! To-day there is one nation and one
only which, following the example of ancient Sparta,
has brought its scheme of life into harmony with its
scheme of education. That nation is the German.
Education in Germany is what education ought always
to be, a lifelong process. The adult citizen is subjected
by the State to constant control and supervision, differing
only in degree from that to which the child is subjected
by his teacher. From the day of his birth till he arrives
at years of discretion he is kept in leading-strings. The
pressure on him is then relaxed, except indeed during
his term of service in the army; but he continues to be
kept in leading-strings till the day of his death. It is
because there is no break of gauge in the life of the
citizen that Germany, as a nation, is in some respects
irresistibly strong. But nations, like individuals, have
the defects of their qualities; and even logical consistency and inward harmony can be bought at too high a
price. It is one thing to bring life as a whole under the
domination of a single ideal. It is another thing to possess
an ideal which is worthy to dominate the whole of life.

The scheme of education on which Germany has based
her scheme of life does not materially differ from that

which prevails elsewhere. In all parts of what we call the civilised world a certain type of education has long been accepted as orthodox. The leading features of this orthodox education are the following: On the part of the teacher, coercive discipline and dogmatic instruction; on the part of the child, mechanical obedience and passive reception of what is taught. These features are familiar to all of us. We are inclined to accept them as inevitable, as rooted in the nature of things, and to regard the scheme of education to which they belong as a dispensation of Providence, which is beyond criticism, and which we can but take and make the best of. But, except in Germany, we do not consciously allow this scheme of education to dominate our adult lives. We think of it as suitable for children; and when we grow up we put it away—such at least is our intention—with other childish things. Insensibly, indeed, it continues to influence us. But that we are in revolt against it is proved by the fact that, directly our education (in the conventional sense of the word) is finished, we free ourselves from the disciplinary control which is of its essence and try to order our lives for ourselves and on other lines. To some of us this day of liberation comes at the age of fourteen, to others at sixteen, to others at eighteen or even later. But sooner or later it comes to all of us; and then, instead of building on the foundations which education has laid, we set to work to reconstruct life on another basis, if not on another site.

It is in this work of reconstruction that nation differs from nation. And it is in adhering to the ground-plan and building on the foundations which education has provided that Germany stands apart from the rest of the world. So wedded is Germany to the conventional type of education that she has not merely accepted it as an adequate basis for her scheme of life, but has even gone so far as to idealise it, in the sense of making the ideal—or despair of an ideal—which is at the heart of it the master principle of her national " Kultur." This would not have been possible if the Germans had not become the most docile people on the face of the earth. For if it be true, as it doubtless is, that the German ideal of life and education tends to confirm and perpetuate the national tradition of ultra-docility, it is equally true that it is the outcome of that tradition, that if, for example, Germany had won for herself a real instead of a sham political constitution, her ideal would have been profoundly modified, if not wholly transformed.

That the Germans are the most obedient of all peoples is unquestionable. They do what they are told to do, and do it unhesitatingly, ungrudgingly, and punctiliously. But their spirit of obedience carries them further than this. They think what they are told to think. They believe what they are told to believe. They say what they are told to say. They even feel what they are told to feel — patriotism, world-ambition, war-fever, hatred of England, or whatever it may be.

How comes it that a people who were once famous for their love of freedom have carried obedience to the verge of servility? The explanation is historical, not racial. Here, as elsewhere, heredity counts for very little, whereas tradition, as determining environment, counts for a great deal. The Germans of to-day are the victims of a tradition which grew up in the Middle Ages and became stereotyped after the Thirty Years' War. The feudal system, which substituted service of a vassal to his lord for service of the citizen to the State, and gave every landholder political power over his tenants, destroyed their domestic freedom. But it did the same in every Western country. Why did Germany alone fail to recover what had been lost? That the Germans have a capacity for self-government the history of their Free Cities abundantly proves. But under the stress of four disruptive influences—tribalism, feudalism, a weakened crown (weakened by the burden of the Holy Roman Empire) and religious strife, culminating in the horror of the Thirty Years' War—their unhappy country broke up into a multitude of independent States, and it therefore became impossible for the people to combine for the recovery of their political rights.

Such a movement as the French Revolution, for example, could not have taken place in Germany. In France the crown had overcome the nobility. In Germany the nobility had overcome the crown. In France there was one master, one country, one people. In Germany three hundred masters had divided the country and the people among them. In France, where the flood of popular indignation had a single wide channel open before it, a national movement against tyranny was possible. In Germany such a national movement was impossible, for the river which flows in three hundred channels is not open to the scouring action of any descending flood. In France the crown, though its wearer had once boasted, "*l'état, c'est moi*," was powerless to resist the will of an awakened people. In Germany the dismemberment of the nation showed that the people had not yet awakened and had no collective will.

When the Thirty Years' War was over, Germany lay in fragments. Three hundred principalities, ranging in size from 30,000 square miles to 30,000 acres, were ruled by three hundred princes or princelings, each of whom was an irresponsible autocrat in his own dominions. And this state of things was accepted with scarcely a protesting murmur. The fatal habit of unquestioning obedience, which had been growing on the German people ever since the rise of feudalism, had now become the central feature of the national character. During the Seven Years' War some of the princes sold their subjects to Frederick the Great, as recruits for his army, at so much a head, as if they were sheep or cattle. Men who could stand such treatment as that could stand anything.

But the princes were not all of one type. Some were benevolent despots who patronised art and letters and learning, and among whose subjects—autocratically but lightly ruled, detached from all that is sordid in politics, and finding in spiritual freedom compensation for the political freedom which they had lost—great men arose, not warriors or statesmen, but poets, thinkers, musicians, scholars, and the like. Others were ambitious rulers, with military gifts and aspirations, who found in their serf-like subjects the raw material of highly disciplined armies, and, having provided themselves with such armies, could not resist the temptation to extend their dominions by force of arms.

Of these two types of ruler, the latter was predestined to stamp his will on Germany. For, whether by conquest or by the establishment of a hegemony, he could give her what the former could not—the political unity and the material strength which would enable her to hold her own against her enemies. It is idle to speculate on what might have happened if Germany had allowed herself to be Weimarised instead of Prussianised. In point of fact she has been Prussianised; and the unity which she has attained to has been forced upon her, and is therefore artificial, material, military, not spontaneous, not spiritual, not genuinely political.

The Germans have a saying that such and such a country possesses an army, but that Germany is an army which possesses a country. They have another

saying that the army made Prussia, and that Prussia
has made Germany. They have yet another saying
that in Germany the army is the nation and the nation
is the army. These sayings point to a fact of vital
importance—namely, that beyond all other countries
Germany is military in the fullest sense of the word,
military in that its slavishly obedient people are pre-
eminently amenable to the discipline of drill, military
in that its ruling classes are all drill-sergeants at heart.
Other nations may be as warlike in temperament; but
in no other nation has the iron of military discipline
entered into the inmost soul of the people, in no other
nation is the organisation of social life essentially military, and in no other nation is the King or Emperor, or
whatever his title may be, primarily the head of an
army, and only secondarily the ruler of a people.

In Germany, then, the army is a great school through
which the manhood of the nation—the larger part of it,
if not the whole—has to pass. In that school the features
of the conventional type of education are reproduced
and intensified. In no other school is the discipline so
severe, the instruction so dogmatic, the obedience of
the pupils so mechanical, the acceptance of what is
taught so entirely passive. But the army is not the
only school which the citizen has to attend. In civil
life he is subjected to a bureaucratic control which is as
inquisitorial as it is despotic, and which becomes more
inquisitorial and more despotic from year to year. His
adult life is the natural continuation of his life as a
child and his life as a soldier. The discipline to which
he was subjected in the school and in the army is indeed
relaxed, but is still severe and strict. His goings are
still ordered for him—ordered to an extent which would
not be tolerated in any other country. Commands and
prohibitions still meet him at every turn. The official

and the policeman take the place of the teacher in the school and of the officer in the army. But there is no essential change.

We owe a debt of gratitude to Germany for having applied to her manhood the coercive discipline and dogmatic pressure which in this and other countries are applied only to the young. In doing this she has made herself the subject of an experiment, the importance of which cannot be overrated. So convinced are we that the prevailing system of education is the only one which is suitable for children and adolescents, that we have lost our power of criticising it, such criticism as we pass on it being confined to details and accessories, and leaving its vital principle untouched. But when the same system is applied, in principle if not in detail, to the manhood of a nation, irrespective of age, we instinctively resume our critical attitude, and it becomes possible for us to forecast the consequences of the system and to estimate its intrinsic worth. For what the system does to the adult it will do, or tend to do, to the child. The unfolding of life is, as has been said, a continuous and lifelong process. The child is father to the man; and to put away childish things in their entirety is to put away human things. It may be contended that ultra-docility, though a vice in an adult, is a virtue in a child. But this is an unproven assertion. The data for the solution of the problem are wanting, a radical reform of education having rarely been attempted and never on a really adequate scale. But such evidence as we possess goes to show that initiative, self-reliance, and self-control, qualities which are incompatible with ultra-docility, are virtues in children as well as in adults.

In Germany, as in a well-regulated school of the conventional type, the pressure of autocratic authority on life is constant and strong. What effect does this pressure produce? There are three things which it necessarily does, or tends to do, to all who come under its influence:

(1) To mechanicalise life.
(2) To externalise life.
(3) To weaken the will, which is the mainspring of life.

Let us consider its action under each of these heads.

(1) It is only by *mechanicalising* life, by substituting machine-like movements for vital processes, that authority, be it incarnate in a teacher, a general, a ruler, or a ruling caste, can bring what it governs under complete control. When we say, for example, that the German army is a perfect machine, we mean that it is moved, both as a whole and in all its details, by a single will. The aim of authority is to regulate life by means of rules, formulæ, plans, schemes, commands, prohibitions, and the like, so as to suppress freedom which always introduces an incalculable element into conduct. The effect of this over-regulation of life is to deaden sensibility, both moral and mental. By *sensibility* I mean that capacity for evolving senses, or faculties of direct perception, in response to the varying stimuli of experience, with which each of us is endowed, and by means of which he steers his way through life, just as he steers his way through the material things that surround him by means of his bodily senses. One objection to undue reliance on rules and plans is that they cannot measure the complexity and subtlety of Nature. The instinctive, intuitive side of us can alone do this. Another, and even more serious, objection is that reliance on rules and plans, by relieving us from the necessity of exercising our senses, actual or potential, either atrophies these or blights them in the bud. The result is that conformity to an artificial standard of efficiency takes the place of conformity to the vital truths of Nature.

Our senses, other than physical, are either intuitive or sympathetic, or both. Or again, they are either moral or mental, or both. These are to some extent cross-divisions, and, so far as they suggest hard and fast boundary lines, they are liable to mislead us. They have, however, their uses, and we cannot wholly dispense with them. As examples of moral senses I may instance conscience, which is the overlord of all the rest; imaginative sympathy; social tact; the sense of honour; the sense of humour; the sense of justice; the sense of duty; and what has been aptly termed " the intuition of totality," a sense which carries us beyond the normal confines of morality into a world of its own creation, the world of religious sentiment and faith. As examples of mental senses, I may instance imagination; judgment; the active intelligence which is the counterpart of initiative, and is therefore to be distinguished from the passive intelligence which merely takes in what is explained to it; the " illative sense," by means of which we reason, in ignorance, and even in defiance, of the rules of logic; the artistic sense, with all its sub-senses ; that range of intuitive faculties which is covered by the words " common sense" and " mother wit"; and those higher intuitive faculties which culminate in genius.

The pressure which deadens *moral* sensibility makes for callousness in the weaker natures, for brutality in the stronger. Hence the savagery of over-disciplined Germany in the field, and her criminality at home. These are strong words to use; but I do not hesitate to use them. We have heard much of late of the savagery of the German soldier, but we hear little of the criminality of the German citizen. Yet the latter, besides serving to throw light on the former, is the graver and more significant phenomenon. Also, it is vouched for by Germany herself in her statistics of crime, whereas the savagery of

her soldiers, however well-attested, is easily denied.
Many years ago, Treitschke, the famous German his-
torian, noted and deplored the prevalence in Germany
of crimes of violence and "crimes of shame." His
words of warning have not been heeded. The statistics
of the past few years show that in Germany crimes of
violence in which "severe bodily injuries" are inflicted
are at least two hundred times as numerous as in England
and Wales, and that crimes of shame which are also
crimes of violence are sixty-five times as numerous.[1]
They also show that among the boys of Germany, below
the age of eighteen, crimes of both kinds are many times
as numerous as among all the inhabitants of England and
Wales.[2] These figures, which make it impossible for us
to reject on à priori grounds the stories of German
atrocities in France, Belgium, and elsewhere, need something more than the deadening of moral sensibility to
account for them; and other causes will in due course
be forthcoming.

The deadening of *mental* sensibility makes for automatism on the lower levels of intelligence, for pedantry
on the higher. In the German army, where the pressure
of authority is at its maximum, it seems to be the fixed
purpose of the General Staff to turn the soldier into
"an automaton with his mind entirely subordinated to
the will of his officer." The author of *The German Army*

[1] It must, of course, be borne in mind that the population of
Germany is nearly double that of England and Wales.

[2] In Germany in the year 1912, 107 boys below the age of
eighteen were tried for murder or manslaughter, nearly 9000 for
unlawful wounding, and nearly 1000 for rape. In England and
Wales, in the year 1913, nine youths below the age of *twenty-one* were
convicted of murder or manslaughter, thirty of unlawful wounding,
and four of rape. (The ratio of convictions to charges in Germany
seems to be about three to four.) Since the war began there has
been a great decrease in crime in this country and, according to
the "official" *Cologne Gazette* and other newspapers, a great
increase in Germany, at any rate among the young.

from Within says that "one important defect in the training of the army is that no chance is given to the men to display initiative. The German character is at no time quick in this direction, and the little that a man may possess when he enters the army is studiously squeezed out of him. On no account may he act and think for himself. He is simply there to do as he is told." The reason for this is obvious. The more machine-like an army becomes, the less room is there for the display of intelligence and initiative by any of its minor constituent parts. If a cog were allowed to think and act for itself, the whole mass of machinery might be thrown out of working order. The pressure to which the citizen is subjected in civil life produces, and is meant to produce, a similar effect. The difference between bureaucratic and military discipline is one of degree, not of kind. Mr. W. H. Dawson, who knows Germany intimately, tells us that "control and regulation at every turn are the lot of all Germans, at least of all North Germans, from the cradle to the grave, with the result that initiative is crippled and men come to regard order and instruction as a necessary part of life."

On the higher levels of intelligence the deadening of mental sensibility makes pedants of men who are worthy of a better fate. Pedantry—undue deference to rules, precedents, and accepted conclusions—is the exact anti-pole to mental initiative; and wherever it prevails, though learning and research may flourish, creative activity wanes. In support of this statement I appeal to the history of modern Germany. During the period of Germany's spiritual and intellectual greatness—1750 to 1870—Prussia, alone almost among the German States, was in the grip of the drill-sergeant, military and civil; and while the rest of Germany was fruitful of genius, Prussia was consistently barren. In the fields of literature, history, music, and thought, out of some twenty to twenty - five men of European fame only two were Prussians, and one of these (Kant) was half a Scotsman, while the other (Schopenhauer) was the least Prussian of Prussians and had but little honour in his own country. Even the statesmen and the thinkers who resuscitated Prussia after her downfall in 1806—Scharnhorst, Stein, Hardenberg, and Fichte—were all non-Prussians. After the war of 1870 Germany as a whole came under Prussian ascendancy; and her creative activities at once began to ebb. In no period of equal length since the middle of the eighteenth century has she done so little for the edification of the human spirit as in the past forty-five years. In music, in which she once reigned without a rival, the sceptre has been wrested from her by Russia; and the greatest of her living men of letters no more belong to the royal line of Goethe and Heine than do her greatest thinkers to the royal line of Kant and Hegel. The mental energies of the nation have been diverted into military, commercial, and industrial channels; and the springs of its spiritual activity are running dry.

(2) The pressure of autocratic authority tends to *externalise* life. The verdict of authority—external, visible, embodied authority—takes the place of the verdict of experience, of life, of Nature. An officer's or a teacher's estimate of worth is accepted as final and decisive. An examiner's certificate determines a man's " station and degree." Class lists, orders of merit, prizes, medals, titles, grades, and the like interpose themselves between the soul and the ultimate realities of existence. Under such a régime the sense of intrinsic reality is gradually lost. What he is reputed to be is a man's chief concern, not what he really is. Now the intrinsically real has another name—the ideal. It is because we feel in our hearts that things are what they are, not what they seem

to be or are said to be, that we embark on the quest of the ideal. And because the ideal, the thing in itself, is unattainable, the quest of it keeps us in touch with the infinite, and so keeps us always immature, always on the ascending curve of life, and therefore truly alive. When external authority takes the place of the real and the ideal, life shrinks within finite limits. Reality is regarded as measurable and ponderable. Standards of value which are outward, finite, and mechanically adjustable, take the place of those which are inward, infinite, and self-adjusting. In other words, autocratic authority idealises itself and expects to be idealised by its victims. " I am sufficient for you," it says to those who submit to it, " do not look beyond me." The consequences of this compulsory narrowing of one's spiritual horizon are far-reaching. He who lives for a self which can be weighed in outward scales and measured by outward standards, lives for a finite self; but to live for a finite self is egoism; and egoism is the beginning and end of immorality. When the vision of an ideal, the sense of intrinsic reality, dies out of a man's life—when the quest of the ideal, the attempt to realise it in himself, by living for it and living up to it, has been abandoned—the master principle of life has been lost, the process of growth has been arrested, and the counter-process of degeneration has begun.

In no other country is the externalisation of life, under the pressure of authority, so complete as in Germany. In no other country is caste-feeling so intense or so all-controlling. In no other country is the cult of the uniform carried to such extravagant lengths. The German nation, said Bismarck, " is a race of non-commissioned officers ; everyone is eager to get the stripes. On an average every man in public life has only that degree of self-reliance which corresponds to his official hall-mark, to the conditions of his official life and to his orders. Exceptions to this are praiseworthy but rare." So deep is the average German's veneration for hall-marks, so much does he care for what he is reputed to be, so little does he care for what he really is, that if you wish to conciliate him you give him a title higher than that which is actually his. " If a German wants the waiter," says Mr. Austin Harrison, " he calls out ' Herr Ober ' (head waiter), or the waiter, feeling himself insulted, refuses to come and rolls his eyes." " This curious vanity," says the same writer, " is characteristic of all classes. If you want to please a German you address him as Von when you know he is a plebeian. You call a youth an ' assessor ' when you are perfectly aware he has not yet passed his examinations . . . if you want to get anything out of a German, by far the quickest and most practical way is to introduce into the conversation such a phrase as ' My dear Count.' "

These are childish follies, of which Germany, though she has more than her share, has no monopoly; but the excessive regard for external authority, with its labels and hall-marks, which they indicate, has a darker side to it. The distrust of human nature, which is at the heart of the German ideal of life, and which has generated the cult of the label and the hall-mark, is ever tending to reproduce and intensify itself. The more thoroughly a man's life is ordered for him, the less capable does he become of ordering it for himself. The standards by which his conduct is regulated—the standards of social, moral, and even spiritual worth—pass under the control of the central authority, and influence him from without instead of from within. If I am to do this thing, if I am not to do that thing, the State, which fences me in with commands and prohibitions, must have reasons of its own for issuing the directions which I have to obey; and those reasons must be determined by standards which are in the keeping of the State, and which have therefore the validity of might, if not of right. And the more the State encroaches on my freedom, the more jealously will it guard its moral weights and measures, and, since willing obedience is worth more to it than enforced submission, the more strenuously will it endeavour to impose those standards on my reason and my conscience, and to regulate my views of life and my consequent aims and ambitions as well as the details of my conduct. Hence it is that in Germany the State takes care to control the Church, the Press, the Universities, and the schools, and, through the medium of these moulds and organs of opinion, to suggest to the people what they are to think, to believe, and to say. And the pity of it is that he whose thoughts, beliefs, and words are habitually suggested—not to say dictated—to him, comes at last to regard those thoughts, beliefs, and words as his own. When this point has been reached, when a man honestly believes that what has been virtually forced upon him from without has come to him from within, the triumph of authority over the inner life of the soul is complete. The pressure of the drill-sergeant is not brought to bear upon the German citizen in civil life. But it is possible that the brutal discipline which makes the German soldier an automaton is less harmful (in the deeper sense of the word) than the insidious pressure on the civilian which enables the State to take possession of his moral and spiritual springs of action.

(3) In the act of mechanicalising and externalising life, autocratic authority *weakens the will*. The truth of this proposition is self-evident. The pressure which makes a man an automaton necessarily weakens his will. So does the pressure which makes a man dependent on

others for his ideals and standards. The former deprives
him of the power of choice at the partings of the by-
ways of life. The latter, at the partings of the high-
ways. And it stands to reason that the man who is not
allowed to exercise his power of choice will lose his
force of will. It stands to reason, in other words, that
the man who is over-disciplined by authority—whether
directly or indirectly matters little—will lose the power
of disciplining himself; for the restraining and directing
forces which come from within will naturally cease to
operate when life is regulated, both as a whole and in
all its details, by systematic pressure from without.

I have said that it needs something more than the
deadening of moral sensibility to account for the abnormal criminality of the German people in civil life, to say
nothing of their savagery in war. We can now see that
other causes have been at work—namely, the corruption
of the first principles of morality which follows when
the State, or any other external authority, takes possession
of the head-springs of a man's inner life, and the loss
of self-control which follows when the will has been
weakened by the withdrawal of the power of choice.
We can also see that all three causes are generated, and
necessarily generated, by the undue pressure of autocratic
authority on life.

The traditional ideal of education may be set forth
in the homely words " Do what I tell you." This ideal
of education Germany has adopted as her ideal of life.
" Do what I tell you " is what the German teacher says
to the pupil, what the German officer says to the soldier,
what the German official says to the citizen, what the
German State says to the people, what the German people
would like to say to the rest of the world. When addressed
to children and adolescents, the formula sounds innocent
enough. We ought to thank Germany for having revealed

to us, on the one hand, what is behind it—what distrust
of human nature, what blind confidence in self, what
arrogance, what intolerance, what want of sympathy
and humanity; and, on the other hand, what it tends
to do to us—to deaden our sensibility, to debase our
ideals and standards, to weaken our driving-power, to
lower our vitality, to make us machines instead of men.
We ought also to thank Germany for having convinced
us that when a ruling caste takes control of a people's
ideals and standards, and concentrates all initiative, intelligence, and driving-power in its own hands, the deteri-
oration of that people, cut off from the central life of
Humanity and Nature, is as certain as the withering of
a branch which has been severed from the parent stem.
The material issue of this war is still uncertain; but in
revealing to the world her ideal of life, Germany has
already ensured its condemnation. It is for us educationists to lay these lessons to heart. If the formula " Do
what I tell you " can do so much to demoralise and devitalise the manhood of a nation, is it likely that it will
leave the youth of that or any other nation unscathed?
The tender, pliant sapling has more to lose from the
pressure that stunts and distorts than has the adult tree,
with its solid trunk and sturdy limbs.

So much for the German ideals of education and life.
We English do not consciously entertain ideals; but so
far as we have an ideal of education, it does not materially
differ from the German. On the other hand, so far as
we have an ideal of life, it not merely differs from the
German ideal, but is directly opposed to it. We think
that the formula " Do what I tell you " is good enough
for the nursery and the schoolroom; but when we leave
the nursery and the schoolroom we substitute for it
the familiar motto " Live and let live "; and we do not
see that the latter formula is the direct negation of the

former. " Live and let live " is a homely and well-worn maxim, but it embodies a profound philosophy of life. We are not a nation of thinkers. Theorising about great matters is not in our line. I mean by this that we do not find it easy to work our way, by the conscious exercise of thought, to large conceptions of life and destiny, and that we have not much inclination to do so. But in our own blind, blundering, instinctive, subconscious way we do sometimes, under the stress and guidance of practical experience, arrive at truth. And when we made " Live and let live " our motto we arrived at a great and vital truth. How did we find our way to it? The typical Englishman is, as we all know, a man of independent character. He rebels against dictation, resents interference, and claims, almost as a right, to be free to order his own doings. How he acquired these characteristics I will not turn aside to inquire. That he possesses them and that they reflect his philosophy of life is, I think, undeniable. Now the man of independent character discovers, sooner or later, that if he is to retain his independence he must respect the independence of others. He must live and let live. If he will not do this he will have to fight perpetually for his own hand, and then there will be social chaos.

It was fitting that the least conscious and most instinctive of all peoples should have allowed its instinct to live to determine its philosophy of life. In doing so it committed itself to the safest of all guides. What our ideal has done and is doing for us in the region of world politics we all know. We owe to it our great Empire, which would have fallen to pieces long ago if " Do what I tell you " had been our motto. We owe to it that when the war broke out our Empire rallied round us almost as if it were a single people. We owe to it the sympathy and good-will of nearly all the neutral nations. We owe to it what is best and most hopeful in our social and political life—the readiness to compromise which makes political progress possible, the tolerance which sooner or later heals all quarrels and effaces all scars, the spirit of comradeship which can on occasion unite all classes and parties in bonds of brotherhood, in defiance of the caste-feeling which is part of our inheritance from feudalism.

What our ideal might do for us in the region of our inner life we have yet to learn. Its emergence as an ideal of life is in itself a victory over egoism—a sub-conscious, instinctive victory perhaps, but one which opens up a vista of endless possibilities. The trust in Nature which is at the heart of it keeps us in touch with the infinite and the ideal; and if it cannot furnish us off-hand with the true criterion of reality and the true standard of values, it can at least tell us where these are to be found. It is the only ideal of life which provides for the diffusion of freedom; and it is only in the atmosphere of freedom that the self-development which is of the essence of life is possible. If we would live, in the true sense of the word, we must let live. Otherwise our own life will be strangled in the coils of an ever-narrowing self. He who wantonly encroaches on freedom imprisons himself behind the walls which he has built for others. He who lets live widens the scope of his own life by going out of himself—(for tolerance is born of sympathy)—into the lives of others.

We see, then, that in our homely ideal of life there are untold possibilities of progress. When shall we be able to realise these? Not, I think, until we have begun to bring our ideal of education into line with our ideal of life. It is here that we are weak as a nation, especially as compared with Germany. The German ideal of education coincides at every point with the German ideal of life. Our ideal of education, so far as we can be said to have one, is opposed to our ideal of life. As educationists we believe in the type of education which Germany has idealised and transformed into a philosophy of life. We believe in dogmatic direction and the discipline of drill. As citizens of a free country, as rulers of a great Empire, we believe in the anti-German philosophy of "Live and let live." From the cradle to the grave Germany stamps her philosophy of life on every German citizen. This is her strength. We are of two minds; and this is our weakness. Germany subjects the child to coercive discipline and dogmatic pressure; and when he grows up, though she loosens the reins that control him, she continues to treat him as a child. We, too, subject the child to coercive discipline and dogmatic pressure; but long before he has grown up we give him freedom and tell him to live his own life and work out his own salvation. Are we wise? Is not the change which we bring about too violent and too abrupt? If we really believe in our ideal of life ought we not to train the young to live up to it? Germany, in her effort to strangle spontaneous life, has arrayed against herself the strongest of all forces, the instinct to live. If that instinct is fighting on our side, the reason is that as citizens and as rulers we have instinctively respected spontaneous life. But have we done so, are we doing so, as teachers?

I am raising a question which has many side issues and which bristles with practical difficulties. I do not wish to dogmatise about it, but I do wish to set people thinking. I wish people to realise that there is a civil war in this country from which Germany is free—a war between two conflicting ideals, the very ideals that are meeting and grappling in the great war which is shaking the whole world. And I wish them to realise that this civil war becomes fiercer and intenser as time goes on. For on the one hand, with the spread of education, our educational ideal is constantly striving to encroach on our adult life. And, on the other hand, with our growing consciousness of the meaning and value of freedom, our ideal of life is trying, in its blind instinctive way, to dominate the education of the young. What part are we educationists going to play in this vital struggle? Some of us, I know, have made up our minds to serve under the banner of freedom, the banner which

> torn but flying
> Streams, like the thundercloud, *against* the wind.

Others hesitate. Others, perhaps a large majority, think that, as we have hitherto blundered along pretty successfully, there is no need for a radical change. I think, on the contrary, that there is need for a radical change. I think that the catastrophe of this terrible war has come upon us in order, for one thing, to compel us to reconsider our ways. Many of the weaknesses which the war has revealed in us are due to our being of two minds about the great issues of life. In particular, the want of discipline, which has manifested itself in strikes, slackness at work, and over-drinking, is due to the fact that the manhood of the nation, which is not disciplined, as in Germany, by a despotic and inquisitorial State, does not learn during the periods of childhood and adolescence to discipline itself. If the war, which is judging us all, will condemn Germany for having adopted a false ideal of life, it will condemn us for having tried to live under two irreconcilable ideals.

The time has come for us to reconsider our ways. *Fas est et ab hoste doceri.* Germany has set us an example of consistency and singleness of purpose which we ought to begin to follow. To follow—but on English, not on

German lines. Let us ask ourselves one crucial question. Are we prepared to bring our ideal of life into harmony with our ideal of education—the ideal of coercive discipline and dogmatic pressure? If we are not, if the bare suggestion of this is abhorrent to us, we must resolutely face the only alternative to it. We must begin to think seriously of bringing our ideal of education into harmony with our ideal of life.

How best to do this, how best to let the rising generation live, how best to help it to unfold its hidden life, how best, in educating it, to harmonise order with freedom, direction with spontaneity, organisation from without with growth from within, is a problem which will give us much to think about for many generations. Perhaps, if I may make one positive suggestion, we might begin by allowing children to let one another live—in other words, by giving them a freer social life than they now enjoy. That would be the thin end of a great wedge—the wedge of comradeship—which might some day cleave this still feudalised world of ours asunder.

DISCIPLINE AND FREEDOM

THE word *discipline*, like the word *character*, is the centre of a never-ceasing whirlpool of cant. By cant I mean insincere talk; and by insincere talk I mean talk which, though not necessarily hypocritical or otherwise dishonest, is vitiated by the talker's inability or unwillingness to think out the matters on which he lays down the law. There is no theme on which men expend so much sound and fury as on the need for discipline in this democratic age, and there is no theme to which they give so little serious thought.

I was recently invited to join the Duty and Discipline Movement, and I said in reply that I could not do so until I knew in what sense the word " discipline " was being used. My letter has not been answered; and I must therefore assume that the leaders of the movement have not yet come to an understanding with themselves as to the meaning of the word which they use so freely. But I am inclined to think that their ideas about discipline do not materially differ from those which are expounded, with much fervour and assurance, by our friend the man in the street—the man in Regent Street, let us say, not the man in a criminal slum. The man in Regent Street, whose dividends have perhaps been imperilled by strikes, is deeply impressed by the restlessness and unruliness of the present generation, by the spirit of independence, or insubordination (as he would call it), shown by the working classes, by the hostility of labour to capital, and other " distressing signs of the times," and he approves of compulsory military service on the ground that a strict course of discipline may teach the "lower orders" to behave themselves, and may thus save the nation from plunging into an abyss of social and economic chaos. The interest which the man in Regent Street takes in the question is in the main personal and financial. The interest which the leaders of the Duty and Discipline Movement take in it is in the main impersonal and ethical. But both parties seem to have a blind belief in strict discipline as the panacea for all our moral and social evils. This being so, may I remind them that in the present war the most strictly disciplined of all the armies has made the whole world ring with the stories of its misdeeds? What do they make of that indisputable fact? If the war has taught us nothing else, it has surely taught us that discipline, as such, does not moralise all who come under its influence, though there may be a particular type of discipline which does.

Let us ask ourselves, then, what we mean by discipline. We mean, in the first place, either a process of training or the result of such a process. It is with the former meaning that we are now concerned. As is the process, so will be the result. Discipline, regarded as a formative process, is defined in the *New English Dictionary*, to which we naturally turn in our perplexity, as "instruction having for its aim to form the pupil to proper conduct and action; the training of soldiers or subordinates to proper and orderly action by instructing and exercising them in the same." In this definition the word "proper" is all-important. Until we know what constitutes propriety of conduct we cannot say whether the discipline which "forms the pupil to proper conduct and action" is a good or a bad influence in his life. Everything depends on the end that the disciplinarian has in view. Fagin, in *Oliver Twist*, was a strict disciplinarian; but the conduct to which he formed his pupils was " proper " only from the point of view of a master thief.

What, then, are the ends which discipline is supposed to serve? There are three ends which at once suggest themselves. The first is to enable one man to make many men the creatures of his will. The second is to secure social order. The third is to enable a man to control his own lower desires and impulses. In each of these cases he who is disciplined has to do or abstain from doing certain things at the bidding of authority. He may or may not wish to do the things which he is required to do. He may or may not wish to do the things which he is forbidden to do. But his wishes are not consulted. He must do what he is required to do. He must leave undone what he is forbidden to do. And the proof of his being well disciplined is that he obeys his orders, whether positive or negative, promptly, exactly, unreservedly, and — in extreme cases — instinctively, and even automatically.

I have said that the first end of discipline is to make many men the creatures of one man's will. This is the discipline which prevails on board a ship, in a school, in a factory, in a house of business, in a Government office, in a fire brigade, in a convent or a monastery, in a gang of smugglers or brigands. It is met with in its strictest form in a well-trained army or navy. There it is a matter of the utmost importance—a matter literally of life and death—that the wishes of the supreme commander, who may be responsible for the welfare of a million men, should be carried out with promptitude and precision; and in order to secure this end it is essential that all who are under command should master their respective parts by means of assiduous practice in obedience to orders.

To this assiduous practice we give the name of *drill*.
The discipline of a well-trained army is pre-eminently
the discipline of *drill*. But in this, the strictest of all
kinds of discipline, there are degrees of strictness. " Until
comparatively recently," says the author of *Drill and
Field Training*, one of our Imperial Army Series, " discipline was developed by methods which aimed at producing a blind mechanical obedience to orders through
habits formed by a monotonous drill, coupled with
severe and even cruel punishments." When this type
of military discipline was the only type, it reached its
maximum of rigour and severity in the Prussian army;
and to-day, while in most armies there is a growing
tendency to relax the rigour and mitigate the severity
of discipline, in the German army, which has inherited
the Prussian tradition, the tendency is, if anything, in
the opposite direction. If the word " discipline " has,
as it surely has, a wide range of meaning—if the idea
of discipline, like most of the ideas which dominate
human life, moves backward and forward between two
antithetical poles, two opposite extremes which limit
the word's range of meaning—one of those poles, the
extreme of dogmatic pressure and mechanical drill, will
be represented by the discipline of the Prussianised
German army. The immediate end and aim of this
" iron discipline " is to make the soldier an automaton.
The ulterior end and aim of it is to make the army
a machine.

That discipline of this sort is not necessarily good for
those who have to submit to it, is a point on which
I need not insist. The man who has become an automaton, the man in whose life mechanical have been
substituted for vital processes and material for spiritual
motives, may be said to have missed his human destiny.
It may be well for the army to which he belongs that

his life should be mechanicalised. It may even be well for his country that he and millions of his fellow-citizens should sink to the level of automata. But it is not well for him. Discipline of the Prussian type makes the force of habit, reinforced by fear, the dominant motive to action; deadens sensibility, both moral and mental; crushes individuality; strangles the freedom without which self-development is impossible; externalises aims; materialises ideals and standards; weakens the will by withholding the power of choice. A private in the German army, who in civil life is (or was) Professor of Latin at a gymnasium, in his diary which fell into the hands of the enemy, sums up the effect of Prussian discipline on character in the following words: " The German soldier has no personality, he is a machine, and that is what he is trained to be; as soon as he is left to himself he is idle, stupid, and a blockhead. He has only one idea, eating and sleeping, and his brutishness is only limited by barbarous punishment. He never knows of his own accord what he ought to do, and everything he does he does with frightful clumsiness." It is not by discipline of this type that human nature is to be regenerated, or society saved from decay.

I do not wish to underrate military discipline. It has its own function to fulfil; and for that particular purpose it is indispensable. Experience, in our own and other armies, has proved that it admits of being humanised and otherwise modified: and that soldiers fight the better, not the worse, for being treated as human beings rather than as puppets and serfs. Experience has also proved that the sinister influence of military discipline on character diminishes in proportion as its severity is mitigated and its rigour relaxed, and that in many cases its influence is, on balance, for good. Those, for example, who have led careless, reckless, lawless, self-indulgent lives, and whose moral fibre has in consequence lost its tone, will be the better for a course of discipline which acts as a tonic on their moral fibre—and every tonic taken in excess is a poison—and so helps them to discipline themselves. So will the youths whom a spirit of adventure, to which lawful outlets had been barred, has led into anti-social practices and has at last landed in the police courts. For those youths have enough spirit and initiative to resist the deadening pressure of the discipline of drill, and they will benefit greatly by having order brought into their lives and by having their energies enlisted under a worthy flag. Those, again, who through lack of self-discipline have become individualists and egoists, and have thus come to regard every command as an insult and every act of obedience as a humiliation, will be the better for being forcibly compelled to realise that they are members of a community—of a company or a regiment, if of no wider community—and must bear themselves accordingly. Those who have learnt to discipline themselves will find in the corporate life of their own military unit a stimulating and vivifying atmosphere, while the drill to which they are subjected, if they do not have too much of it, may prove as helpful to their mental nerves and muscles as a self-imposed course of physical exercises might prove to their bodily frames. All this can be said for military discipline; but it is not enough to justify the extravagant claims that are sometimes made on its behalf. Its own immediate end—to make many men the creatures of one man's will—is not intrinsically desirable; and to say that its highest function is to help men to discipline themselves is to subordinate the discipline of drill and compulsory obedience to the discipline of self-control.

I have called the first type of discipline the discipline

of drill. Other names for it are the discipline of compulsion and the discipline of positive direction. The second type of discipline is that which aims at securing social order. If military discipline is mainly positive, the discipline of social life, so far as it is enforced by external authority, is mainly negative. The soldier is told what he is to do, and is compelled to do it again and again, the essence of drill being the repeated performance of definite movements in obedience to the word of command. The citizen, who in this matter is the lineal descendant of the child in the nursery, is told what he is not to do, and is threatened with pains and penalties if he does it. In other words, the discipline to which he is subjected is enforced through prohibitions rather than through commands. What is its value? For an answer to this question we must again turn to Germany. There the discipline of prohibition, like the discipline of positive direction, reaches its maximum of dogmatic pressure. The life of the German citizen is hemmed in with innumerable prohibitions. The warning word " Verboten "—the equivalent of the " Don't " or " No! No! " of the nurse or mother—meets his eyes at every turn. The objection to this type of discipline, as to that which prevails in the German army, is that it is based on distrust of human nature, and that it leaves too little to the intuition, the volition, or the initiative of its victim. The legal and administrative system which takes for granted that the average citizen has little or no sense of social propriety or power of self-control, tends to atrophy that sense and that power, so far as they do exist, by forbidding their possessor to exercise them. Also it tempts him to assume that whatever is not forbidden is lawful and right, from which he readily passes on to the further assumption that, so far as his life is not covered by legal enactment or administrative direction, he is free to do whatever he pleases. The anti-social tendency of this assumption makes it necessary that prohibitions shall be multiplied so as to cover all possible cases of anti-social conduct. But to this process there are no assignable limits; for the more guidance the State gives to the citizen by means of its formal enactments, the more it tends to dull and deaden his moral and social intuition; and as his intuition weakens he becomes more and more dependent on authority for his knowledge of right and wrong, being thus involved in a vicious circle from which it is hard to escape.

In its extreme form, then, the discipline of prohibition or repression is an actively demoralising influence. What is valuable in the laws and bye-laws by which the social life of a community is regulated is that they point out to the individual how best, under existing conditions, he may serve the community by the exercise of self-control. If they give him too much guidance his sense of social propriety will, as I have said, be weakened; but a reasonable amount of guidance, based on a rational consideration of the general interest, will be of value to him, and the pains and penalties by which that guidance is enforced will have no terrors for him so long as he is able and willing to discipline himself.

Thus the discipline which makes for social order, like the discipline which makes for military efficiency, is far from possessing the intrinsic value which those who bewail the laxity and lawlessness of the present age believe all discipline to possess. If carried to excess, both kinds tend to demoralise those who submit to their pressure. If kept within reasonable limits, they have their merits, but only because they subserve, or may subserve, and only so far as they do subserve, a higher type of discipline—the discipline of self-control.

This is the third type of discipline. It has one thing in common with the other types. Obedience is of its essence. But it differs from them in respect of the authority to which obedience is due. And this difference is all-important. For the value of any type of discipline depends on the character of the authority which claims the right to regulate our lives. It may be expedient that in certain matters a man should obey the will of another man. It is desirable that, within limits, he should obey the will of the community to which he belongs. But it is absolutely and eternally right that he should obey the will of his own higher self. The man who controls his impulses to selfishness, sensuality, self-indulgence, cowardice, indolence, and the like, not because he is commanded to control them, not because he has been drilled into controlling them, not because he is threatened with pains and penalties if he does not control them, but because they belong to his lower self and are therefore unworthy to dominate his life—this man has attained to self-discipline; and we can see from his manner of living that, as regards morals and character, self-discipline is the only type that really counts. The soldier who, when his company advances into a zone of deadly fire, keeps his place in the ranks from force of habit, reinforced by fear of punishment, is inferior as a human being to the man who keeps his place because he has mastered his impulse to run away. The former, if not constitutionally fearless, bears himself bravely because he has been drilled into automatic steadiness. The latter, if not constitutionally fearless, bears himself bravely because he has learnt to discipline himself. That the courage of the latter is of a higher order than that of the former, and that it is therefore the product of a higher type of discipline, will, I think, be universally admitted; and what holds good of courage holds good of all the other virtues which discipline is supposed to produce.

But how is the discipline of self-control to be achieved? Without attempting to give an exhaustive answer to this question, I may point out that only in an atmosphere of freedom can a man or child learn to discipline himself. The truth of this statement is, I submit, self-evident. If we want a man to do things by himself we must, within reasonable limits, leave him free to do them. If we order all his goings for him we cannot expect him to acquire the power of ordering them for himself. If we control his lower impulses for him, either by the compulsory formation of countervailing habits or by bringing the fear of punishment to bear on him when he falters, we undermine his power of controlling them for himself. So vital is the connection between freedom and self-discipline that each in turn may be said to imply, and even resolve itself into, the other. As there is no self-discipline without freedom, so there is no freedom without self-discipline; for he who is in bondage to his own lusts and passions is the most abject of slaves. And as in self-discipline the compulsion to orderly conduct comes from within, being imposed by the higher on the lower self, so what differentiates freedom from servitude is not that in the former there is no compulsion—for wherever there is action there is compelling force—but that the compulsion comes from within, in the sense of being imposed by the higher on the lower self.

Now, if compulsion from within, in this sense of the phrase, is to become possible, we must try to diminish the deadening pressure of compulsion from without. So one instinctively argues; and if due stress is laid on the word *deadening*, the argument is sound. But it is a mistake to suppose that compulsion from without can be dispensed with or that its pressure is necessarily

deadening. The popular belief that freedom means
release from all external constraint is a dangerous delusion. The individual develops himself by resistance, as
well as by response, to the pressure of his environment;
and if that pressure were withdrawn he would cease to
develop himself and his life would cease to expand.
Nay, in the last resort, he would cease to live; for reaction to pressure is of the very essence of life. It is only
when the pressure is mechanical rather than vital, when
the source of it is outside the will and the desire of its
victim, when reaction against it is difficult if not impossible, when its impress is therefore as deep and
lasting as that of the potter's hand on the clay that he
handles—it is only then that discipline deadens and
freedom disappears. But disciplinary pressure of this
—the Prussian—type is a misapplication of the formative
forces of Nature. The true relation between the individual and his environment is more than geometrical
and other than mechanical. The environment centres
in and acts on the individual; but the individual, if,
and so far as, he can react to his environment, goes out
into it and interpenetrates it and assimilates it to himself. And the relation between the two is reciprocal.
The pressure from within which we call self-discipline,
and which we may with equal propriety call freedom,
is pressure from without, co-ordinated and organised and
vitalised by the personal medium through which it passes.

But how is this change effected? How does pressure
from without transform itself into pressure from within?
Through the social or communal instinct of the individual, is an answer to this question which, though
obviously inadequate, is correct as far as it goes, and is
therefore sufficient for my present purpose. It is because
the individual tends to identify himself with the community that the pressure of the community on his

personality tends to transform itself into pressure of his higher on his lower self. But if his communal instinct is to have fair play, if the disciplinary pressure to which he is subjected by the community is to be transformed by him into self-discipline, that pressure must, as far as possible, be indirect rather than direct, informal rather than formal, suggestive rather than coercive, held in reserve rather than exerted to the full. In other words, it must be exerted by the community as a whole rather than by a ruling caste of officers and officials. It is true that officers and officials, as executants of the will of the community, cannot be dispensed with. But it is also true that the less the pressure of the community on the individual is controlled and directed by them—in the interest, perhaps (for this often happens), of their own self-love and self-will—and the more it emanates, like a subtle exhalation, from the community as a whole, the less likely it is to awake resentment and opposition in the individual, and the more likely it is to immingle itself with his buried or subconscious life, to appeal to his latent spirit of comradeship and sense of corporate unity, and thus to transform itself into pressure from within. It follows that the community in which the discipline of drill and the discipline of prohibition exert the minimum of pressure will be most favourable to the development of the discipline of freedom and self-control. The size of the community, let me say in passing, is a matter of minor importance. The community may be a great nation or it may be a small school.

If we are to compare the merits of the three types of discipline, we must ask ourselves which of them best serves the end—the supreme end—to which discipline is the appointed means. That end is an inward end, the edification and consequent well-being of the human spirit. But an inward end, which is necessarily elusive and incalculable, expresses itself in outward ends; and the well-being of the human spirit expresses itself in the well-being of the community, in social happiness and social order.

The value of discipline, then, is determined by its bearing on morality and, through morality, on social life. The immediate purpose of discipline is to generate order; and discipline is good or bad according as the order that it generates is social or the reverse. The discipline of compulsion makes for military order, for the organisation of a community as a machine under the control of one dominant will. For its own purpose this type of discipline may be highly effective; but as its avowed aim is to mechanicalise life both in the community and in the individual, it is obvious that if it were forcibly applied to a civil community it would speedily strangle its social life. The discipline of repression is supposed to produce social order; but the prevalence in all civilised countries of crime, misery, social injustice, and social discontent proves conclusively that repression alone cannot vitalise a community and that the semblance of order is quite compatible with social disorder, and even with social decay. From the social point of view, then, the first type of discipline is mischievous, and the second is largely ineffective. What of the third? I claim that self-discipline, or the discipline of freedom, fosters the growth of social feeling and of self-control, and so makes the best possible provision for the outgrowth of a healthy social life.

That this estimate of the respective merits of the three types of discipline is fairly correct, is proved, as it seems to me, by what is now happening in this country and in Germany. In this country the discipline of compulsion and the discipline of repression exert their minimum—in Germany, their maximum of pressure. In this country crime has decreased to a remarkable extent since the war began. In Oldham, for example, an English industrial centre which has a population of more than 150,000 and is not supposed to be the most refined and civilised of English towns, there was not a single case for trial at the Quarter Sessions which were held there at the beginning of this year. In Germany, on the contrary, crime has increased to an extent which has alarmed the authorities and given rise to serious comments in the more responsible newspapers. The following paragraph appeared in a recent issue of the "official" *Cologne Gazette*:

Crime has increased among young people—in the industrial districts particularly—to a really alarming extent. In the case of one single local tribunal the number of sentences passed on young men, as well as young women, rose from 58 in 1913 to 183 in 1914, and to 254 during the first ten months of 1915. Among the offences, fraud, robbery with violence, attempts at murder, and actual manslaughter figure very largely, the youngest offenders being from sixteen to twenty years of age, while none of them was older than twenty-six. It is a truly terrifying picture which casts a deep stain on German Kultur.[1]

In order to realise the full significance of these figures we must remind ourselves that before the war broke out crimes of violence in Germany had been appallingly numerous and the ratio of juvenile criminality had been abnormally high; and that since the war broke out the number of young men in that particular district must have been greatly reduced by death in battle and absence at the Front.[2]

[1] This is no isolated indictment of German crime and immorality by a German newspaper. See Dr. Arthur Shadwell's article, "Victory and the Alternative" in the *Nineteenth Century and After*, February 1916, p. 283.

[2] The recent increase in juvenile delinquency in this country—the delinquents being mostly boys of twelve and thirteen—is, I need hardly say, an entirely different thing from the increase in serious crime in Germany, among young persons between the ages of sixteen and twenty-six, which has taken place since the war began.

This lurid picture of the demoralisation of the most strictly disciplined of all peoples sets one thinking. From the facts and figures which the *Cologne Gazette* has recorded the inference is unavoidable that neither the discipline of compulsion nor the discipline of repression can moralise or socialise mankind, and therefore that if salvation is to be achieved by discipline it must be by the third type of discipline—self-discipline, the discipline of freedom, the discipline of self-control.

If this is so the question arises: Can self-discipline be begun at too early an age? I do not think it can. I think that from their very tenderest years such a measure of freedom should be given to children as would make it possible for them to begin to discipline themselves. I think that it has been our cardinal mistake, as educators, to impose on the young during the periods of childhood and adolescence the discipline of compulsion and the discipline of repression (especially the latter), to the exclusion of other formative influences, and then expect them to impose on themselves the discipline of self-control. And I think, further, that no small part of what is unsatisfactory in our social life, that much of the prevailing disorder and discontent, that many of our acute social maladies are due to the inability — the sheer inability — of those who have been forcibly disciplined for the first fifteen or twenty years of their existence, to take themselves in hand at a moment's notice, and control their own anti-social desires and impulses, and regulate their own lives.

But can we give freedom to children; and, if so, in what way and to what extent? I have said that the essence of freedom is compulsion from within, and that compulsion from within is really pressure from without — in particular, the gentle pressure exercised by a community as a whole on each of its members—co-ordinated and organised and vitalised by the personal medium through which it passes. The question now arises, Is it possible for freedom, in this sense of the word, to be enjoyed by children? Is it possible for them to have a communal life of their own—a communal life which has not been imposed on them by any autocratic authority, but which they have spontaneously evolved for themselves? For unless they can evolve such a life, it is a dangerously rash experiment to give them freedom. The answer to this question is that the social instinct is strong in children, and that if they are provided with suitable occupations and interests and allowed to lead a communal life they instinctively form themselves into happy communities, which are self-governing, in some sort and some degree, without possessing any machinery of government. The experiment of giving freedom to children has seldom been tried, and when tried has not always been successful. Where it has failed, the cause of failure has been the teacher's inability to efface himself, which has resulted in his dominating the social life of the children, in the sense of making it centre in himself, with the further result that he has taken back with one hand what he has given with the other. As far as my experience goes, those who have been successful in giving freedom to children have so given it as to provide for the outgrowth of a communal life in the given school or class. To this rule I know of no exception. It is safe to give children as much freedom as will allow of the outgrowth of a communal life; for that life, as it grows out, furnishes the necessary safeguards against the abuse of freedom, by applying to each child in turn a steady pressure, which, when responded to by him, and subjected to some quasi-chemical process in his inner being, transforms itself, through his readiness to identify himself with the community, into sympathy and self-control.

I have seen this transformation take place again and again, in schools and classes for older children, and in Montessori classes for infants. One of the great merits of the Montessori system, as it seems to me, is that by giving the child freedom of choice, so far as his occupations are concerned, it exposes him to social influences and social trials. For the Montessori apparatus is not dealt out to the children. When the time comes for it to be used, the children go to the cupboards, and each child takes out whatever he wishes to occupy himself with. Does not this give rise to squabbling and general disorder? There are never more than three or four replicas of any item in the apparatus; and there is no reason why ten or twelve children should not have set their hearts on the same item. What would happen in such a case? Would there not be a general scramble for possession? Would not the older and stronger children lay violent hands on what they wanted? And would not the younger and weaker children have to go to the wall? Experience has proved that this is not what happens. In response to the social pressure which a communal life, when they are allowed to lead it, exercises on children, the Montessori child speedily learns the greatest of all social lessons—learns that he must let live as well as live; and as his will has been duly developed by the freedom of choice which has been given him, he finds no difficulty in practising the amount of self-control that is needed for the application of that lesson. On this point my own testimony, though based on a fairly wide and varied experience, might be regarded with suspicion. So I will call into court an unprejudiced witness, whose words will, I think, carry weight. Professor Earl Barnes, whose work among the teachers of

London is still remembered, having visited Miss George's Montessori school in America, has set forth his impressions of it in the following words:

I knew that in the school they [the children] were given every opportunity to express themselves freely, to show and develop their individual tendencies. I was sure, therefore, that I would see evidence of egotism, selfishness, and rudeness; that there would be children idling, disturbing each other, and being disorderly. I knew it had to be so, because that is the way children are in the aggregate when left to themselves in the ordinary school. I have seen thousands of schools, and I have never known an exception until to-day; but this is the miracle I have now seen. In a room where fourteen [1] children were free to occupy themselves as they pleased, where there was no formal order for order's sake, there was absolutely no disorder. During the whole morning there was no exhibition of selfishness, or temper, or egotism; no idling. A child crossing the room would pause to look at what another was doing as an older person might without interfering. I did not see any one child strike another or push another. What was perhaps more remarkable was that there was among those children, free to do as they pleased, no idling. They were all voluntarily busily engaged in self-chosen occupations. Dr. Montessori has brought to us a re-interpretation of the whole educational process.

Dr. Montessori has done more than bring us a re-interpretation of the whole educational process. She has also brought us a re-interpretation of human nature. What Professor Earl Barnes saw was no miracle. It was a natural phenomenon, the product of natural forces which had been allowed—for once—to have their way. Man is by nature a social being; and when children who have been encouraged to follow their social instincts begin to control their self-seeking impulses and become unselfish and sympathetic, they are obeying the dictates of their nature as surely as when they eat and drink.

[1] Had there been forty, or even fifty, children, instead of fourteen the same " miracle " would have happened. The larger the Montessori class (within reasonable limits) the busier and the happier is the community.

The state of things which Professor Earl Barnes thought miraculous ought to be the universal rule. If school-children, when left to themselves, are rude, selfish, idle, and disorderly, the fault is ours—for we deliberately de-socialise their lives—not theirs.

Some day or other we shall begin to realise that social reform, for which we are all waiting, is to be achieved, not so much by legislation as by the transformation of character; and that the transformation of character, which is another name for the evolution of character, must begin in the nursery and the schoolroom. When that day comes we shall look back with gratitude to the great pioneers who, inspired by faith in the child's latent capacity for good, taught us how best to give freedom to children, young and old—such a measure of freedom, duly arranged for and safeguarded, as would provide for the outgrowth on the one hand of independence, self-reliance, and self-control, and, on the other hand, of sympathy and good-fellowship, and would thus make it possible for the child, in all the stages of his development, to discipline, and moralise, and socialise himself.

July 1916.

DRUDGERY AND EDUCATION

A DEFENCE OF MONTESSORI IDEALS

A NEW and revolutionary system, such as that which
Madame Montessori has worked out in the sphere of
education—a system which goes deep into life and
covers a large surface of life—is bound to become the
target of much unfair, irrelevant, and unintelligent criticism. For the world into which it comes has long been
dominated by certain ideals and standards; and the new
system must expect to be judged by reference to these,
and to be accepted or rejected according as it conforms
or fails to conform to them. But as its own *raison d'être*
is to protest against the validity of those ideals and
standards, the criticism to which it will be exposed will
be an elaborate begging of the question, and the arguments advanced by its detractors will be as illogical as,
though possibly less effective than, the mediæval arguments—familiar to the students of religious controversy
—of the rack and the stake.

The world into which the Montessori system has
come has been dominated for more than a thousand
years by one fundamental principle—distrust of human
nature. As the mainspring of the Montessori system
is trust in human nature, it is obvious that the old order
of things will not easily come to an understanding with
the new. Official Christianity teaches, as one of its
fundamental doctrines,

original sin,
The corruption of man's heart.

It also teaches, in the doctrines of the Incarnation and
the Holy Spirit, the potential divinity of man. But

whereas the doctrine of Original Sin has been taken very seriously, the antidotal doctrines—with the immense demands which they make on human nature and the immense responsibilities which they lay on it—have as a rule either been ignored or turned over to the theologians to deal with. It is possible that the explanation of this mystery is to be found in the spiritual indolence, the instinctive resistance to the expansive forces of Nature, which is man's besetting weakness, and which may conceivably have its equivalents in other grades of life. But that is a question which I must not allow myself to discuss.

The religious or quasi-religious distrust of human nature which has resulted from the acceptance by the average man of the doctrine of original sin and his tacit rejection of its sublime antidotes found, and still finds, its secular counterpart in feudal contempt for the mass of Humanity. Feudalism, as a political system, has long since passed away, but as a scheme of life it still dominates in greater or less degree the world in which we live. The delegation in feudal times of political power and administrative responsibility by a supreme over-landlord to his tenants and sub-tenants, led to the permanent association of power and position with property —first with landed property, and then with property in general. The consequent political disfranchisement and social degradation of the landless and unpropertied masses generated in the upper classes a sense of mental and moral, as well as of social and economic, superiority to the lower, an attitude—alternately arrogant and condescending—which still persists, and which, as the lower orders form by far the larger part of every community, readily translates itself into a radical underestimate of human character and capacity, exceptions of course being made in the secular, as in the religious, world in favour of the elect. Allying itself with the traditional belief in man's congenital depravity, and descending from stratum to stratum of the social pyramid, this quasi-feudal feeling has gone far towards determining and, though no longer at the zenith of its influence, still helps to determine, our whole attitude towards life.

As is our attitude towards life, so will be our attitude towards education. In a feudalised society we must expect the school to be the first and last stronghold of feudalism. The child being comparatively helpless and ignorant, those who are responsible for his education naturally adopt a despotic, dogmatic attitude towards him, which readily harmonises with the prevailing distrust of human nature and underestimate of human character and capacity. Hence the tendency, which has long characterised education, both in the home and in the school, to regard the child as a potential rebel and criminal, and also as perversely stupid, and to deal with him accordingly. It is true that the rigour of this attitude is being gradually relaxed; but even where it has been abandoned in theory, its practical influence is still very strong. There is still a widespread belief—a belief which is by no means groundless, though the explanation of it is not that which is usually given—that education is, and ought to be, repugnant to the child, and that he must therefore be drilled and coerced into accepting it. The cane, the birch, the tawse, the imposition, and other instruments of punishment, the use of which is by no means extinct, bear witness to the teacher's conviction that he has to work against the grain of the child's nature. So do prizes, merit marks, class lists, and other instruments of bribery and corruption, by which the teacher tries to rouse the child to intellectual exertion. That the child does not take kindly to education, that he dislikes lessons, that mental work is drudgery to him, that the end of the term, or even of the daily session is a happy release, is the fundamental postulate on which the orthodox system of education in this, if not in other countries, has long been based.

To those who are so well accustomed to this state of things that they have come to regard it as of divine dispensation, the sight of a class of children who are heartily enjoying their lessons, and seem to be thoroughly happy in their school life—in school as well as out of school—must be disconcerting in no small degree. The feeling that children ought not to be happy in their school life, that they ought, for their own sakes, to be working against the grain of their natures, is strong amongst the men and women—especially the women—of my own generation. When I describe the Montessori system to my friends and tell them how happy the children are who are working under it, I am often met with the rejoinder—made in perfect good faith and without any suspicion of its savouring of paradox—" Oh, but isn't that a bad preparation for the drudgery of life ? " I have lately come into possession of a pamphlet issued under the auspices of the " Duty and Discipline Movement." The name of the pamphlet is *Anarchy*; it belongs to what is called the " Patriot Series "; and the writer is a Mrs. Colvill. I have not yet succeeded in discovering what the leaders of the " Duty and Discipline Movement " mean by the words *Duty* and *Discipline*: but I have reason to think that some of their supporters regard the " movement " as a buttress to the tottering fabric of Feudalism; that the " Duty " which they have in mind is the duty of the lower classes, as they call them, to order themselves lowly and reverently to all their betters; and that the " Discipline " which they have in mind is the coercion of the lower classes by the upper, and in general of the weak by the strong. To such persons any serious departure from feudal ideals and the feudal scheme of life is anarchy. Mrs. Colvill seems to be one of these. At the beginning of her pamphlet she tells us that one day she caught herself saying to a friend of hers, " England is going downhill; going to destruction like the Gadarene swine. You and I see the beginning of the end; our children will be in at the death." An unfortunate prophecy this, to which the events of the past two years have given the lie direct. The spirit in which this country is waging the greatest of all wars is not that of a dying people; and our army in France and elsewhere—an army of millions drawn from all classes of the community, including that class which Mrs. Colvill, in characteristically feudal fashion, speaks of as " the dregs of the population "—can scarcely be described as a herd of Gadarene swine. But I have no doubt that many of the supporters of the " Duty and Discipline Movement " think, as Mrs. Colvill seems to do, that from impatience of swaddling clothes to desire to dance the *carmagnole* there is but a single step.

That a writer who takes this reactionary view of life should see in the introduction of the Montessori system into this country one of the signs of our decadence and approaching downfall, is what we have every right to expect. Mrs. Colvill tells us that Madame Montessori has announced her intention of reforming education from the children's point of view; and as the words " from the children's point of view " are printed in italics, one knows, without going further, what is the writer's own attitude towards education. Her comments on the Montessori system are for the most part meant to be jocular, and are scarcely worth quoting. But towards the end of her discourse she becomes serious, and delivers herself of the following criticism:

Seriously, in all this new system I question whether unwilling children ever really gain the power of doing something they don't want to do, of learning something they don't want to learn. This power can be gained; for instance, I mastered the Scales—with pain and grief, I admit—but their early conquest, quite apart from its benefit to my future playing, became an object-lesson to me for all my life. If the children don't learn to do the things they don't want to—and incidentally to submit themselves to their betters—what will their subsequent lives be? The good, the intelligent, ones will no doubt grow up reasonable and disciplined, though I should expect even these to be "soft." But what about the children who are naturally insubordinate, mischievous, dull, perverse, perhaps vicious? I think they will end as they have begun—Anarchists.

Here we have the familiar drudgery argument, emphasised, elaborated, and extended. The Montessori system, which gives children freedom for development, and encourages self-help and self-reliance, is a bad preparation for the drudgery of life; and the Montessori school, in which the children are admittedly busy, happy, and well-behaved, is a training-ground for Anarchists.

What is the value of the arguments which lead to this paradoxical conclusion? And to begin with, What is drudgery? To drudge is to do monotonous, laborious, and distasteful work. This will, I think, be generally admitted. But what do we mean by *distasteful*? Is drudgery distasteful because it is monotonous and laborious? Or must some other element be added to it if it is to rise—or sink—to the level of true drudgery? That monotonous and laborious work is distasteful to the old Adam—"the natural man," as we miscall it—may perhaps be admitted. But what is distasteful to the old Adam is not necessarily distasteful to the new. The work of rescuing imprisoned miners in a coal-pit is monotonous and laborious in a high degree; but not one of the rescuers would call it drudgery. The end, the saving of their comrades from death, sanctifies and transfigures the means; and the rescuers, one and all, throw themselves into the work of rescue with all their heart and with all their will. If monotonous and laborious work is to be worthy of the name of drudgery, another element must be added to it. The work must be done under compulsion from without. The galley-slave in bygone days was a drudge, in the true sense of the word. His work was monotonous, laborious, and distasteful; but an overseer, armed with a whip, stood near him and compelled him to ply the oar, the slightest relaxation of effort being visited with the lash. Yet rowing hard, even for hours at a stretch, is not necessarily drudgery. When the galley which carried the message of reprieve to the condemned men of Mitylene was racing against time, it is probable that even the slaves who manned it, inspired by the occasion, did more than was required of them, and did not count their toil as drudgery. And it would be an insult to the athletes who train for the University Boat-race, through weeks of toilsome practice, to speak of them as drudges.

But we have not yet fathomed the lowest depth of drudgery. The work done may be monotonous, laborious, distasteful to the average man, and compulsory, but so long as it serves a useful end, so long as the drudge can see a meaning in it, his cup of bitterness has not been filled to the brim. But let the work be meaningless, or even seem to be meaningless, and the last drop—bitter with the bitterness of poison—will have been added to the cup, and the martyrdom of the drudge will be complete. The Russian novelist Dostoieffsky, in his book on convict life in Siberia, has truly said that the most terrible punishment which could be inflicted on a human being—a punishment from the prospect of which even the most hardened criminal would shrink with horror — would be that of compelling him, day after day, to do useless and meaningless work, such work, for example, as that of digging a pit to-day and filling it up to-morrow.

If, then, monotonous, laborious, and distasteful work is to be accounted drudgery, in the fullest and strictest sense of the word, it must be done under compulsion, and must either be intrinsically useless and meaningless, or must seem so to the worker. These two features are closely allied, as closely as are will and reason; and together they constitute the differential element in drudgery. When they are absent, drudgery rises to the level of ordinary work. Now it is highly desirable that drudgery should, as far as possible, be transformed into ordinary work. The life of drudgery is not the ideal life. To do monotonous, laborious, and distasteful work under compulsion, and without seeing a meaning in what one does, is not the best possible way of passing one's time. On the contrary, it is a bad way, bad for the worker, and bad for the work that has to be done. On this point all the critics of the Montessori system, including— I venture to hope—Mrs. Colvill, will agree with me. But if I am right, if the life of drudgery, in the strict sense of the word,—the life of a galley-slave, for example, or of the convict who takes exercise on the treadmill— is at best an unsatisfactory life, then two things are clear. *The best possible preparation for the workaday life of the adult*—I will not say for the drudgery of life, for that phrase begs the question—*is that which gives the worker the power of transforming drudgery into ordinary work. And the worst possible preparation is that which leads the worker to regard all work as drudgery.*

That being so, let us ask ourselves what preparation for the drudgery of life, if we are to continue to use the phrase, was made by education in its pre-Montessori days.[1] I do not think I am exaggerating when I say that it was the fixed aim of the educator to make his pupils regard all work as drudgery. Take what subject you will, and call to mind how it was taught. Was it Writing? The child filled whole copy-books with strokes and pot-hooks and hangers before he was allowed to form a single letter. Was it Reading? The child began by learning the alphabet, and was then launched on a course of a–b, *ab*. Was it Arithmetic? He began with rules and tables and abstract numbers. Was it Geography? He began with definitions, and went on to lists of capes and bays, of countries and towns. Was it a Language? He began with declensions, conjugations, and vocabularies. Was it Music? Her life—for the pupil was probably a girl—was made a burden to her with what an admirer of the old régime calls " beastly scales." Was it Drawing? In our Infant Schools, at any rate, the child began by drawing straight lines, followed by arbitrary arrangements of straight lines, and went on to simple curves, followed by arbitrary arrangements of curves. Was it Woodwork? The boys in our handicraft centres spent weeks in planing and weeks in chiselling before they were allowed to do any constructive work. And so on. And so on.

It was through this dreary portico that the child was supposed to be ushered into the hall of learning. Can we blame him if, after a long sojourn in the portico, he lost himself in its gloomy corridors, and thenceforth could see nothing but meaningless monotony wherever he looked? No appeal was made to his reason. No appeal was made to his will, except indeed

[1] By pre-Montessori days, I mean the days before Montessori ideals began to impregnate the atmosphere of education. There were Montessori teachers — teachers whose aims and methods were dominated by Montessori ideals—long before we first heard of Madame Montessori.

the brutal appeal of " Do what I tell you or take the consequences." No attempt was made to consult his tastes and inclinations. No attempt was made to discover his latent capacities. No attempt was made to interest him in what he did. The work which he was set to do was drudgery in the fullest sense of the word. It was monotonous. It was laborious while it lasted. It was compulsory. And, as far as he could see, it was meaningless. No wonder that if he was vivacious and high-spirited he rebelled against its deadening pressure, and sought refuge from it in pranks and escapades of his own contriving. And no wonder, let me say in passing, that his pastors and masters, obsessed as they were with the idea of the congenital depravity of human nature, attributed the child's reluctance to learn to the old Adam of naughtiness in him, instead of to the old Adam of ignorance and stupidity in themselves.

But the child was at least compelled to drudge, and so formed the habit of drudgery, a habit which stood him in good stead in after-life. So it will be said. But did the habit stand him in good stead in after-life? What of the vivacious and high-spirited rebels whose spirit of rebellion survived the pranks and escapades of childhood and lived on into adolescence and manhood? What of the many children, including some of the brightest and most vigorous, who, when they grew up, were swept away by the impetus of their instinctive protest against senseless drudgery into paths of lawless activity in which they lost themselves and came hopelessly to grief?

It is true that some of the rebels sought out paths of useful activity for themselves, and did good and even original work on lines of their own. It is also true that a few of them, men of the type of Robert Clive and Captain Cook, when they went out into the world, found appropriate spheres for great talents which their education had failed to discover and done its best to repress, and so were able to " ride with the great adventurers." The old régime may, if it pleases, take credit to itself for these successes; but in doing so it will pronounce its own doom, for the system of education is manifestly unsound which does its highest work and produces its best results by provoking a fierce reaction against itself.

And what of those—perhaps a more numerous class than the foregoing—who got into the way of regarding work as drudgery, and, in their not unnatural recoil from the latter, became work-shy for the rest of their lives？

And what of the majority？ What of the milder, more submissive, less vigorous, less imaginative, less reactive victims of the old type of education who yielded to its pressure, and settled down to a life of dull routine？ Were they the better for having learnt to regard all work as drudgery, and yet, under the numbing influence of a compulsorily-formed habit, resigned themselves to drudge？ Were they the better for having been forcibly disciplined into drudgery instead of having been encouraged to discipline themselves？

Here we come to the parting of the ways, to the point at which the new régime diverges from the old. It is right that children should learn to do work which is monotonous and laborious and even distasteful to the natural man. Let this be freely admitted. They will have to do such work when they grow up, and it is right that their education should prepare them for their adult life. But are they to be constrained to drudge—if I may continue to use that word " without prejudice "—or are they to constrain themselves？ Need we be at a loss for an answer to this question？ Is it not an accepted principle—accepted in theory even by those who flout it in practice—that if a child is to do a thing well, he must learn to do it for himself? Let us apply this principle to the problem that faces us. If the child is to drudge well —and to drudge well means to transform drudgery into ordinary work—he must discover for himself the meaning and value of drudgery, and so, when the need for drudgery arises, must be willing and able to impose it on himself.

But how is this to be done? The first thing to do is to let the child see the meaning of what he is doing. In demanding blind faith and mechanical obedience from children we are overstraining human nature. And we are asking for what is of no value. Faith is less than faith if it is blind; and obedience is less than obedience if it is mechanical. It is only by forcible measures, by threats and punishments, that we can secure such faith and such obedience; and what is given in response to force is a tax, an exaction, not a gift. Nature has endowed the child with reason. The desire to understand, to see the meaning and purpose of things, is strong in his soul. Let the teacher appeal to his reason rather than to his fears. In doing so he will inaugurate an alliance between himself and the child which will probably be fruitful to both. But if the child's reason is to come into play, if he is to see a meaning in what he is doing, his work must be related to some desirable end. And the child must see for himself that the end is desirable. In other words, it must be an object, or capable of becoming an object, of his own desire. We cannot expect him to take a far-sighted view of things. We cannot expect him, for example, to realise that something which he is asked to do now and which he dislikes doing will be useful to him when he grows up. We may tell him this, but it will produce no impression on him, for we are asking him to look too far ahead. We must set before him ends which appeal to him now, and then trust him, under our guidance, to take the appropriate means, at whatever cost to himself.

One or two examples will help me to explain what I mean. In a magazine called *Science Progress* I recently came across the following paragraph, written by Mr. Usherwood, teacher of handwork at Christ's Hospital:

> Woodwork is commenced. Not that formal woodwork which has been condemned because it demands the expenditure of much time on mere " exercises," and through reliance on established schemes has degenerated into mere formal routine work; but of a freer, less restricted type which appeals to the boy's innate tendencies to construct and to manipulate, and leads naturally—through the actual manufacture of models which do not require much refinement, much detail—to recognition of the reasons underlying this and that formal method, of the steps which led to the invention of certain tools, and their importance.

Here we have the teacher setting a desirable end before the pupil, and the pupil responding by recognising for himself the necessity for drudgery if skill is to be acquired and the end achieved. And we may be sure that the pupil, intent on acquiring skill, would drudge away contentedly without knowing that he was drudging; in other words, would see in the exercises which he had to go through, not drudgery, as the word is usually understood, but obviously useful, even though laborious, work. It is the same with the practice of " beastly scales." The writer of an interesting paper on the teaching of music says that " the dull mechanical practice of scales, arpeggi, and five-finger exercises is the deadliest impediment to progress ever devised by the conscientious teacher." But scales are not necessarily "beastly." The pupils of Dr. Yorke Trotter, the well-known teacher of music, who are encouraged to express themselves freely, and even to do original composition from a very early age, practise their scales (within reasonable limits) with due diligence, but, strange to say, do not find them " beastly "; for they instinctively realise that without such practice they will not be able to go far along the path of self-expression.

These examples are typical. They prove conclusively that drudgery ceases to be drudgery when it is seen to be the means to a desirable end. Shakespeare, who went to the root of most matters, went to the root of one of the most vital of educational problems when he wrote:

> No profit grows where is no pleasure ta'en:
> In brief, Sir, study what you most affect.

We need not say to the child, " Study what you most affect, and that only." But we ought to encourage every child to study what he most affects—to study it, not to dally with it. For in studying a subject which attracts him the child will find himself pursuing congenial ends, and will be under the necessity, if he is to compass those ends, of devising the appropriate means. In this way he will get an insight into the heart of his subject, will be able to profit by and assimilate the experience of those who have studied before him and studied more deeply than he has, and will see a meaning in and realise the necessity for the laborious and even monotonous work by which skill is to be acquired and difficulties overcome. And having once learnt this lesson—having learnt for himself what study means and what it involves —he will be able to apply it, if he is judiciously handled, when the time comes for him to give his mind to other subjects.

Now one of the great merits of the Montessori system is that it does for the very young child what Dr. Yorke Trotter and the Christ's Hospital teacher of woodwork do for older children and adolescents—it coaxes him into many paths of self-development, and leaves him free,

within certain limits, to study what he most affects.
And the result of this is that, in response to the teacher's
trust in him, the Montessori infant drudges away at
what he takes in hand, and finds happiness and even
joy in doing so. Two years ago, when I was in the
North of England, I visited a school in which one of
the classes did Montessori work for one hour a day;
and a little girl was pointed out to me who, having
mastered the difficulty of tying a bow, had tied and untied
bows without a break for nearly a week. She wanted to
perfect the skill which she had acquired, and of her
own accord did what another child would have accounted
drudgery—and did it day after day for nearly an hour
at a time. So too Madame Montessori tells us of a little
girl of three who was so deeply absorbed in the work
of placing wooden blocks and cylinders in a frame, that
though she was moved—arm-chair, frame, blocks, cylinders and all—from the floor on to a large table, and though
the rest of the children in the room were invited to sing,
she continued her work undisturbed, and did not pause
until she had repeated the set of exercises forty-four
times. This was laborious work for a child of three,
and it was highly monotonous, but it was not drudgery,
for it had a meaning for the child, and she did it of her
own accord. Like the Christ's Hospital boys when they
practise planing and chiselling, like Dr. Yorke Trotter's
pupils when they practise scales and other monotonous
exercises, these little children drudged without knowing
that they were drudging, and they thus transformed
drudgery into interesting and enjoyable work.

Another merit of the Montessori system as a preparation for adult life, is that it encourages activity
and perseverance, whereas the ordinary Infant School,
through no fault of its teachers, discourages both. If
you will go into a large Infant School, as I happened

to do the other day, you will be struck by two things —the inactivity of the children during the greater part of the session, at any rate while the " 3 R's " are being taught, and the shortness of the lessons. A writing lesson is being given to forty children. Much time is spent in giving out copy-books at the beginning of the lesson and collecting them at the end. The teacher writes a letter or word on the blackboard and talks to the children about it. The children copy it. The teacher goes round and looks at the exercise-books, and comments on what the children have done. This occupies some minutes, during which the children sit still. Then the teacher writes another letter or word, and the same performance is repeated. As the lesson must not last more than from fifteen to twenty-five minutes, for fear of over-tiring the more delicate members of the class and overboring the rest, the order to close copy-books is given long before the children have really got into their stride. It is the same, *mutatis mutandis*, when Reading or Arithmetic is being taught. What is the value of such a lesson? I have elsewhere told of the little boy who, after his first morning in a kindergarten class, said to his parents when he got home that his time in school had been all interruptions. Forced inactivity during the greater part of the lesson, and then forcible interruption of the children's efforts at the end of some twenty minutes or so—is that the best possible preparation for the work of life? Do not blame the teachers for these follies. Blame the system under which they have to work. If young children are to be taught in large classes, if all the children in a class are to do the same work at the same time, if the teacher is to be the chief centre of activity, if she is to spend her time in issuing commands, giving instruction, and doling out information, if no regard is to be paid to the child's inclinations, if nothing is to be left to his choice, then short lessons, during the greater part of which the child does nothing, must needs be the order of the day. Contrast with this the free activity of the Montessori child and his freedom to persevere in what he is doing, and then ask yourselves which system of education makes the better preparation for the work, or, if you will, for the drudgery of life. The noise of a Montessori classroom has been happily likened to the hum of a busy hive. Who will be the better worker in the future, the child who is reared in a busy hive, or the child who spends much of his school life in sitting silent and still?

There is another aspect of the Montessori system which is perhaps the most important of all from our present point of view. Being allowed to have free intercourse with one another, even in school hours, the children in a Montessori class spontaneously develop a social or communal spirit, which cannot be expected to flourish in the schools of the orthodox type, where all eyes are fixed on the teacher and intercourse with one's neighbour is a punishable offence. Where this social spirit grows up, where the sense of belonging to a community and sharing its successes and failures is strong, the feeling that in doing one's own work well one is in some sort serving the community, comes into existence and, though not consciously realised by the children, becomes a real element, however subtle and volatile it may be, in the atmosphere of the school. The transforming influence of this feeling on the attitude of the child towards work cannot be overrated. When to pleasure in one's work is added the sense of service to the community, when the joy which is generated by unimpeded energy, or rather by the energy which triumphs over impediments, becomes a " joy in widest commonalty spread," the slowest and most backward member of the little community will be a willing worker, not a drudge. The Montessori infant is not too young to catch the infection of this happy spirit; but in schools for older children of the Montessori type, the sense of comradeship enhances, and even transfigures, the pleasure of doing congenial work, and the air is in consequence electrical with happiness and goodwill.

But that, it will be said, is precisely where the Montessori system breaks down. The child is actually happy in his school life. He is not working, as he ought to be, against the grain of his nature. Critics of Mrs. Colvill's school come back to this point again and again. What are we to make of the philosophy of education, or rather of the philosophy of life, which underlies their criticism? Is it a deadly sin to enjoy work, to enjoy the use of one's faculties, to enjoy overcoming difficulties, to enjoy doing what is right? When I was an undergraduate at Oxford I studied a certain history of philosophy in which I came across two doggerel couplets which have remained in my memory ever since. They were made in Germany in the days when the doctrine of the Moral Imperative was in the ascendant, and they are characteristically German in their pathetic loyalty to the demands of logic and their sublime indifference to the demands of right reason and common-sense. A disciple who is in trouble about his soul says to his master:

> Willing serve I my friend, but do it, alas! with affection;
> And so gnaws me my heart that I'm not virtuous yet.

To which the master replies:

> Help except this there is none: thou must strive with might
>   to contemn him,
> And with horror perform then what the law may enjoin.

To obey the moral law with horror of heart, to hate your neighbour in order that your service to him may count as righteousness—that is the high-water mark of virtue. To obey your teacher with horror of heart, to hate your work and yet to do it under compulsion—that is the proof of being a well-educated child. Is it really so? Is it of the essence of goodness to hate to do what is right? Is it of the essence of a sound education to make children hate work and then compel them to do it? When Mrs. Colvill hears that Montessori children put things in their places, enjoy washing, and are distressed (at their own awkwardness) if they upset chairs, she exclaims, " Good heavens! " She expects children to be naughty and troublesome. She even seems to wish them to be naughty and troublesome, so that she may be free to coerce them into reluctant submission. Then they will be well-educated. Then they will be well prepared for the battle of life. To provoke rebellion and, having provoked it, to deal with the youthful rebels as Prussia deals with her subject peoples, that is the educational ideal by reference to which Montessori ideals are judged and condemned. If the product of this feudal type of education had so strong a will that he could compel himself to do right even while he hated doing it, there might be something to be said for his up-bringing. But you do not strengthen the will by breaking it. On the contrary: what coercive education, when it achieves its end, does to the child is to substitute in his character the force of habit for the force of will. This is what Prussian discipline does to the perfectly dis-ciplined soldier; and Mrs. Colvill and her friends seem to have made Prussia their model in more ways than one. Mrs. Colvill expects the best products of the Montessori system to grow up " soft." The current confusion between " softness " and natural goodness, like the kindred confusion between high spirits and naughtiness, throws a lurid light on the type of education which has long passed as orthodox. Southey, in his poem *The Inchcape Rock*, says of Sir Ralph the Rover:

> His heart was mirthful to excess,
> But the Rover's mirth was wickedness.

Educators of the repressive school seem to think that when children are mirthful to excess, their mirth must needs be naughtiness. That is a profound mistake. Mirth, or high spirits, may become naughtiness if all natural outlets are closed against it. But I have visited schools in which, thanks to their being rationally and sympathetically educated, all the children were full of high spirits, and in those schools naughtiness was practically unknown.

In conclusion. The supreme merit of the Montessori system is that it is based, as I pointed out at the beginning of my paper, on trust in human nature. Some day or other the medical profession will, I hope and believe, take a serious interest in education. When it does, it will tell us, if I am not greatly mistaken, that the right education is that which vitalises, that the wrong education is that which lowers vitality, and that joy— which is another name for the sense of well-being—is at once the proof and the source of health of body and soul. Now nothing is so vitalising, so inspiring, one might almost say, as to be trusted. And nothing is so depressing as to be distrusted. This is as true of adults as of children. The education which is based on distrust of human nature, if carried out in practice to its logical conclusion, does undoubtedly enfold the child's life in an atmosphere of gloom. But to suppose that in doing so it fits the child to face the gloom of adult life is to make a fatal miscalculation. Just as the orthodox education, by teaching the child to regard all work as drudgery, gives him the worst possible preparation for the workaday world in which he will have to play his part, so, by making his childhood gloomy, it predisposes him to take a gloomy view of life, and therefore to carry gloom with him wherever he goes. The child who has been allowed to develop freely and naturally, and to lead a life of rational and happy activity, and whose consequent sense of well-being has been subconsciously realised by him as joy, will no doubt, when he grows up, have his full share of trials, troubles, disappointments, and sorrows. But he will neither anticipate these nor fear to face them. Why should he disquiet himself about them? He will wear an armour which is proof, in the last resort, against their slings and arrows. For there will be a song in his heart as he goes through life which will never die down into silence.

April 1917.

THE REAL BASIS OF DEMOCRACY

THERE are three chief types of Government: (1) Autocracy, or Government by one; (2) Oligarchy, or Government by a few; (3) Democracy, or Government by all. As the work of governing a country is the most important that a man can take in hand, as it demands the very highest qualities both of intellect and character, it is clear that in an ideal world the rulers, whether one or few or many, would be the very best men that could be found. When the King of Prussia, at his coronation, puts the crown on his own head, he implies that he is the best man in the land, that he is the chosen of God, that he is the supreme ruler by right as well as by might. So, too, in an oligarchically-governed country, when the ruling classes call themselves the aristocracy, they say in effect that the Government, which happens to be in their hands, is in the hands of the best. But what of democracy? We cannot all be the best; but there is no inherent reason why we should not all be equally good. If supreme merit in a ruler is the real—or ideal—basis of autocracy, if the superior merit of a ruling class or caste is the real basis of oligarchy, the real basis of democracy must be the fundamental equality of all the citizens in the State.

But are men fundamentally equal? Is it conceivable that they should ever be so? Is not society based on inequality, on a bewildering diversity of gifts, attainments, and achievements, on inequality in material possessions, in social position, in influence, in education, in learning, in culture, in mental ability, in aptitudes, in accomplishments, in moral qualities, in spiritual gifts? So some of my readers will protest; and I will say in reply that they have not overstated, and cannot possibly overstate, their case. In what sense, then, do I use the word equality? In the sense in which it is used by Christianity when it teaches us that all men are equal in the sight of God—equal because they have immortal souls to be lost or saved. The notation in which this teaching is set forth may not commend itself to all of us, but the psychology which underlies it is, I think, profoundly true. When we say that all men are equal in the sight of God, we mean, I imagine, that they are intrinsically equal, equal by reference to an absolute and infallible standard of worth. And they are intrinsically equal because they all have immortal souls to be lost or saved. What does this mean? It means, I imagine, that in each of us there are infinite potentialities waiting to be realised; that so far as we realise these we save our souls, in the sense of finding them; that so far as we neglect to realise them, we lose our souls, in the sense of failing to find them. By comparison with these infinite potentialities, the actual inequalities in which life abounds, and of which we make so much, shrink to zero, and men are seen to be fundamentally equal. And if men are fundamentally equal, the right to share in the government of the community to which one belongs, and to that extent to shape one's own destiny, to give effect to one's own ideals, to order one's own goings, is obviously inherent in the right to live one's own life and realise one's own soul.

How comes it, then, that the Christian doctrine of equality in the sight of God has counted for so little in the social and political life of Christendom? Chiefly, I think, because the unhappy distinction between what is religious and what is secular in life, between the Church

and the world—itself the outcome of the yet more fundamental distinction between the Supernatural and Nature
—has led us to think of the immortal soul as something
quite apart from the ordinary human being, something in
fact which belongs to another life and another world,
and to think of salvation—which for many centuries
meant, and for many minds still means, escape from
hell-fire—as an end to be achieved by almost any means
but that of living one's everyday life as a member of a
social community and a citizen of the world. And so
we have been content to say that men are equal in the
sight of God because of their immortal souls, and yet
to emphasise their " inherent and congenital inequality "
in all the things which really matter, and to base on this
supposed inequality our social and political systems and
the whole view of life which those systems at once
express and control. But if men are unequal, inherently
and congenitally unequal, in such matters as mind,
character, judgment, taste, manner, and so forth, what
is the value of that thing in respect of which they are
supposed to be equal—the immortal soul? If we are to
think of the immortal soul as a shadowy something, far
removed from our daily life, if the things which affect
its welfare are matters with which the Government of a
country need not seriously concern itself, shall we not
at last, as our daily life gains in interest and complexity,
cease to concern ourselves with the shadowy something and even come to regard it as non-existent?
Then the doctrine of inequality will have triumphed
both in theory and practice, and the doom of democracy
will have been pronounced.

But surely the immortal soul, if there is such a thing,
is not a shadowy something belonging to another life
and another world, but on the contrary the supreme
reality of this life and this world—the unity and totality

of the various aspects and manifestations of man's many-sided being. Surely it is this and even more than this. In our attempts to rehabilitate, or rather to resubstantiate the soul, we are faced by a difficult problem. If the soul is the unity and totality of man's being, how are we to reconcile our presumed equality in respect of it with our actual inequality in respect of mind, character and the other vital aspects of man's being? So far as I can see, there is but one solution of this problem—a solution which has already been provisionally suggested. The soul is something more than the unity and totality of man's being. It is also—and above all—its infinity. Life is self-realisation. Actually we are finite. Potentially we are infinite. We realise self in different directions and different degrees. In respect of these we are unequal. But we have limitless reserves of potentiality to draw upon; and in respect of this we are equal. And this equality, being rooted in the infinite, overpowers and effaces our inequalities, which are always measurable and finite. It is this principle of infinitude, and therefore of equality, in men which the great seers of the world have discerned and affirmed, and in affirming which they have boldly taught, not shrinking from the apparent paradox, that all men are equal in the sight of God.[1] Nor have they, in calling upon men to realise their august destiny, raised inequality itself, as some might think, to a higher power. Differences of achievement will always be finite and measurable; but in the supreme achievement, when the finite expands into the infinite, the category of the equal and unequal will be finally effaced. I mean by this that between the finite and the

---

[1] Nowhere in the range of literature is the inherent infinitude of the individual soul proclaimed with such sublime audacity as in Emily Brontë's magnificent couplet:

" The earth which wakens *one* human heart to feeling
Can centre both the worlds of Heaven and Hell."

infinite there is no such thing as equality or inequality —an arithmetical conception which holds good only of differences within the limits of the finite. If a man could realise his infinite potentialities and so find his true self, he would know that he was one, vitally and essentially one, with all his fellow-men. The idea of being greater or less than others would therefore have no meaning for him. That point of view, that way of looking at things, would have passed for ever out of his life.

I will now try to show that the principle of infinitude which we call the soul is no elusive phantom, but an inexhaustible fountain of potentiality, on which we are always drawing, and in realising which, as we take it up, little by little, into our conscious being, we carry on all but the purely physical processes of our life; a fountain from which spring unceasingly all the higher energies which are characteristic of man as man— thought, reason, judgment, insight, emotion, desire, wonder, aspiration, devotion, hope, faith, love; a fountain of latent capacity, latent versatility, latent power, latent character, latent will.

I will try to show that this theory of the soul holds good of what we call, for lack of a fitter phrase, the " average man." Let us first think of the average man as a new-born child. At a very early age the child will begin to talk. In what language will he express himself? That will entirely depend on where and by whom he is reared. He has it in him to speak a hundred different languages. A friend of mine has brought up an Italian child who was rescued, as a baby, from the earthquake of Messina. That child speaks English like a native. Had there been no earthquake, she would now be speaking an Italian *patois*. Had she been adopted by a Russian, she would be speaking Russian. By a Frenchman,

French. By a Chinaman, Chinese. By a Negro, a Negro dialect. In brief, she had a capacity for learning any language or any dialect that happened to be spoken by those who surrounded her. And so has every normal child. And as every language and every sub-language —*patois*, dialect, or even provincial accent—has behind it a particular way of thinking and feeling, a particular outlook on life, we may safely conjecture that every child has it in him at birth to adapt himself to as many ways of thinking and feeling, and to adopt as many outlooks on life, as there are languages and sub-languages in this world of ours.

As the child grows up, the choice of a vocation for him will devolve upon his parents or guardians. What will they do? Will they examine his pedigree in order to see for what calling his inherited tendencies have specially fitted him? No, they will look to his environment, past and present, rather than to his lineage. They will look to their own means, to the way in which he has been educated, to the opportunities for continuing his education, to the possibilities of his being trained for a profession, to the possibilities of his being apprenticed to a trade, to the local demand for labour, and other such matters; and they will make their choice for him by reference to these considerations, unless indeed he has some strongly pronounced inclination, of which they approve and which they are in a position to gratify. They will take for granted that if he is of average ability and is reasonably industrious, he will be able, sooner or later, to become proficient at almost any craft, or trade, or profession, for which his circumstances, including his education, past and prospective, have fitted him. They will take for granted that he has it in him to make himself at home in a multitude of different callings, and that it must in the main be left to circumstances to

determine which of these he is to adopt. It is true that
aptitudes vary. We cannot all do all things equally well.
There is no one who is not better fitted for some pursuits
than for others. But there is no one who cannot, if he
chooses, make himself tolerably proficient at any one of
a large number of different pursuits. And if the average
adolescent, in spite of the cramping pressure to which
he has, almost inevitably, been subjected, has it in him
to earn his livelihood in so many different ways, does it
not follow that his inherent adaptability is practically
unlimited—in other words, that he has practically unlimited reserves of potentiality to draw upon? Since
the present war began our army has expanded to ten
times its previous strength. How has this been done?
By men going into it out of a hundred different callings,
and learning what was a new trade for each of them, the
trade of war. But though some of these apprentices
were doubtless apter pupils than others, so well has the
average Englishman, of whatever class or calling, learnt
this new trade, that our vast army is now as efficient
as it is resolute and brave. What better proof could be
given of the inherent versatility of human nature, of the
infinite resourcefulness of the soul?

Let us now make an imaginative experiment. Let us
arrange for a hundred babies belonging to a certain
country—Germany if you will—to be born and reared
in ten foreign countries, ten in each—say in England,
France, Russia, Spain, Italy, Sweden, Holland, the
United States, the Argentine, Brazil. Let us divide the
inhabitants of each of these countries into ten social
grades—landowners, peasants, merchants, shopkeepers,
clerks, manufacturers, artisans, civil servants, professional men, ministers of religion. And let us arrange
in each country for the babies to be brought up in these
ten social grades, one in each. Above all, let us arrange,

in each case, for German influences to be excluded from the baby's life, if not from the day of its birth, then from as near to that date as possible. Let us then look forward some twenty or thirty years. What will have happened? Can anyone doubt that a large majority of the German babies will have become loyal citizens of their adopted countries and respectable members of their respective social grades? Some failures there will have been among them. But probably not a higher percentage than if they had belonged by birth to the various countries which I have specified, and been born into the social grades in which I have placed them. The chances are that each of them will have accepted the " Kultur " of his particular country and (whether nominally or really) the religion of his particular foster-parents, and will have adopted the prejudices and general outlook on life of his particular social grade.

Consider what this means. Each of the babies had it in him to play a hundred different parts, the part of an English squire, of a French artisan, of a Russian peasant, of an American manufacturer, of a Dutch merchant, of an Italian priest, of a Swedish official, and so on. What vast potential resources he must have had at his disposal! Which particular part he was to play was decided by what we call chance. But potentially he was equal to all the parts and to as many more as we might choose to assign to him. His adaptability in fine reflected that of the whole human race, and the range of his latent capacity had no limit.

In this respect, if in no other, man stands apart from all other living things. Even his friend and companion, the dog, who probably comes next to him in mental and moral development, is separated from him, as regards adaptability, by an impassable abyss. It is true that the dog family can play a great variety of parts. But this has been made possible, as anyone can see at a glance, only by very strict physical differentiation. Hence the supreme importance of breeding, from the dog-fancier's point of view. Vocation, among dogs, is handed down from father to son, not as a tradition, but as a tendency "in the blood." No amount of training could convert a Newfoundland puppy into a sheep-dog, or enable a bulldog to course hares. With man it is entirely different. In spite of the distinctions of colour, with all that they imply, and in spite of a host of minor variations in face or figure, there is but one dominant human type. And that one type, besides being able to adapt itself to all climates and to a vast range of material conditions, can take up an unlimited number of different interests and pursuits. The average baby has it in him, as we have seen, to speak a hundred languages, to belong to a hundred nations, to learn a hundred trades and professions, to play a hundred parts in life.

And the infinitude of the inheritance which he brings with him into the world is of many dimensions. The religious phenomenon known as " conversion," with the sudden transition which it sometimes effects from the very worst in a man to the very best; the winning of V.C.s and other rewards of courage and self-sacrifice by criminals and other " detrimentals " on the field of battle; the upsurging in seasons of supreme crisis of heroism and self-sacrifice from unsuspected abysses in some seemingly commonplace soul; the sudden melting of a hardened heart in the sunshine of sympathy and kindness; the transforming influence of the passion of personal love on a man's whole attitude towards life— these and other phenomena of a kindred nature, which though necessarily rare (for only exceptional combinations of circumstances can produce them) are not therefore to be regarded as abnormal, seem to show that the unfathomed depths of man's generic nature are as illimitable as its lateral range.

It is a wonder [writes one of our war correspondents] that never palls, but is always new: the spirit which these men of ours possess, from no matter what corner of the Empire they may have come. One wonders where the grumblers, the cowards, the mean people whom one thought one met in ordinary life, have gone. They are not here. Or, if they are, they are uplifted and transfigured. They doubtless, many of them, could not explain or express it, but some wind has blown upon them, the inspiration of a great cause has come into them, some sense of comradeship and brotherhood inspires them, something has made true soldiers and gallant men of them all.

The transfiguration of the " plain average man " which is described in this passage proves conclusively that there are immense reserves of spiritual vitality in his soul, and that though for the most part these forces lie dormant and undreamed of, they can awake and energise when some great crisis makes its mute appeal to the man's highest self.

What is the explanation of this fundamental paradox? Why is it that whereas on the physical plane our racial inheritance seems to be strictly limited, on the higher levels of our being infinitude seems to be of its very essence? The answer to this question may be given in a single word: *Consciousness*. What consciousness is, how we have acquired it, into what fundamental factors it admits of being analysed, we cannot say.[1] What we can say is that though foreshadowings and weak beginnings of it are to be found below the level of human life, consciousness is a distinctively human endowment, or rather it is *the* distinctively human endowment, the

[1] We may say, if we please, that consciousness is the self-awareness of the soul, or again, that it is the self-awareness of life. But no definition can enable us to fathom its fundamental mystery. If we would know what consciousness is we must turn for instruction to consciousness itself, and open our hearts and minds to its dawning light.

feature which, more than any other, differentiates us
from all other living things and is therefore characteristic of man as man. Now consciousness, by enabling
man to look before and after and also to look all round
an ever-widening horizon, throws open to him all the
resources of the Universe, and in doing so reveals to
him, or begins to reveal to him, corresponding resources
in himself. In other words, it raises, or tends to raise,
" to infinity " all his powers and tendencies which are
not merely physical. Thus it transforms instinct into
reason, blind purpose into self-determining will, feeling
into fellow-feeling, perception into imagination, sensuous
enjoyment into the quest of ideal beauty, carnal desire
into spiritual love, communal devotion into the " enthusiasm of humanity," the instinct of self-preservation
into the thirst for eternal life. In the awakening of
consciousness life begins to be aware of its own limitless
possibilities. Before consciousness awakes, the current
of life flows blindly and instinctively in a narrow channel,
between containing walls which it may never overpass.
As consciousness awakes, the channel begins to widen,
and a tidal wave flows up it fraught with

> murmurs and scents of the infinite sea.

I have said that the real basis of democracy is the
equality of all men in the sight of God. When we say
that men are equal in the sight of God, we mean that
there is an equalising element which dwarfs to nothing-
ness all the differences and distinctions to which we
cling so fondly. We can now see that this equalising
element—the infinite in man—is no metaphysical abstraction, no shadowy mystery, but an ever-present
reality, " closer " to us " than breathing," blinding us
to its presence by its very excess of light, the medium
in which and through which we live and move and have

our being, the source of all the energies, capacities, and activities which differentiate man from the rest of living things. If men are equal in this sense of the word, democracy, as a principle of government, is founded on a rock. For the right to share in the government of one's country means the right to control the environment in which a man lives and into which his children are born; and if every man, without regard to class or position or property or any other source of inequality, has unlimited reserves of potentiality in himself, and if the realisation of potentiality is effected through reaction to environment, the claim of the lowliest of men to regulate the affairs of the particular community to which he happens to belong is as strong as the claim of the mightiest.

But before we pronounce in favour of democracy, let us examine the title-deeds of the rival types of Government. If equality is the basis of democracy, supreme merit must be the basis of autocracy, and superior merit —in a class, or some other governing circle—of oligarchy. What, then, has autocracy to say for itself? Is there anyone to-day, except perhaps the German Emperor, who seriously believes in the divine right of hereditary monarchs? And may there not be moments when even he, the last champion of autocracy, begins to wonder whether supreme merit is always transmissible from father to son? But if it is not so transmissible, how is the succession in a line of autocrats to be provided for? Adoption gave the Roman Empire a sequence of wise and able rulers, but when Marcus Aurelius *chose* his *son* Commodus as his successor, his error of judgment, which was irretrievable, revealed the inherent weakness of both systems. Election would resolve itself into a contest between rival caucuses or juntas, and would end by placing a party nominee on the throne. If by some

divine chance there were a man in this or any other
country who was really qualified by wisdom and force
of character for autocratic rule, it would be impossible
to devise a system by which his supreme merit could
be recognised, and the crown placed on his brow. Moreover, if there were such a man, and if he could be
discovered and the crown offered to him, he would either
decline it or accept it temporarily and provisionally, for
he would be the first to realise that for their own sakes
the people must learn to govern themselves.

The case for autocracy is hopeless. The case for
oligarchy may seem to be stronger, but chiefly because
we are apt to assume that *oligarchical* and *aristocratic*
are interchangeable terms. The current use of the word
aristocracy begs a large question. If men are fundamentally unequal, it is right that government should be
placed in the hands of the *aristoi*, or best. But are the
ruling classes, in this and other countries, really the
best? Are they really superior to the rest of the community? And if they are, is their superiority inherent
or accidental? That the "upper classes," in whose
hands political power is mainly concentrated, have a
serious belief in their own inherent superiority, is certain. Comparing themselves with the "lower orders,"
as they call them, they claim that they have a higher
degree of culture, more refined tastes, better manners,
a wider range of interests, and a larger outlook on life.
This claim may perhaps be conceded. But the upper
classes believe that their superiority in these matters is
inherent and congenital, instead of being due, as might
reasonably be contended, to the advantages which a
happier environment has given them, especially in the
periods of childhood and adolescence.

This self-flattering assumption may well be challenged.
But it has lately received support from an influential

quarter—that of biological science. Professor Bateson, the eminent biologist, in his Address to the British Association in Australia, having laid down that the biological theory of " strain " is as applicable to human beings as to plants and animals, goes on to assume, as a self-evident truth, that in modern society the upper classes are of a superior strain to the lower, from which premises he logically concludes that democracy is a vicious type of government. He admits indeed that if the upper classes may be regarded as plums and the lower as bullaces, many plums have been sown among the bullaces and some bullaces among the plums; but this admission does not make his political views the less anti-democratic, for he is careful to explain that the present " instability of society is due, not to inequality, which is inherent and congenital, but to the fact that in periods of rapid change like the present convection currents are set up such that the elements of the strata get intermixed and the apparent stratification corresponds only roughly with the genetic "; and though he approves of the statesmanship which " aims at helping those who have got sown as wildings to come into their proper place," he adds, " let not anyone suppose such a policy democratic in its ultimate effects, for no course of action can be more effective in strengthening the upper classes, while weakening the lower "; and his final contribution to political science is, as might be expected, that " in all practical schemes for social reform the congenital diversity, the essential polymorphism of all civilised communities must be recognised as a fundamental fact; and reformers should rather direct their efforts to facilitating and rectifying class distinctions than to any futile attempt to abolish them."

The theory which Professor Bateson has expounded must surely have originated in Germany. One can

imagine with what gusto the Hohenzollerns and the
Prussian Junkers would lay its flattering unction to their
souls.   One might even conjecture that the professor
who elaborated it, if of " bullace " origin, was raised
to the " plum " level by royal mandate and made a " *von*"
in recognition of his newly-acquired superior strain.
But what is the value, what is the meaning of the theory?
When one remembers by what methods the upper classes,
in this and other countries and in this and other ages,
have gained the upper hand, one begins to wonder what
are the qualities, superiority in which differentiates the
high-born aristocracy from the low-born populace.   Are
they, for example, the qualities which Christ pronounced
blessed in the Sermon on the Mount?   I doubt it.   As
I turn the pages of history I find that again and again
the ungodly flourished like a green bay tree, flourished
so triumphantly that he was able to bequeath his ill-
gotten prosperity to the third and fourth and even to
the tenth generation of his descendants.   In such a case
did the successful scoundrel bequeath his character as
well as his position and wealth?   According to Professor
Bateson he must have done so.   But if he did, there is
surely a flaw in his descendants' title to social and
political ascendancy.   Professor Bateson has raised an
interesting and difficult question.   Will he help us to
answer it?   Are his upper classes an aristocracy of
physique, of intellect, of morals, of spirituality?   That
they are " inherently and congenitally " superior in
all four directions is a proposition which those who are
well acquainted with both classes will laugh to scorn,
and which even Professor Bateson will scarcely have
the hardihood to maintain.   Were the Robber Knights
of the Rhine, are the arrogant barons of East Prussia
and the Baltic Provinces, " high-born "?   Are the Fran-
ciscan brothers and sisters, whose ideal of life has always

been diametrically opposed to that of knight or baron, " low-born "? The pedigree of a dog or a horse is recorded in certain unmistakable features. In what features, inward or outward, does Nature record the pedigree of the high-born or the low-born man? This is a point on which Professor Bateson would do well to enlighten us, but on which he prefers to keep silence.

Let us try to answer the question which he has left unanswered. That his theory of " strain " is wholly incompatible with the hypothesis of man's inherent infinitude, goes without saying. But let us waive that argument for the moment and ask what positive evidence can be brought forward in support of his theory, or rather of its applicability to human nature. He seems to take for granted that the upper classes in this country —the nobility, gentry, and members of the liberal professions, let us say—are mostly plums, and that the lower classes—the peasants, miners and artisans, let us say—are mostly bullaces. Wherein, then, do the upper classes show their inherent and congenital superiority to the lower? That they are of superior physique may perhaps be admitted; though even in this respect the difference between the two classes at birth is comparatively small, the physical superiority of the average adult specimen of the upper classes being largely due to healthier surroundings and better food. That they are superior in mental power is disputable, to say the least. The adult peasant is no doubt less cultured and less intellectual than the average " gentleman," but he has been exposed from his birth, both at home and in school, to much less favourable influences, and it is to this rather than to any inherited inferiority that his shortcomings, cultural and intellectual, are probably due. What the inherent and congenital mentality of the lower classes really is, or how it compares

with that of the upper classes, we do not know. What
we do know is that the peasant, the miner, and the
artisan are born into a cramping and depressing environment, the product of social and economic causes, from
which they cannot easily escape, and in which it is as
difficult for their mental powers to unfold as for a tree
to thrive in an exposed situation or a poor soil. This
fact invites imaginative conjecture as to what might be
or might have been. The psychology of Gray's *Elegy*,
which wisely limits itself to " perhaps " and " may," is,
I believe, absolutely sound:

> Perhaps in this neglected spot is laid
> Some heart once pregnant with celestial fire;
> Hands, that the rod of empire might have sway'd
> Or waked to ecstasy the living lyre.
>
> But Knowledge to their eyes her ample page,
> Rich with the spoils of time, did ne'er unroll;
> Chill Penury repressed their noble rage,
> And froze the genial current of the soul.
>
> . . . .
>
> Some village Hampden, that with dauntless breast
> The little tyrant of his fields withstood;
> Some mute inglorious Milton here may rest,
> Some Cromwell guiltless of his country's blood.
>
> Th' applause of listening senates to command,
> The threats of pain and ruin to despise,
> To scatter plenty o'er a smiling land,
> And read their history in a nation's eyes,
>
> Their lot forbade.

Some such epitaph as this might be written on many
a nameless grave in country churchyard or urban ceme-
tery. It was said that in the Napoleonic armies every
soldier carried a Field-marshal's baton in his knapsack;
and it is a fact that some of the ablest of Napoleon's
lieutenants rose from the ranks. Why? Because in
Republican France the superstition of the congenital

inferiority of the lower classes had been temporarily swept away by the Revolution, and because the Republican tradition had been inherited by the Empire and respected by the Emperor, whose own genius had raised him from obscurity to supreme power, and who was on the look-out for talent in the armies that he led. In the British Army, where the soldiers fought " under the cold shade of aristocracy," the private who, had he been born in France, might have become a Field-marshal, would probably have won his stripes, or at best become a subaltern, and gone no further. The constitution of things was against his rising to the height of his deserts. " His lot forbade " his advancement.

The experiment which the Republican War Ministers initiated and which Napoleon carried on is of lasting interest and opens up a wide vista to speculative thought. Professor Bateson will perhaps contend that the marshals who rose from the ranks were plums which had got " sown as wildings." But no: a Field-marshal is, *in his own line*, a super-plum, not a plum; and where there is one super-plum there must be thousands and tens of thousands of plums. In the Napoleonic armies, as in the Republican, there was a temporary relaxation of a deadening pressure. If that concession could enable many soldiers who would otherwise in all probability have lived and died in obscurity, to rise to the very highest grade of all, what might not a general equalising of conditions do in the way of raising the lower classes to the mental level of the upper? This is the question which the romantic stories of such men as Murat, Lannes, Ney, Hoche, Augereau, Junot, and other great commanders, compel us to ask ourselves. In our attempts to answer it we can, I think, pass beyond the limits of mere conjecture. A village schoolmistress, to whose work I have elsewhere tried to do justice, was the first to convince me that under favourable conditions, foremost among which is an attitude of trust and encouragement on the part of the teacher, the village boy or girl can easily hold his own with the child of the upper classes in all-round mental capacity, in resourcefulness, in initiative, in versatility, in intellectual power, in literary and artistic taste. Other teachers have since taught me the same lesson. Not long after my discovery of the village which I called " Utopia," the headmaster of an elementary school in the East of London showed me some admirable drawings done by his pupils. I asked him what proportion of his pupils could reach that level. He answered: " Had you asked me that question a year ago I would have said 5 per cent., but now I can say 95 per cent." As a teacher of drawing he had recently changed his aims and methods. Had he not done so he would have continued to take for granted that 95 per cent. of his pupils had little or no capacity for drawing. More recently I was shown some thirty or forty poems written by girls in a higher-standard elementary school in one of our Northern manufacturing towns. The high level of feeling and expression reached in these poems astonished me.[1] The head-mistress explained to

[1] Here is one of the poems:

Late October.

Patter of fitful rain,
Shiver of falling leaves,
And wail of wind that has left behind
The glory of fruit and sheaves.

Mist on the crowning hills,
Mist in the vales below,
And grief in the heart that has seen depart
Its summer of long ago.

A similar and equally successful experiment has been made by Miss Ruth M. Fletcher in the Lower Form of a Girls' Municipal High School. " Original poetry by children," writes Miss Fletcher,

me that, being in need of " copy " for the school magazine, she encouraged the girls to try their hands at
writing verse. The girls, who had long had access to a
good school library containing many volumes of poetry,
responded with alacrity. The teacher added that " our
poetry is only a very small part of our literature scheme,[1]
the carrying-out of which is to the children pure joy;
and these poems are only first attempts." Similar dis-
coveries of latent taste and talent in the average elementary
school-child are constantly being made. They point to
serious defects in our system or systems of education,
which do so much for the child, of whatever social
grade, and leave so little to his spontaneous activity,
that his mind is still in large measure an unexplored
land. If education could be reformed in the direction
of setting children free to develop individuality and
realise latent capacity, it would, I think, be found that
the mental ability of both the upper and the lower
classes was much greater than we had imagined it to
be. But it would not be found that the mental ability
of the upper classes was appreciably greater than that
of the lower. Such at least is the conviction which my
recent educational experiences and my reinterpretation,
in the light which they cast, of former experiences,
have forced upon my mind.

The idea that the upper classes are by nature morally
and spiritually superior to the lower is a dangerous

" is an interesting subject, but space forbids full discussion here.
Enough to state that I have experimented independently in this
direction, and am amazed and delighted at the result. I believe
that most intelligent children of this age have within them, mostly
latent, a vein of poetry, simple and rhythmical, and need only right
stimulus to use and delight in the powers." Most of Miss Fletcher's
pupils would be of " bullace breed," some being ex-elementary
scholars and others the daughters of lower middle-class parents.

[1] This is quite true. The prose efforts of the children are as
remarkable as their poems.

delusion, of which, for their own sakes, those who belong to the upper classes would do well to rid themselves. If the lower classes fill more than their share of our prison cells, the reason is that many of them are born into and reared in criminal surroundings, that they are beset by temptations to dishonesty and other forms of lawlessness to which the upper classes are not exposed, and that, in spite of the desire of our legislators to do justice to all classes, there is still one law for the rich and another for the poor.[1] Criminality is not viciousness. The lower classes may be more criminal than the upper, in the sense of being more frequently convicted of offences against the law, but they are certainly not more vicious. If anything, they are less selfish and less worldly. But this too can easily be explained. The disadvantages of environment are not all on the side of the poor. The rich are exposed to temptations from which the poor are largely, if not wholly, exempt. It was said of old by One who taught with authority that it is easier for a camel to go through the " eye of a needle " than for a rich man to enter into the Kingdom of Heaven. Did not Christ mean by this that material prosperity, with its temptations to self-indulgence—a hydra-headed vice— to worldliness, with the perversion of ideals which it involves, and to arrogance, with its acceptance as final of an outward standard of value, is ever tending to distract the prosperous from the inward life? Bearing these things in mind, let us hold the scales even between the two classes and say that on the moral and spiritual planes neither class is inherently superior to the other. The present war has proved to demonstration that there are vast reserves of heroism and self-devotion in human nature, and that in this respect the upper classes are not more richly endowed than the lower, nor the lower

See Judge Parry's book *The Law and the Poor*, passim.

classes than the upper. One of our officers, writing from the Front, says of his men:

I'm not emotional but . . . since I've been out here in the trenches I've had the water forced into my eyes, not once, but a dozen times, from sheer admiration and respect, by the action of rough, rude chaps whom you'd never waste a second glance on in the streets of London, men who, so far from being exceptional, are typical through and through, just the common street average. . . . Under the strain and stress of this savage existence those men show up for what they really are under their rough hides; they are jewel all through . . . and the daily round of their lives is simply full of little acts of self-sacrifice, generosity and unstudied heroism.

And our men at the Front have often written in equivalent terms of their officers. The truth is that, in response to the stimulus of this tremendous war, sublime qualities are ever awaking which exist as possibilities in those hidden depths of our nature where distinctions of class and breeding are unknown, and which are therefore, in the real meaning of the phrase, characteristic of man as man. In the Kingdom of Heaven there is no such thing as " strain."

Far from shaking my faith in the fundamental equality of all men, Professor Bateson, the apostle of human inequality, has indirectly confirmed it, for he has led me to examine the evidence for his anti-democratic assumption, with the result that the " inherent and congenital " superiority of the upper to the lower classes, which he takes for granted, has resolved itself into a doubtful superiority in physique. This is but a slender basis on which to build a claim to political supremacy. On the higher levels of human nature such phrases as *well-born, high-born, well-bred, good birth, good breeding,* and their opposites have no meaning. Or rather, so far as they have a meaning, they indicate superiority or inferiority in respect of environment, not of breed. The infinitude, which is of the essence of human nature, is as much the birthright of the peasant or the miner as of the plutocrat or the peer. The biological theory of strain, when applied to human beings, may lend its countenance to the arrogance of those who are born into high places. But that proves nothing except that, like the arrogance which it seems to countenance, the theory, as an interpretation of human nature, is profoundly materialistic at heart. The philosophy of life which resolves psychology into biology is vitiated by one fundamental fallacy. It ignores the transforming, expanding, sublimating power of consciousness. It ignores the soul.

So much for the theoretical basis of democracy. What is the practical basis? When I use the word " practical " I am not thinking of the activities of politicians; I am not thinking of caucuses, conventions, unions of democratic control, or other such contrivances. These things belong to the machinery of political organisation; and it is possible for the machinery of democratic organisation to have been ingeniously contrived and to work smoothly and effectively, and yet for its chief function to be that of enabling ambitious and unscrupulous demagogues—true descendants of the robber knights of the Middle Ages—to exploit the people, in the sacred name of democracy, for their own selfish ends. The practical basis of democracy is the spread of the democratic spirit—the spirit of fundamental equality—among men. Till that spirit has permeated the people, we may elaborate and over-elaborate the machinery of democratic government, but we shall not arrive at democracy.

And we are still far from that goal. Centuries of political progress are behind us; but the feudal rather than the democratic spirit is still in the air that we breathe. The tenacity of feudalism, its survival of its own apparent dissolution, is due in part to its being the logical development of a great philosophical principle. If trust in human nature, recognition of the infinite in man, is at the heart of the philosophy of democracy, distrust of human nature, denial of the infinite in man, is at the heart of the philosophy of feudalism. The infinite, as feudalism conceives it, is outside man, outside Nature, outside the world of our experience, enthroned in an unimaginable world of its own. From that supernatural source authority is delegated to the overlords of the earth, from whom it descends by a process of devolution from grade to grade —from emperor to king, from king to duke, from duke to count, from count to knight—till we come at last to the mass of the people, whose sole political privilege is to obey. Under the feudal system authority was inherent in the ownership of land, the supreme landlord being the supernatural God; and where the ownership of land ceased, political power and responsibility ceased with it. With the decay of feudalism as a political system and the development of commerce, manufacturing industry, and urban life, the contrast between the landowning and the landless classes reproduced itself in the field of industrial activity as the contrast between capital and labour, and in general broadened out into the contrast between the haves and the have-nots, between the rich and the poor. Feudalism, as a political system, has long since passed away; but the after-effects of an order of things in which authority descended from the apex to the base of the social pyramid, and was held to be inherent in the ownership of property, are with us still. The worship of rank, of riches, and—on a lower level—of respectability, the tyranny of class-distinctions, the thirst for material possessions as the ultimate source of political power, of social influence, of well-being, and even of happiness, are as strong to-day as they ever were. Materialised ideals, outward standards of value, undue regard for appearances still rule our hearts. And as the able and ambitious men in every grade are not unnaturally consumed with a desire to struggle upwards to higher grades, and as the association of power and position with property encourages a general scramble for possessions, we cannot wonder that competition, rather than co-operation, is still the master principle of our social life, or that, if we do co-operate, our motive in doing so is too often competitive, our forces being united for purposes of aggression or defence. So long as this spirit is in the ascendant, democratic institutions, whatever form they may take, will prove but a mockery or a fraud. Class may array itself against class, labour against capital, the landless against the landlords, and so on; but so long as these movements are dominated by competitive selfishness, so long as our attempts to redress inequality are controlled by the avowed desire for an impossible outward equality or by the secret desire to establish a new inequality, so long as we are the victims of the delusion that equality is a matter of outward possessions rather than of inward life, we may get revolutions of various kinds but we shall still fall far short of democracy.

If we wish to arrive at democracy, we must, I repeat, cultivate the democratic spirit. What, then, is the democratic spirit? In answer to this question the historical formula " Liberty, Equality, Fraternity," rises of its own accord to my lips. In this formula the key word is *Equality*, which is properly placed in the middle. If that word is rightly interpreted, the formula is transcendent sense. If it is wrongly interpreted, the formula is worse than nonsense. If the equality of which we dream is outward and material, if it is to be achieved, for example, by the forcible spoliation of the rich, we must not be surprised if the man of property gives us, as his version of the formula: " Anarchy, Robbery, Conspiracy." But if the equality of which we dream is inward and intrinsic, if its source is the principle of infinitude, the divine spirit in man, then the supporting words—*Liberty* and *Fraternity*—will discover in themselves new depths of meaning, and the formula as a whole will become the expression of a glorious ideal of life.

Liberty, Equality, Fraternity. If we are to have equality we must have liberty; and if we have equality we shall have fraternity. Let me try to explain what I mean. If the equalising element in us is to have fair play, if we are to begin to realise our infinite possibilities, we must have freedom for self-development. For self-development means development by self as well as of self, and the business of growing must in the main be done by the thing that grows. When we say that our reserves are infinite, we of course imply that no one, in the space of one brief life, can hope to realise them. The baby has it in him to speak a hundred languages; but the chances are that he will speak only one. The adolescent has it in him to play a hundred parts in life; but the chances are that he will play only one. What a man can do and should aim at doing is to keep alive and even develop his capacity for self-development. It is in this respect that men are unequal, man differing from man, and class from class. The differences between man and man are partly congenital, mainly environmental. The differences between class and class are, as far as I can see, wholly environmental. The upper classes may have a greater capacity for self-development than the lower; but we have no evidence that their superiority, whatever it may amount to, is congenital, whereas we have ample evidence that they have been born into and reared in a larger, freer, and less monotonous environment. This will account for their greater adaptability and their wider outlook. We are all creatures of habit, and we are all apt to get into grooves and stay in them; and therefore the stronger the pressure that is applied to us, and the narrower the surface on which it operates, the more likely we are to yield to it, and in doing so to stunt our growth and contract the scope of our life.

Let me take an extreme case. In ancient days civilisation was based on slave labour. What chance had the slave of developing or even keeping alive his capacity for self-development? If you insist on ordering a man's goings for him, he will gradually lose the power of ordering them for himself. The slave had all his goings ordered for him. From morning to evening, from day to day, from year to year, he was subjected to the maximum of disciplinary pressure; and his environment, which was wholly under the control of his master, was narrow, rigid and monotonous. A Stoic, like Epictetus, or a Christian devotee, might be able to retire from this tyranny into the fortress of his inmost soul, and there find freedom and life. But the average slave could scarcely fail to succumb to the tremendous pressure which was brought to bear on him; and we must not blame him if at last he fell below the level of normal manhood and became little better than an animated machine.

Slavery has passed away, but the liberty which makes for equality has not yet come. One cannot spend much time in the deep and dreary slums of our great industrial centres, without feeling that the dwellers in those regions, though they may be free and independent electors, are in bondage to a social and economic pressure which is hurtful to their higher interests and from which they find it hard to escape. They pass their lives in dull, ugly, sordid, depressing surroundings. They spend, as a rule, ten hours a day in monotonous and mechanical work. The quickening and illuminating influences of nature, literature, and art are in large measure withheld from them. At any rate, they are not at their doors. If growth is brought about by reaction to stimulus, what kind of growth can men who are doomed to live in such an environment be expected to make? All honour to those among them who have kept their capacity for self-development unimpaired. If they are a minority, the majority are to be sympathised with, not blamed. Sympathised with, and still believed in. The iron has entered into their souls, but it has inflicted no mortal wound. Their reserves of potentiality are still limitless; and a supreme crisis would probably reveal the latent greatness of their souls. But their power of drawing on their reserves has been seriously impaired, and both as citizens and as men they have suffered from the undue restriction of their liberty by a social system which is economically and therefore politically unsound.

If we are to realise our inherent equality, we must have freedom for self-development, we must be relieved, as far as possible, from cramping, stunting, deadening constraint. And in proportion as we realise our inherent equality, the sentiment of fraternity will grow and spread among us. For the infinite in man is something more than the source of equality among men. It is also the source of unity. It is the one sure solvent of individualism. The individual can keep many things to himself, claim them as his own, speak of them as his property, and exult in the possession of them. But he cannot keep the infinite to himself. That, the greatest of all his possessions, is his on condition that he shares it with all other men. No man, not even the German Emperor, has proprietary rights in God. The more fully a man realises his latent infinitude, the more successful he is in finding his own soul, in making good his claim to the prize which is worth more to him than the whole world, the stronger is his sense of being one, in it and through it, with all other men. The sentiment of fraternity is the sense of equality worked out to its legitimate conclusion by the logic of the heart—the sense of equality touched with emotion, transformed into an enthusiasm, a passion, a glow of sympathy, a flame of love. With the acceptance of equality, not merely as a philosophical principle or as a psychological truth, but also and more especially as a personal experience, the individual ceases to live to himself; but this is a gain to him rather than a loss, for he renews his life on a larger scale by merging it in the life of his kind.

The democratic spirit, then, is compounded of three elements, the sense of equality, the desire for liberty, and the sentiment of fraternity; and these three are not three, but one. But how are we to get the democratic spirit into the various classes of our still feudalised society? For it must dominate all classes if the day of democracy is to come. Alas! as I have already confessed, we are still deep in our old grooves. We still worship our old idols—position, property, power. The spirit of competition is still in the ascendant, the very efforts that we make to co-operate being largely under its control. The old watchword, the battle-cry of individualism—" Each for himself and the devil take the hindmost "—still retains, in practice if not in theory, some measure of the black magic of its charm. Living in this sinister tradition, breathing this polluted atmosphere, what shall we do to be saved?

Well, if we adults are past praying for—I do not say that we are, nay, I am very sure that we are not, but in any case—why should we not begin where we ought always to begin, and where we ought to have begun long ago—with our children? Nothing astonishes me so much as the indifference of the average English parent to the social aspect of the education which his children are receiving. Such interest as he takes in the matter is, as a rule, merely snobbish, being limited to the desire that his children should consort with those who are above rather than below his own social status. With the socialising influence of education on his children he does not concern himself in the slightest degree. The democrat is well content that his children should attend schools which are still dominated by the feudal tradition of devolved authority, inherent inequality, and personal ascendancy. The socialist is well content that his children should be taught by men who can think of no better way of rousing their pupils to exertion than that of appealing to their competitive instincts, with the baser passions— envy, jealousy, vanity and the like—which are implicit in these. The democrat does not see that the feudal spirit is as antagonistic to the democratic in a school as in a political community, and that when the child becomes a citizen he will probably cling to the tradition in which he was reared. The socialist does not see that those who, as children, are forced to compete against one another will be reluctant to co-operate with one another when they go out into the wide world.

Education, as it is conducted to-day in most civilised countries, seems to be at open war with the democratic ideal of liberty, equality, fraternity. The children who attend school are despotically governed and compulsorily disciplined, instead of being helped to govern and discipline themselves. In this way violence is done to their natural and quite legitimate desire for liberty, a desire which is generated by their inborn instinct for self-development. They are compulsorily instructed instead of being helped to instruct themselves. A cut-and-dried curriculum is imposed on them, with or without their consent, and no attempt is made to discover, or help them to discover, in what directions their talents really lie. The result is that an arbitrary standard of intellectual worth is applied to them, by reference to which glaring inequalities among them speedily reveal themselves, inequalities which are accepted by both teachers and taught as congenital and inherent, and therefore as ultimately decisive of destiny, and which are duly registered by the teacher, and even numerically appraised. In this way violence is done to the sense of equality which is latent in all children, and which is ready to assert itself whenever it is given fair play. And as the régime of compulsory discipline and compulsory instruction is distasteful to the healthy child, in order to induce children to exert themselves they are urged and even compelled to compete against one another for prizes and other marks of distinction, and are thus taught to regard their classmates as rivals instead of as fellow-workers and friends. In this way violence is done to the nascent spirit of fraternity—the spirit of comradeship, of co-operation, which has made possible the communal life of man.

The reform of education, then, in the direction of relaxing unnecessary pressure, removing unnecessary restrictions and, in general, giving the child space to grow in and fresh air to breathe, must precede that diffusion of the democratic spirit which is to prepare the way for the advent of democracy. Feudalised education leads of inner necessity to the ascendancy of the feudal spirit in society; and so long as that spirit is in the ascendant, it will either thwart or misdirect whatever movements we may make towards the realisation of the democratic ideal. Therefore, if we are really devoted to the cause of political and social reform, our first aim must be to de-feudalise education. How is this to be done? We must begin by recognising that the ultimate source of authority in education is not the will of the teacher, but the unfolding spirit of the child. Let this fundamental truth be realised, and reforms which embody it will follow of their own accord and in their own good time. Instead of basing our whole educational system on profound distrust of the child's nature we shall gradually learn to base it on faith in the inherent sanity of the great forces which are at work in his expanding life, in the limitlessness of his unrealised reserves of capacity, and in the general orientation of his nature towards good. We shall then relax the rigour of a discipline which takes for granted that the child is a potential rebel and criminal, and which therefore does its best to crush his spirit and mechanicalise his life. And we shall relax the rigidity and formality of a system of instruction which takes for granted that the child is as stupid and helpless as he is ignorant, and which, by forcibly cramming him with information, does its best to starve his desire to win knowledge for himself. And in general we shall relax the dogmatic and dictatorial attitude which reflects our traditional conviction that the mind of the child is at best a blank page waiting to be written on, and that his character is at best unkneaded clay.

If we will make the experiment of giving freedom to the child, and persevere in it in spite of inevitable mistakes and failures, results will follow in due season which will surprise us. Relieved from the deadly pressure which was paralysing his natural activities and therefore either arresting or distorting his expansive tendencies, free at last to obey the laws of his own being rather than the arbitrary commands of his teacher, the child will begin to make healthy and harmonious growth; and his consequent sense of well-being will be realised by him as joy. In the vitalising atmosphere of joy his deeper nature will begin to reveal itself. His secret desire for liberty having been gratified, the sense of equality will begin to awake in him. By this I mean that his competitive instinct, which we, his seniors, have so basely exploited, will be gradually swamped, and at last wholly submerged, by the rising tide of fellow-feeling and goodwill. Instead of measuring himself against his classmates and either envying their prowess or priding himself on surpassing them, he will learn to regard them as his fellow-workers and comrades, as sharers with him in the life and well-being of a social community, and will therefore learn at last to take as great a pride in their achievements as in his own. This is no mere dream of what might be. It is a prophecy, based on experience of what has actually happened in more schools than one. In the village school which I have already mentioned, prizes, marks of distinction, orders of merit, and all their pernicious kindred, were entirely unknown, and any attempt to introduce them into the school would have been strongly resented by the children themselves. If a child had a special gift for drawing or any other subject, his reward for doing good work at it was to be allowed to help those who were less proficient than himself, and, if possible, raise them to his own level. And as no artificial standard of measurement prevailed in the school, and as all the children were encouraged to cultivate their natural tastes and aptitudes, the clever draughtsman—let us say—was free to remind himself that, if he was strong where some of his class-mates were weak, he might well be weak where some of his class-mates were strong.

Looking back to the days which I spent in that school, I can say, without hesitation, that it was a perfect social community, in which the spirit of liberty, equality, and fraternity was fully realised, in which each lived for all and all for each, in which the development of the children was in the highest degree healthy, vigorous and many-sided, in which the prevailing atmosphere was one of sympathy, good-will, and joy.

I have visited other schools in which the same spirit was producing similar results. If schools of that type were the rule instead of the rare exceptions, the social Kingdom of Heaven, which is also the spiritual Kingdom of Heaven, would be at hand.

The spread of the democratic spirit among the young is not the only preparation of democracy which the reform of education may be expected to make. I have said that actually, though not congenitally, the upper classes have a greater capacity for self-realisation than the lower. I do not think they owe this superiority, such as it is, to their school education. At any rate, they owe it in a far higher degree to the general advantages of their environment, especially in the days of childhood and adolescence—to their homes, their surroundings, their friends, their opportunities for travel and self-improvement, and above all to the leisure which makes it possible for them, through the medium of books and periodicals, to get into touch with all the ages and with all parts of the world. Taken as a whole, their environment is larger, more varied, more stimulating, and therefore more educational, in the deeper and truer sense of the word. If the poor cannot secure these advantages for their children, there is the more reason why the education given in our elementary schools should be of such a character as to keep alive and even foster the child's natural capacity for realising his latent possibilities. Now, as it happens, the type of education which will best secure this end coincides at every point with the type of education which will best promote the growth of the democratic spirit in the rising generation. Give a child freedom for self-development, release him from the cramping and deadening pressure of autocratic

authority, rigid discipline, and mechanical instruction—
and two things will happen. The spirit of liberty,
equality, and fraternity will begin to germinate in his
heart, and his capacity for realising capacity, for making
the most of his natural aptitudes and inclinations, will
at least be kept alive. With such a school life behind
him, he will be animated, when he grows up, by the
true spirit of democracy, and he will also be ready to play
his part as a useful and efficient member of the community,
and to take a hand in the great work of governing the community, and the still greater work of governing himself.

The psychology from which I have deduced my
political philosophy may seem to some of my readers
fantastic and even paradoxical. Yet it ought to be familiar
to all who call themselves Christians. For I have but
taken seriously two of the leading tenets of the Christian
faith. The doctrine of the Incarnation and the doctrine
of the Holy Spirit proclaim, each in its own way, the
potential divinity of man. The essence of the doctrine
of the Incarnation is that Very Man is Very God. The
essence of the doctrine of the Holy Spirit is that the
indwelling spirit of God is the life of our life and the
soul of our soul. The seers and sages of Ancient India
proclaimed the same truth in other words when they
taught that the soul of the universe, the " unbeholden
essence " of all things, is the true self of each of us.
We do not take this great truth seriously. We give a
formal assent to the doctrines which enshrine it, and
then leave these for the theologians to deal with, while
we devote ourselves to secular pursuits. The doctrines
may have a meaning for us—so we seem to think—
between certain hours on Sunday, and for our children
during the first half-hour of morning school on week-
days. But they do not otherwise concern us; and we

take good care that they shall not enter into and dominate our daily lives. The consequent loss to our daily
lives is immeasurable. If the true self of each of us is
infinite and even divine, ought not self-development—
the unfolding of our latent powers, the realising of our
limitless possibilities, the opening of our hearts to the
creative spirit of God—to be the central purpose of our
lives, the basis of our culture, the basis of our morals,
the basis of our social organisation, the basis of our
political aims? In the light of this master principle
should not we who believe in democracy see a deeper
meaning in *liberty*, without which self-development is
impossible, in *equality*, which reflects the presence of
the infinite in our souls, in *fraternity*, which is the natural
outcome of our oneness with and oneness in God? I ask
that we shall take this truth, if it is a truth, away from
the theologians and bring it into our daily lives. When
once the leaven of it has begun to work in our hearts,
new vistas will open before us, and ideals which we
had thought impracticable will come within the compass of our forethought and our will. I am no prophet,
and I will not pry into the future; but I must be
allowed to dream that one of the ideals which will then
begin to materialise will be the reconstruction of society
on a genuinely democratic foundation.

But even in our dream of that possible millennium
we must remind ourselves again, and yet again, that without the democratic spirit no democratic institution can
serve its purpose or endure. If the theoretical basis
of democracy is recognition, the practical basis of it is
realisation of the divine element in man. The Kingdom
of Heaven is a community as well as an inward state;
but if we are to realise it as a community we must also
realise it as an inward state.

August 1917.

FREEDOM AND GROWTH

I BELIEVE that human nature, in all its length and breadth
and depth and height, comes under the master law of
growth. I also believe that the spirit of man is, ideally
and potentially, free. How can I reconcile these beliefs?
Do they not flatly contradict one another? Is not growth
a movement towards a predetermined form? And if the
goal of growth is predetermined, what place is there
for freedom in the process? There is only one way of
escape from this impasse. I must so interpret each belief
as to show that it is dependent for its own inner meaning
on the truth of the other. I must devise a theory of
growth which will countenance and even postulate the
idea of freedom. And I must devise a theory of freedom
which will countenance and even postulate the idea of
growth. If each of these ventures is successful, the two
will no doubt converge on a common goal. Meanwhile,
as I cannot embark on both simultaneously, I will begin
with the problem of freedom.

With consciousness comes the sense of freedom; and
with the sense of freedom comes the sense of responsibility.

Antithetical to and correlative with the idea of freedom
is that of necessity. As consciousness, in the life of man,
seems to be slowly emerging from the depths of uncon-
sciousness, so freedom seems to be slowly extricating
itself from the enveloping network of necessity.

To think rationally about freedom is well-nigh impossible. For the function of reason is to discover the
all-pervading, all-controlling order in Nature, which it
begins (unknown to itself) by postulating; and freedom

introduces into human life—the highest plane of Nature that is known to man—an element of apparent disorder, or at any rate of incalculableness, which threatens to stultify all the operations of reason, all its efforts to understand the world. The result is that reason can find no place for freedom in its provisional scheme of things, and is therefore subconsciously prejudiced against it even before it begins to examine its title-deeds. Hence the inherent futility of the arguments against—and for —freedom. The history of philosophy tells us that the problem of freedom is at the centre of one of those whirlpools of controversy which are ever changing their scope and their position, but which continue to rotate with unabated energy and which seem as if they would never whirl themselves to rest. The problem has been again and again re-stated, but the solution of it has not been found. Each thinker in turn tries to untie the knot, and ends by cutting it. One subtle and insidious fallacy vitiates every argument that has ever been employed in this most barren of logomachies—the assumption that the question is open to discussion. One might as well try to prove or disprove the existence of colour on purely *a priori* grounds as ask, in disregard of the direct testimony of consciousness, whether freedom is or is not a vital attribute of the soul of man. All the arguments for freedom, though they may fill volumes, amount to no more than this: I feel that I am free; therefore I am free. And all the arguments against freedom, though they may fill hundreds of volumes, amount to no more than this : I can find no place for freedom in my theory of things; therefore I am not free.

Can the defender of freedom do more than plead the cogency of the sense of freedom? To defend freedom on metaphysical grounds, to pretend to fit it into a reasoned scheme of things, is to play into the hands of the determinists (as they call themselves). What really happens in the free-will controversy is that the sense of freedom holds the key to the position against a beleaguering host of theoretical objections. The argumentative defence of freedom should therefore limit itself in the first instance to an attempt to expose the fallacies of the determinists. Out of a critical study of their arguments a theory of things may evolve itself which will countenance freedom on dialectical grounds. But to begin by trying to prove that men are free agents is to assume by implication that the question is open to discussion, and in doing so to weaken the authority of the sense of freedom, and therefore to invalidate our claim to be free.

That the question cannot be discussed on its own merits is proved by the fact that in nine cases out of ten the corresponding controversy turns out to be a mere episode in the larger strife between the materialistic and the idealistic tendencies of human thought. The Calvinist and the Mussulman, whose sole concern is for the power and glory of their supernatural God, do indeed regard man as the victim of a compulsion which is at once spiritual and quasi-mechanical. But, with these exceptions, determinism deprives man of freedom in the interest of material forces and physical laws. For, as a rule, the determinist approaches the problem of freedom from the standpoint of physical science. In doing so he necessarily prejudices the question; for physical science finds it needful to deprive the world of freedom (which would introduce utterly indeterminable factors into its problems) before it can even begin its appointed work. But it is not freedom only that physical science finds it needful to withdraw from Nature—or rather from that abstraction which it miscalls Nature—but every spiritual quality. The result of this is that the triumph of determinism is as barren as it is cheap. The aim of determinism is to bind man's will in the chains of mechanical causation; but in the very act of being seized and fettered its victim escapes from its grasp. For the arguments by which it deprives me of freedom prove nothing except that I— the self, the living soul, the living will (for will is soul on the threshold of action)—have ceased to exist.

Even the determinism which, without actually breaking with the popular psychology, tends to regard every action as the resultant of motives, is, or at least may be, as destructive of man's personality as is the doctrine of human automatism. We do not need determinists to teach us that no man can act except from motives. The question is: Where do these motives come from? From external sources only, or also from the inner life of the man who acts? The new English Dictionary defines determinism as " the philosophical doctrine that human action is not free but necessarily determined by motives which are regarded as external forces acting on the will." In this definition the word *external* is of cardinal importance. " External forces." Are any of the forces that act on the will wholly external to it? Can they be? Is it possible for a force to remain external to the will and yet to act on it? I doubt it. One knows from experience that every influence which comes or seems to come to a man from without is coloured and otherwise modified by the man's personality. Indeed, it is only by entering into quasi-chemical combination with a man's personality that an external influence can transform itself into a motive. And the same influence can transform itself into a thousand different motives by entering into combination with a thousand different minds. The sight of a bottle of brandy is a strong temptation to one man, a matter of indifference to a second, a source of disgust to a third. It follows from these premises that if all motives are, as determinism assumes, external to *me*, *I* do not exist. For something of me (so vital is my connection with my environment) has immingled itself with each of the many motives that govern my conduct; and that something is abstracted from me whenever the motive in question is regarded as wholly external to my will. Therefore, when all my motives have been transformed by determinism into external forces of which I am the supposed victim, nothing of me remains. But if *I* do not exist, it is a waste of time to debate the question of my freedom. My will is an essential aspect of myself. If I am nothing but a shorthand symbol, my will is obviously non-existent, and as such can neither be bond nor free.

There is one aspect of the problem which the disputants on both sides are apt to lose sight of. As freedom and necessity are antithetical and therefore correlative terms, the vanishing point of either idea must needs be the vanishing point of the other. It follows that if there is no such thing as freedom in Nature, there can be no such thing as necessity. Determinism deludes itself when it claims to have demonstrated the unreality of freedom. What it has really done, if its arguments are as conclusive as it believes them to be, is to cancel an entire category of human thought. But its arguments are inconclusive, in the sense that, the more triumphant is their vindication of necessity, the more effectually do they safeguard freedom. For wherever there is necessity there is constraint, and wherever there is constraint there is a constraining power. This power may itself be the victim of a higher necessity; but the chain of effect and efficient cause must lead us at last (ideally, if not actually) to a power which, having nothing beyond or outside it, is self-constrained and therefore free. Thus acceptance of the idea of necessity

compels us, sooner or later, to recognise the *a priori*
possibility (not to say necessity) of freedom.

Now, it is obvious that if the *a priori* possibility of
freedom be conceded, Nature in the cosmic sense of the
word, Nature in her totality, is free. For since her
limits are presumably illimitable, since her being is presumably the all-in-all of existence, it is clear that she
cannot be controlled by any superior power and that the
end of her activities cannot be alien to herself. Though
all lesser things be the victims of necessity, she at least
is free. She at least is the arbiter of her own destiny,
the orderer of her own goings, the lord and giver of
her own life.

But when we study the universe, detail by detail, the
freedom that belongs to the whole seems to vanish from
our sight. No one would dream of saying that a cloud
was free because it moved across the sky; that a stone
was free because it rolled down the mountain side; that
a flake of snow was free because it floated down to the
ground; that a plant was free because it put forth leaf
and flower and fruit. Nor need we go far to seek an
explanation of what common-sense accepts as an obvious
fact. For, in the first place, each detail in the complicated
machinery of material existence acts under the stress
and pressure of the whole. The proof of this statement
rests with physical science, which is ever discovering
new links in the chains of causation that bind each thing
to all and all things to each. And, in the second place,
the ends for which each particular thing is working lie
beyond the scope of its own individual existence. Indeed,
the ultimate end of its action may be said to coincide
with the ultimate end of the universe. Nor is it only
in the lesser details of material Nature that necessity
reigns supreme. As science advances from effect to cause,
and from cause to law, freedom flies before it and finds

no rest for her feet. The Dryads have long since left
the woods, and the Naiads the streams; and the physical
forces that have taken their place are to the full as blind
and helpless as are even the least of the phenomena that
are supposed to have been produced by their agency and
to be governed by their laws. There are no limits to this
process. Potentially, if not actually, science is master
of the whole material universe. There are islands and
continents which it has not yet had time to conquer;
yet even on these it has landed and hoisted its flag, the
flag of mechanical necessity and physical law.

Where, then, it will be asked, is freedom to be found?
I answer, " At the heart of the universe." The true
self of Nature, the world seen as it really is, is free.

But what is at the heart of the universe? What is
the true self of Nature? What face does the world
wear when seen as it really is? I have said that the free-
will controversy is a mere episode in the larger strife
between the materialistic and the idealistic tendencies of
human thought. We can now see that this is so. The
mind of man is so constituted that, if it tries to think of
Nature as a whole, it must needs bring her being, just
as it brings every typical aspect of her being, under the
great law of polar opposition. What are the poles of
Nature's being? The history of philosophy tells us that
there are two main systems or tendencies of speculative
thought, whether quasi-scientific or popular—materialism and idealism. The right name for idealism is of
course spiritualism; but that word has unfortunately
contracted other associations. The two philosophies
agree on one point—that matter and spirit are the antithetical poles of Nature, and that one or other of these
is the pole of intrinsic reality. Materialism holds that
matter is real, and spirit phenomenal. Idealism holds
that spirit is real, and matter phenomenal. If we are

asked what we mean by *matter* and *spirit* respectively, we must say in the first place that we mean by each the opposite of the other. And if that answer is considered unsatisfactory, we must go on to say that, when we make our own experience our starting-point, the path of analysis takes us towards what is material, the path of synthesis towards what is spiritual. This is equivalent to saying that by matter (in the final sense of the word) we mean what is ultimate in analysis; by spirit (in the final sense of the word) what is ultimate in synthesis. For materialism, what is ultimate in analysis is absolutely real; for idealism, what is ultimate in synthesis is absolutely real.

What is ultimate in analysis? Who can say? At one time we flattered ourselves that we had got to bedrock, that in the atoms of the physicist we had discovered what we called " the bricks of the universe." But of late years the bricks of the universe have shown a tendency to melt away into electrons, into whirls of energy, into no one knows what. This, however, does not seriously disconcert the materialist. For materialism is the philosophy of the average man, so far as he is a conscious thinker, just as idealism is the philosophy of his buried life; and, as a conscious thinker, the average man, who is as a rule sense-bound, is content to believe in a general way that the path of analysis—analysis of his own sense-experience—is the pathway to reality, and to leave it to his confederate the physicist to follow that pathway to its goal. It might bewilder him to find that the more penetrative is our analysis of matter, the more immaterial (in the negative sense of the word) does matter tend to become. But, strong in his naïve belief in the intrinsic reality of the outward and visible world, he averts his eyes from the vista which scientific research, since the discovery of radium, has opened up to speculative thought.

In the idealistic philosophy the corresponding problem admits of an obvious though somewhat paradoxical solution. What is ultimate in synthesis is the universe itself, Nature in her totality, the All of Being, or whatever else we may please to call it, conceived of as an organic whole. Belief in the reality of spirit is belief in the organic unity of the universe. Idealism stakes everything on the universe being, in the last resort, a Cosmos, an ordered and unified whole; just as materialism stakes everything on its being, in the last resort, a Chaos, a dance of atoms, a whirlpool of force.

It would be beside my purpose to argue for or against the idealistic conception of the universe. Suffice it to say that it is the only conception which countenances the idea of freedom. For materialism, the world of our experience is a complex of machinery; and in a mechanical world there is no place for freedom. But a mechanical world, though infinite in all its dimensions, is less than the universe. For machinery is always the product and expression of a mind outside itself. Materialism knows nothing of a mind outside the world of our experience; but, in its place, it subjects the world to a blind force which it calls Necessity. Whether the complex of machinery in which we live and move is under the control of mind or in the grip of necessity, matters little from my present point of view. In either case it is less than the whole. And when we speak of the universe we mean the whole, or we mean nothing. If the universe is really the universe, if it is really the All of Being, it must be free.

I have said that if there is such a thing as freedom—and if there is not, there is no such thing as necessity,—then Nature, by which I mean the totality of existent things, is free—free in the sense of being all-inclusive and therefore, *ex hypothesi*, exempt from external constraint. I have also said that if we study the internal economy of Nature we can find no trace (apart, of course, from our own sense of being free) of the freedom which we must needs predicate of the all-inclusive whole. I have asked, then, " Where is freedom to be found? " And I have answered, " At the heart of Nature." Nature, seen as she really is, is free. By the light of the idealistic theory of things I can now see that what is at the heart of Nature is the unified totality of her own being; that what is real in Nature is the spirituality, the soul-life, in virtue of which she is not a Chaos but a Cosmos, not an aggregate but a whole. And here let me say that, when I use such words as *spirituality* and *soul-life*, I always have in mind the definition of spirit as what is ultimate in synthesis, and am therefore thinking, not of what is immaterial, ethereal, imperceptible by our gross senses, and so forth, but of the principle of unity, the principle of wholeness, whether in an individual organism or in the Infinite Whole. I am thinking of this, and perhaps of something more than this. The soul of the world is something more than the principle of cosmic unity: it is the Cosmos in its ordered totality; it is the One in the Many, the world itself seen by itself, seen by its own all-penetrating, all-embracing vision.

This, I say, is free. The heart of the universe is the fountain-head of freedom. What follows with regard to man? In what sense and to what extent is he free? He is free, with the full freedom of unfettered Nature, so far as he can draw life into himself from the heart of the universe, so far as he can live in the infinite and the eternal, so far as he can make the soul of Nature his own. So far as he can do these things, or rather this one thing—for the one thing has many facets,—he is free. Let us for the moment assume that he can do this

thing in some sort and some degree. Let us assume that
he can draw into himself some measure of life from the
heart of the universe. How he may be able to do this
is a problem which we will consider presently. Meanwhile let us assume that he can do it; and let us go on
to say that so far as he can do it he is free. So far—
but no further. Absolute freedom is an infinitely distant
and wholly unattainable goal; yet every step that takes
us towards it brings its emancipative influence more and
more fully into our lives. We are apt to divide things
into the bond and the free. But in this, as in other
matters, our static, dualistic view of things leads us
astray. For freedom is an ideal rather than a possession,
a process rather than a state. The germs of freedom are
present in the germs of spirituality, wherever these may
be found; and the degree of freedom is measured by
the degree of spirituality, from the first stirring of mere
vitality up to the highest imaginable development of
spiritual life. Thus (to take obvious examples) adults
are freer agents than children; men of culture than
savages; human beings than animals; animals than
plants; plants than machines or stones. If necessity
is the law of the world without us, freedom is the law of
the inner life of man. Compulsion from within, spiritual
compulsion, the pressure on one exerted by one's own
highest and widest self, is freedom.

It is well that we should sometimes remind ourselves
that freedom is an ideal rather than a possession, a
prize to be won rather than a privilege to be paraded
and enjoyed. For it is as easy to overestimate as to
underestimate the degree and the range of human freedom. Orthodox Christianity, for example, has always
been too ready to assume that the will of man is absolutely and unconditionally free, and that his shortcomings
are therefore due to perversity rather than to infirmity of

will. And there are modern thinkers who seem to share this view. Dr. Schiller, the Oxford philosopher and critic, in support of his contention that "there is no natural law of Progress," says: "Surely we shall never find our way to God unless we realise how entirely free we are to go to the Devil, and how imminent and constant is our danger of going there." But are we entirely free to go to the Devil? In the abstract perhaps we are. But what of this man or that man? The average man is as little able to go, at will, to the Devil as to enter, at will, into oneness with God. If anything, he is less able to go to the Devil, for his natural tendency is towards good and therefore towards God. A man must be high in development, must have won a quite exceptional measure of freedom, if he is to qualify for admission either to Heaven or to Hell. The average man is no automaton; but he is, at best, partially, provisionally, and (in the main) potentially free. Inherited tendencies, inherited traditions, compulsorily-formed habits, dictated rules of conduct, prescribed ends of action, prejudices of various kinds, his own childhood, his own youth, press in upon him on all sides and seriously restrict his freedom. To suppose that he can at will free himself from the pressure of these influences and go straight to God, or the Devil, as the case may be, is to ignore the teaching of experience. Let a man use such freedom as he possesses to win more freedom, and let him co-operate as best he may with his natural tendency towards good. We can ask him to do as much as this, but we cannot in reason expect him to do more.

In order to test the worth of this theory of freedom, let us confront it with one or two of the difficulties in which any such theory is bound to involve itself, and see how it deals with them.

There is a point of view from which, even in the

sphere of moral action, man seems to be under the dominion of irresistible forces and inexorable laws. History is ever teaching us that the ends of human conduct are immeasurably larger than man himself intends or conceives them to be. Again and again, as we study the records of the past, we are forced to confess that men are, as it were, instruments in the hands of some wide and mighty power — the "Providence" of the Christian, the "Destiny" of the Mussulman, the "Nature" of those who can call it by no other name. We aim at this or that immediate object or personal end. Later on, we or those who come after us are able to see that in working for it we were working for ends which we never dreamed of compassing, ends which transcended the range of our desire as far as they transcended the limits of our sight. It sometimes seems as if our impulses, our tendencies, our instincts, desires, and passions, our very lusts and propensities to evil, were all being used by Nature for secret purposes of her own. When this feeling takes possession of us we are tempted to say, with Renan, "Il y a quelque part un grand égoïste qui nous trompe"; "Nous sommes exploités"; "Quelque chose s'organise à nos dépens; nous sommes le jouet d'un égoïsme supérieur." At any rate the feeling of helplessness in the hands of Nature is a real feeling; and the wider our experience and the larger our view of things, the stronger does it tend to become.

But when it leads us to think of our Lord and Master (whoever he may be or by whatever name we may call him) as a "great egoist" who is exploiting us for purposes of his own, and of ourselves as

impotent pieces in the game he plays,

then the spiritual theory of freedom comes to our rescue

and provides us with an antidote to our specious but shallow pessimism. For it tells us that inasmuch as freedom is the counterpart of spirituality, both in Nature and in us, we have but to spiritualise or integrate ourselves in order to share in Nature's freedom, and to make our destinies coincide, potentially and ideally, with hers. The slave who toils at the bidding of another has no part or lot in the fruits of his labour; but man, even when he seems to be a passive instrument in the hands of Nature, is toiling for ends which he may, if he pleases, make his own. The sense of helplessness that sometimes overwhelms him is really the sense of the pressure to which the central tendencies of things are subjecting him; but this despotic pressure is the very source of his freedom, for Nature (so far as she reveals her purposes to him) realises her own destiny by spiritualising his life; and the end for which her central tendencies are working is the evolution of his soul (which is also hers) and its consequent emancipation from the forces that fetter its freedom and impede its growth. That I am clay in the hands of the potter matters nothing, for it is only in the mould of spiritual freedom that my true self can be shaped. As I expand my being in response to the pressure of Nature's vital forces, I draw those forces little by little within the scope of my own inner life, and at last absorb them all into myself.

There are other experiences in the sphere of moral action on which this conception of freedom seems to throw light.

There is one in particular which no one who studies his own feelings can fail to observe. In yielding to a lower impulse—to the passion of anger, for example, or to a fleshly lust—we feel as if we were scarcely free agents. We yield, either because we are the slaves of an acquired habit, in which case we are no longer free, or because the impulse comes upon us like a whirlwind and constrains us, as it seems, from without. On the other hand, when we surrender ourselves to the pressure of a higher motive we feel that we are free; and the higher the motive, the stronger does our sense of freedom become. I find it difficult to account for these feelings except on the hypothesis that freedom is spiritual necessity or compulsion from within. The man who does right is constrained by a higher impulse. But the higher impulses belong to the spiritual side of man's nature, or in other words, to the true self; and action that is initiated by one's true self is obviously free. Moreover, the ends of righteous action always coincide with the ends of the true self. The man who habitually does right has allied himself with the real or spiritual tendencies of Nature, and in virtue of this high partnership has placed himself (potentially, if not actually) at the centre of the universe, the point from which all the energies of Nature radiate and to which they all return; and so he controls the aboriginal sources of his own action and reaps its ultimate results. The bad man, on the other hand, is acted upon from without. The lower impulses which issue in wrong-doing belong, for the most part, either directly or indirectly, to that more animal side of our nature in respect of which we belong to the material universe and are therefore in bondage —in some sort and some degree—to physical necessity. And the ends towards which they move us are always foreign to our true life and adverse to our higher interests, as is proved by the fact that we curse ourselves for having gained them. Nay, the sources of the motive power that constrains the vicious are external objects which act upon the lower self as a magnet acts upon steel. Thus the drunkard is constrained by the brandy-bottle;

the profligate by a seductive face or figure; the thief or the miser by the glitter of gold.

> How oft the sight of means to do ill deeds
> Makes ill deeds done!

Yet there are times when even the best of men become conscious, perhaps more vividly conscious than the rest of us, of their helplessness in the hands of mightier powers; and while this feeling lasts, they, if not the rest of us, are ready to disown their freedom and glory in their bonds. Religion, speaking as the interpreter of man's spiritual experiences, tells us that when we do right it is not we who do it but God who dwelleth in us. Is this " constraining grace " of God compatible with the freedom of man? If the vicious are slaves to their own lusts, and the virtuous to the grace of God, are not all of us the bondsmen of necessity? No, for the pressure of the Divine Will is a source of freedom, not of bondage. In the last resort, indeed, it is the only source of freedom. For to be constrained by God, who, being the spiritual pole of the universe, dwells in each human soul as its unattainable ideal, is to be constrained by one's best and deepest self; and to be self-constrained (in the deepest sense of the word *self*) is to be free.

The difference between virtue and vice shows itself most clearly in the reaction of conduct on character. By yielding to lower impulses men form bad habits, and so forfeit their freedom. By responding to higher impulses they gradually acquire a mastery over the lower self, and so free themselves from the trammels of necessity. In brief, freedom is lost or won by conduct. This fact—for we know from experience that it is a fact—is easily accounted for on the hypothesis that freedom is the counterpart of spirituality. For to be virtuous is to live to the spirit; and to live to the spirit is both to be and to become free.   The vicious man, on the other hand, by degrading his life to the level of its own material subsoil, gradually accustoms himself to the yoke of physical necessity, and in so doing forfeits his birthright and degenerates into a slave.

It follows from these premises that the man who does right without an effort, and therefore without any apparent exercise of volition, is really freer than the man who feels that his will has been in battle and that resistance has been met and overcome.   The moral struggle is at heart a struggle against coercion and therefore for freedom: with the gradual acquisition of freedom, the tension of the struggle diminishes; and if freedom should ever be fully and finally won, the struggle would have ceased.   Those who do right because they cannot help themselves, because the compulsion from within is overwhelmingly strong, are the freest of men.

Thus there is an intimate connection between virtue and freedom and between vice and necessity.   Yet nothing short of the total extinction of my freedom can absolve me from responsibility; and when my freedom has been finally extinguished, I, the self, the ego, shall have ceased to exist, and the question of my responsibility need no longer be discussed.   So long as *I* survive, I am potentially free; and the presence of this germ of freedom suffices to condemn me when I do wrong.   When necessity has finally triumphed, nothing will be left for it to coerce.   When freedom has finally triumphed, I shall know at last that all the while I——the real I—have been free.

Having tried to justify the conception of freedom as spiritual necessity, by showing that it resolves difficulties and throws light on obscurities in our ethical experiences, I will now conclude my defence of it by interpreting it in terms of my own instinctive feelings and

secret convictions. On one point I have never wavered.
I am as free as I feel myself to be. This feeling is its
own guarantee; and no argument that draws its premises from a lower level of experience can invalidate it
in the court of reason or shake my faith in its authority.
But my sense of freedom, though it never sinks to zero,
is an exceedingly variable quantity. Sometimes I feel
as if my freedom were absolutely unfettered. Sometimes
I feel as if I were the plaything of world-wide forces, as
helpless—almost—as a straw on a rushing stream. The
truth is that the question as to my freedom resolves itself
into the question as to the limits of myself. If I am nothing
but a " conscious automaton," I am obviously the helpless victim of mechanical necessity; but in that case
there is no I to be victimised. If, on the contrary, I am
a spiritual being, freedom is my birthright, and the
degree of my freedom varies directly with the extent
to which I have developed my potencies of spiritual
life. In other words, the expansion of myself is accompanied and progressively measured by the expansion of
my freedom. It is the movement of the stream of spiritual
life through the channel of my being, on the way to its
own ocean source, that endows me with freedom; and
it is the self-same movement that is developing my spirit
and making me what I really am. I become free by
becoming myself, and I become myself by becoming
free. I am not I, in any sense of the word, until I have
won some measure of freedom. I am not I, in the true
sense of the word, until I have made all the forces that
constrain me my own. It follows that the question,
" Am I free? " is so far from admitting of a definite
and final answer that it has to receive a fresh statement
and a fresh answer, and perhaps also an ever-changing
answer, in the case of each individual man. The terms
of the question are always fluid and unstable, and the

answer is always moving forward—with the movement of
the human spirit—in the direction of its own ideal, the
direction of an unqualified and all-embracing " *Yes.*"

Here, then, we have a theory of freedom which not
merely countenances the idea of soul growth, but postulates it and bases itself upon it. If man is free because,
and just so far as, he is at one with the supreme source
of freedom, with the heart of Nature, with the soul of
the universe; if the degree of his freedom is measured
by the degree of his spirituality, by the progress that
he has made in integrating himself, by his nearness to
the spiritual pole of existence—then it is certain that
if man is to win freedom he must follow the path of
soul-growth. For it is only by growing (in the fullest
sense of the word), by continually expanding the scope
and raising the level of his existence, that he can hope
to attain to oneness with the life which is all-in-all and
therefore wholly free. His potentialities are infinite. If
and so far as he can realise them, he will live in the
infinite, and the fetters of necessity will therefore fall
away from him. If and so far as they remain unrealised,
he will remain in bondage to his own limitations, constrained by forces which act upon him from without
because he has not been able to make them his own.
But to realise potentiality is to grow.

Yes; but to grow is to fulfil destiny, to move towards
a predetermined form. How, then, can growth eman-
cipate the growing soul? How can a man, by yielding
to a relentless pressure—for what pressure is so relentless as that of growth?—become able either to resist that
pressure or to intensify it? How can self-determination
be predetermined? How can the very stress of necessity
set its victim free?

We are up against the central paradox of our existence. A paradox it will always remain. Yet it may

be possible so to deal with it that it will " comfort while it mocks."

We have worked our way to a theory of freedom which countenances the idea of growth. What we now need is a theory of growth which will countenance the idea of freedom. Such a theory is at our service if we will not shrink from the immense demands which it will make upon us. We have seen that if by freedom we mean exemption from external constraint, there is one thing and one thing only which is absolutely free—the soul of the universe, the living whole. If this—the fountain-head of all freedom—is the true self of each of us, the self which each of us, so far as he fulfils his destiny, is predestined to realise, and if it is by growing on all the planes of his being, by bringing all his latent powers to maturity, that one fulfils that high destiny, then the ideas of freedom and predetermined growth are reconcilable through the paradoxical conception that man is predestined to become free. And if this is indeed his destiny, then, while he is fulfilling it, he must be winning freedom through his fulfilment of it, and must therefore be free either to thwart it or to ally himself with it. And as, by using his freedom to thwart his destiny, he will gradually forfeit his freedom and become the slave of his own lower desires and impulses—the hereditary enemies of his spiritual growth,—so, by using his freedom to co-operate with his destiny, he will win an ever fuller measure of freedom, thereby fitting himself for the work of co-operating, in an ever higher degree. Indeed, there is a stage in his development beyond which his destiny cannot fulfil itself without his active co-operation. Thenceforth, the more effectively he co-operates, the more willing is destiny to hand over to him the duty and responsibility of directing his own growth. At last, in the fullness of time, he will become his own destiny, and predetermination and self-determination will become one. From this point of view one sees that in man, as in every other living thing, the process of self-realisation is the fulfilment of a destiny, the evolution of a latent life, and yet that the individual soul is free—not absolutely, as Dr. Schiller seems to suggest, but within ever-varying limits—to go to God or go to the Devil, to make or to mar itself.

On one point we must make our minds quite clear. The goal of self-realisation is oneness with the One Life. This, and nothing less than this. The idea of self-realisation is all too easily misinterpreted; and to misinterpret it is to invert its meaning. If the universe is a living whole, the only way for each of us to integrate himself (and so win freedom), without disintegrating it, is to become one with it. He who thinks to win freedom, not by growing into oneness with the living whole, but by becoming a living whole on his own account, by integrating himself independently of the supreme integer, by separating himself from the cosmic life and finding the fullness of life in a little world of his own, has renounced his high birthright in the act of laying claim to it prematurely, and has become a disintegrative and morbific influence in the body politic of the great world to which, in spite of himself, he still belongs. Separatism, individualism, aggressive egoism, self-realisation, with the stress on the word *self*, is the sin of sins, the malady of maladies, the exact equivalent, in the pathology of the soul, of the disease of rebellious and therefore malignant growth which we call cancer in the pathology of the body. And the end of it is not freedom, but imprisonment in an ever-narrowing self.

We can now see that the theory of freedom which countenances the idea of soul-growth and the theory of soul-growth which countenances the idea of freedom are one. It sometimes happens that ideas which are irreconcilable and even mutually exclusive on the normal levels of experience and thought, admit of being reconciled and even harmonised into a higher and more comprehensive idea on that super-normal level which we indicate by the formula " at infinity." And it certainly seems as if the apparently irreconcilable ideas of freedom and growth ceased to be irreconcilable when viewed from the standpoint of the ideal and ultimate identity of the individual with the Universal Soul. Realising, then, as I do to the full, that the supreme mystery will ever remain mysterious, I must henceforth be content to find rest (such rest as it affords, the rest of eternal motion) in the conception to which the central experiences of my life—the sense of freedom and the sense of predestination—as I follow them out in thought, direct my mind—a conception which is a paradox in itself and paradoxical in all its developments—the conception that to universalise myself, to become one with the soul of all things, is my ideal destiny; and that I can either thwart that high destiny, in the strength of the freedom with which it invests me, and so become the thrall of a lower destiny, or escape for ever from thraldom to destiny by striving to fulfil my own.

July 1919.

RELIGION AS THE BASIS OF SOCIAL
RECONSTRUCTION

THE war has revealed to us the hollowness of the materialistic civilisation on which we had prided ourselves.
The social order which our armies and police forces
had maintained is breaking up. In many lands settled
government is giving place to anarchy, and the semblance
of prosperity to the reality of misery and want. Even in
those which are more fortunate the turmoil is great, and
there is a growing sense of insecurity, and a vague fore-
boding of disaster. We are being borne hither and
thither by swirling cross-currents of hatred, jealousy,
greed, ambition, and self-will. There are other currents
than these—larger, deeper, saner, purer. But in this
world-wide crisis the more turbulent currents have risen
to the surface, and human society has become a mael-
strom, strewn with the wreckage of many institutions
and traditions, and threatening shipwreck to many more.

No wonder that the idea of social reconstruction is in
the forefront of our thoughts. The theme is one which
touches many interests and attracts all classes and all
types of mind. Those who have suffered under the old
order of things clamour for a new order. Those who
have profited by the old order are beginning to realise
that things cannot go on as they were and that their
own tenure of " the good things of life " is, to say the
least, insecure. Politicians promise us a better and a
happier world. Statesmen are busy with schemes of
practical reform. Each clique, each party, each group of
enthusiasts or faddists—Trade Unionists, State Socialists,

Guild Socialists, Syndicalists, Anarchists, Individualists, Teetotalers, Tariff Reformers, Currency Reformers, Land Reformers — has its own formula for reconstruction. Opinions and proposals are many and various; and such features as they have in common are negative rather than positive. In particular, there are two factors in the great problem which all the rebuilders seem to have agreed to ignore — Education and Religion (the essentials of each, not the externals). Yet to reconstruct society without regard to education is to build without laying foundations. And to reconstruct without regard to religion is to build without a plan.

How can we best repair these vital omissions? Let us begin with religion. Religion controls all things, including education. Without a ground-plan of our proposed edifice we cannot so much as stake out its foundations. When I speak of building without a plan, I am thinking of an architect's plan, not of a speculative builder's. The speculative builder works to a plan, no doubt, but his plan is planless. His aim, in running up a house, is to sell it at a profit as soon as possible and then forget all about it. The plan as such does not interest him. What does interest him is to get a quick return on his money. For the architect, on the other hand, if and so far as he is an artist, the plan is everything. His aim, in designing a house, is to realise an ideal—an ideal of comfort, convenience, durability, inward harmony, outward beauty. If our reconstruction of society is to be successful, we must work as architects, not as speculative builders. We must not be content to meet immediate demands, to satisfy conflicting claims, to provide this thing here and that thing there. We must try to embody an ideal in our social structure—a spiritual ideal, a dream of a perfect world.

Now our architectonic ideals are all in the keeping of

religion. For what is religion? From one point of view, a struggling science. From another, a struggling art. The subject-matter of religion, as a science, is supreme reality, the popular name of which is God. When man's vision of supreme reality becomes the object of his desire, rather than his thought, it transforms itself into his ultimate ideal. And to realise ultimate ideals is the function of religion, as an art.

Religion, then, whether we accept or reject it, whether we reckon with it or try to ignore it, is in command of the whole situation. If and so far as our religion is false, our vision of supreme reality will be defective, our ultimate ideal will be inadequate, and the structure of our social life will be badly planned. But the structure will be still worse planned if we do what we are now intent on doing—if we ignore religion in our attempts at social reconstruction, and think to dispense with its inspiration and guidance. For then we shall be building without a plan, building as speculative builders, not as architects. And the result of our labour will be an ill-built, inconvenient, insanitary, perishable structure, not the realisation of a high ideal, not an enduring monument of vision and forethought and skill.

That the existing social structure was badly planned, that it embodies an inadequate ideal, is proved by its present collapse. If the ideal which it embodies is inadequate, the architect's vision of supreme reality must have been defective, and the central conceptions of his creed must have been at fault. These considerations point to one momentous conclusion. The reconstruction of religion must both precede and accompany the reconstruction of society.

What form will the reconstruction of religion take? Let us go back to first principles. We mean by God supreme reality. So I have ventured to assume. And my assumption will, I think, commend itself to all who believe in God. Those who regard what is ultimate in analysis—atoms, ions, electrons, or whatever else the *primordia rerum* may prove to be—as supremely real will decline to grant it, but only because their own vision of reality does not kindle aspiration or love. We can think of supreme reality as outside the world of our experience, and outside our own inner life. This is the transcendent God. Or we can think of supreme reality as at the heart of the world of our experience, and at the heart of our own inner life. This is the immanent God. We have hitherto worshipped, or tried to worship, the transcendent God. We have thought of God as the supernatural creator and therefore as the autocratic ruler of the universe. We have thought of the world of our experience, and of ourselves who dwell in that world, as bereft of his presence, and therefore as fallen, ruined, accurst. But we have also thought of him as entering at his own good pleasure into relations with the world of our experience, with ruined nature, with fallen man; and as choosing for the purpose of his self-revelation special prophets, a special people, a special church. And this idea of a special revelation we have interpreted, as might have been expected, in our own favour. The votaries of each religion in turn believe that their God is the true God. In particular, we who call ourselves Christians are convinced that we dwell in the light of God's countenance and that the rest of mankind sit in darkness and the shadow of death.

We have gone on to believe that blind obedience to the revealed will of the transcendent God is the beginning and end of virtue, the only means of salvation, the only passport to eternal life. And we have accepted all the sinister consequences of this fundamental assumption. From the materialism in the region of imaginative thought, which has blinded us to the inward light, we have passed on to literalism in our interpretation of God's message, to externalism in morals and in our general attitude towards life, to individualism in our scramble for God's favours. We have approached the throne of God as servile courtiers, petitioning him, each for himself, first for the boon of salvation (which depends on his nod or his frown) and then for secular blessings and privileges (which, as an omnipotent wonder-worker, he can provide and distribute at will). We have paid homage to him as the overlord of a feudal hierarchy, which is secular as well as spiritual; as the guarantor of the " divine right " of kings and princes—and multi-millionaires; as the fountain-head of authority and patronage; as the arbitrary dispenser of power, position, property, and privilege; as the controller of our various destinies; as the orderer of our various estates. Above all, the " Haves," the favoured few, have persuaded themselves, and tried to persuade the " Have-nots," that social inequality and injustice are divinely ordained and must therefore be accepted, if not with gratitude, at least with pious resignation.

This is the conception of God which has embodied itself in the existing social structure. That structure has long shown signs of decay, and is now falling to pieces. The " Have-nots " are ceasing to accept social inequality as of divine dispensation, and, having found strength in union and organisation, are preparing to claim their share of the " good things of life," even if this should involve the forcible spoliation of the " Haves." The old order of things is passing, and the days of propping and patching are over. If we are to rebuild society we must work to a new plan, we must have a new social ideal, a new conception of God.

In trying to enter into direct relations with the

transcendent God we have attempted the impossible. Relationship and absolute transcendence are incompatible ideas, incompatible in the logic of words and thoughts, incompatible in the deeper logic of experience and life. The idea of divine transcendence will always haunt us; and it is well that it should do so. But if we allow the idea to materialise, we shall run the risk of profaning the most sacred of all mysteries. The transcendent God reveals himself in the immanent God, and we must accept that revelation and ask for no other.

Let us worship the immanent God, then, and know that in doing so we are offering the transcendent God the only tribute which he desires or will accept. Let us worship the immanent God, and try to live up to our faith in him. The immanent God is at the heart of nature and therefore at the heart of man. He is the life of man's inmost life, the soul of man's inmost soul. As such he is the ideal self, and therefore the true self, of each of us—of the worst of men not less than of the best, of the least of men not less than of the greatest. To realise the ideal self, to become one with the indwelling spirit of God, is the purpose of man's life. And the purpose of life determines the meaning. The end determines the way. Destiny determines duty.

Divine immanence has its counterpart in human equality. Because God is the true self of each of us, we are all potentially equal; and this potential equality, being rooted in the infinite and the ideal, overpowers and dwarfs to nothing all the actual differences of which we make so much. Equality, in this sense of the word, is the ideal basis of our social and political life. Because God is the true self of each of us, we are able to come together as brothers, as comrades, as fellow-men, as " members one of another," as sharers in a common life, as inheritors of a common destiny. And this is not all. The path of self-realisation is the path of self-development, of growth. It is by growing, by expanding our being, by bringing our powers and capacities to maturity, by making the most of our limitless possibilities, that we find—or, at least, set out to find—the ideal self. And growth, in the case of man as of every other organism, is carried on through adaptation and reaction to environment. Now the environment of the individual is to a large extent under the control of the social community to which he happens to belong. It follows that the right to share in the government of the community, and to that extent to shape and control his own environment, is inherent in his right to realise his ideal self. In this two-fold right, which is also a two-fold duty, we have the real basis, and the only durable basis, of democracy.[1] To democratise our social life on any other basis than this, is to build (or, in the present crisis, to rebuild) on shifting sand.

The relation of the individual to the community may be looked at from another point of view. The path of self-development is the path of self-emancipation, of escape from bondage to self. In any process of growth there is a conflict between the ideal and the actual, between the universal and the individual self. If a man is to realise his high destiny, he must make growth of soul as well as of body. And as his potentialities are limitless, the growth of his soul must never cease. But

---

[1] Am I taking too much for granted when I use the word "democracy"? I do not think so. Autocracy proper has recently committed suicide; and the inverted autocracy of Bolshevism is a devastating fire which will sooner or later die out for lack of fuel. Society must therefore be democratised if it is not to be abandoned to anarchy. Democracy has long been coming. It has now come —and come to stay. How long it will stay depends on what conception Demos forms of the meaning and purpose of life. Will he sow seed for his own harvesting only? Or will he try " to sow the seed the fruit of which shall feed the world "?

if his soul is to grow and keep on growing, he must overcome the resistance which his actual self, in every stage of his development, offers to the expansive forces that are making for the evolution of his ideal self. This resistance never ceases. If it did, the demand upon him to bring his reserves into action, to realise his latent potentialities, would cease also, and his soul would cease to grow. But if there is need for continuous resistance to the forces that make for growth, there is still greater need that the resistance should be continuously overcome. At whatever cost, man must conquer self, and keep on conquering it. He must break, again and again, the chains in which it seeks to bind him. He must escape, again and again, from the prison of finality in which it seeks to confine him, into the infinitude of the divine ideal.

Now the first and most obvious way of escaping from self is that of living in the lives of others, and in particular of giving disinterested service to whatever community has a claim on one's loyalty. This is the first way of escaping from self. It is also, as it happens, the last way. For the service *must* be disinterested: in other words, it must always have at the heart of it devotion to a wider community than that to which it is consciously given—devotion therefore, in the last resort, to the widest community of all. Absolutely disinterested devotion is an unattainable ideal. The pursuit of it must therefore be worthy of the goal. The man who serves a community because its material interests coincide with his own, and who regards such service as an end in itself, has but exchanged individual for collective selfishness, and is therefore still in bondage to self. The devotion of a robber to his gang may reach a high level of zeal and self-sacrifice. The loyalty of a swindler to his confederates may be unimpeachable. But in each case the communal sentiment is criminally selfish at heart; and its underlying selfishness must needs be a potent principle of social disintegration, for men who are held together by regard for their own material interests will always be ready to quarrel among themselves. Of all organised communities the one which does most for its members and has the strongest claim on their service is one's country. Yet even patriotism, if it has in it no vivifying germ of pan-humanism, will end by demoralising the patriot. In Germany, for example, the State, by claiming the whole of the loyalty and devotion of its citizens, and by teaching them to regard the material well-being of their country as the supreme end of their aims and efforts, has made them partners in its own inhumanity and selfishness, and so gone far towards corrupting their character and their morals.

Disinterested devotion, then, is the beginning and end of communal life. In this fact we have a key—perhaps *the* key—to the problem of social reconstruction. The *raison d'être* of the community is, first to enable each of its members to live securely and happily, and then—since happiness depends on health, and health on vigorous and harmonious growth—to help each of them to grow to the fullness of his ideal stature, to outgrow and keep on outgrowing self. If and so far as the community does this for the citizen, it renders the best possible service both to him and to itself. To him, because it helps him to fulfil the end of his being. To itself, because the better the man, the better the citizen, and the more effective his service. Its own claim for service will lead him into the path of self-realisation through self-sacrifice. But if the path is not to become a blind alley, the claim for service must be an unselfish claim. From first to last the community must try to qualify its members for the service of a community which is higher and wider than itself. This must be its τέλος τελειότατον, the final end for which it lives and works.

One's country, for example, must train one for the service of humanity; and the human commonwealth, when it has been organised, must train one for the service of the cosmic commonwealth, for citizenship in the kingdom of God. When the spirit of the community rises to the level of this high ideal, the relation between all and each will be one of complete reciprocity and therefore of perfect harmony. For their respective interests will wholly coincide, and yet—if I may be allowed the paradox—will be wholly disinterested. And in every case devotion to the larger community will safeguard the well-being and guarantee the integrity of the lesser. The patriot will be a better patriot when devotion to mankind takes precedence in his heart of devotion to his country. And the philanthropist will be a better philanthropist when love of God takes precedence in his heart of love of man.

I have said that disinterested devotion—devotion, in the last resort, to the immanent, the universal God—is the beginning and end of communal life. As the end of communal life, it gives us a general plan for the recon-struction of society—an ideal which each architect is free to realise by ways of his own. As the beginning of communal life, it gives us the cement in which the foundations of the social structure are to be laid, and by which, as it rises, its component parts are to be held together. But if the cement is to be well made and well laid, we must teach the lesson of disinterested devotion to our children as well as to ourselves. Or rather we must teach it to our children even more than to our-selves. For, in the first place, the child is father to the man. And, in the second place, it is as easy for him to learn the lesson as it is hard for us. He has little or nothing to unlearn. We have much. We have " grown hard," if not " in our viciousness," at least in our self-love. To ask the adult to make a radical change in his inner man—the change from selfishness to selflessness —is to set him a task of almost superhuman difficulty. " Conversion "—the sudden transformation of the inner man—is a very rare phenomenon. It presupposes an exceptional combination of circumstances. It is not always a healthy movement. It is sometimes hysterical or otherwise morbid. And the new life does not always endure, the violent change being sometimes followed by an equally violent reaction. If a change in the inner man is to be permanent and effective, it must be evolutionary rather than revolutionary, the outcome of a secret process of growth, rather than of a sudden reversal of the current of one's being. We adults are not past praying for. But if the reconstruction of society is to wait till most of us have been " converted," it will have to wait for ever.

It is in the nursery, then, and the schoolroom that the building of the new world must be begun. But it will not be begun until our educational ideals are reconstructed in harmony with the proposed reconstruction of religion. For if the cult of the transcendent God has been the evil genius of religion, it has been in no less a degree the evil genius of education. The parent and the schoolmaster have played the part of the God whom they worshipped, in the little worlds which they ruled. And they have reproduced in the life of the child, and therefore of the man, all the evils which the tyranny of the omnipotent autocrat has wrought in the life of mankind. They have applied to the child—applied, that is, to the growing man at the time when his growth ought to have been most vigorous, when the sap of his life was running most strongly—a steady and relentless pressure which has had behind it a heavy weight of ignorance, prejudice, and " will to power." The result of this pressure has been, in part to arrest, in part to warp his growth; and as growth, if healthy and harmonious, is the most emancipative of all forces, as it concentrates in itself all emancipative forces, the further result of the pressure of dogmatic education has been to imprison the child in himself. And as the child, animated by the instinct to live, has passively resisted this deadly pressure, the autocratic controllers of his destiny have tried to overcome his resistance by alternating rewards with punishments, bribes with threats. In doing this they have lowered the whole plane of his effort and activity, and de-idealised his whole outlook on life. And when bribes and threats have failed them, they have gone further along the path of compulsory demoralisation. Having killed the child's interest in his work by their blind faith in their own stereotyped methods, and their want of insight into his real needs, they have tried to revive it by forcing him to compete with his classmates for prizes and other marks of distinction. They have thus tempted him to regard his comrades as his rivals and possible enemies, to pride himself on his petty achievements, to look down on those—his equals, perhaps, or even his superiors in many ways—whom he may have happened to surpass in this or that branch of his narrow curriculum. In other words, they have deliberately exploited his selfishness, his ambition, and his vanity. They have done more than this. They have made him dependent on themselves for instruction and guidance, and have thus paralysed his faith in himself. They have weakened his will, partly by trying to break it, partly by giving him no opportunity for the exercise of self-discipline and self-control. They have made him blind, or at least dim of vision, by assuming that he could not see. They have sterilised his intellectual, his artistic, and his constructive capacities by wilfully narrowing the field of his development; and when his tastes and powers have died of inanition, they have taken for granted that they never existed, that he was by nature as stupid and helpless as he was vicious and perverse. They have taught him to look without instead of within for his ideals, his motives, his standards of value, his tests of reality, his proofs of failure or success. And, as the crowning injury, they have thought to make him religious, not by helping him to discover and follow the light that lighteth all men, but by compelling him to take part in ceremonial observances which have no meaning for him, and by forcibly dieting him on their own scriptures and creeds.

The whole scheme of his education seems to have been framed for the express purpose of turning him out into the world with few or no interests which can take him away from himself; the victim of arrested, or at best of one-sided, mental and spiritual development; imprisoned in a narrow and conventional morality; dominated by the prejudices of his own social class; absorbed in selfish aims and ambitions; destitute of any sense of human fellowship; a materialist; an individualist; an externalist; asking from life too much of comfort and pleasure, and too little of that deeper happiness which will be given to him freely if he will but claim it. There are many lessons which his pastors and masters have omitted to teach him. But there is one which they seem to have deliberately prevented him from learning—the lesson of disinterested devotion, of self-realisation through self-forgetfulness, of losing the world that he may find his soul.

Yet he was ready to learn that lesson before they took him in hand. The pioneers in education who have based their schemes of education on trust in the natural goodness and all-round capacity of the average child, have proved this to the full. There are schools in this country which are ideal social communities—schools in which the children, released from needless constraint, allowed to express themselves freely in many ways, allowed to develop themselves in many directions, have found, in the joy of "unimpeded activity," the sense of oneness with their fellows through partnership in a common life; schools in which material rewards and punishments are unknown; in which honest effort is its own reward; in which the success of each is a matter of rejoicing for all; in which the spirit of comradeship has killed the spirit of competition; in which the whole atmosphere is electrical with life and happiness and goodwill. At present such schools are few in number; but if the basis of education could be changed, they would multiply, and as they multiplied there would be a corresponding change in the basis of our social life.

The cult of the transcendent God, involving as it does profound distrust of human nature, is, I repeat, the evil genius of education. Let us now base education on the cult of the immanent God, and on the inexhaustible trust in human nature which is at the heart of that cult. It is not for me to suggest how this is to be done. The immanent God "fulfils himself in many ways"; and in the sphere of education, if in no other, exclusive devotion to any "one custom," however "good," will sooner or later "corrupt the world." The orthodox type of education has been a failure, not only because its aims and ideals have been at fault, but also because of its uncritical acceptance of traditional methods, which it has forced on the teacher as well as on the child. In this it has been true to its own master principle; for if the immanent God fulfils himself in many ways, the transcendent God—if those who speak in his name are to be believed—reveals himself in only one. Let the new education be equally true to the master principle which is inherent in its faith in divine immanence. At present the new education is a heresy. Let it take care that it never degenerates into orthodoxy. Let it give freedom and responsibility in generous measure to the teacher, and through the teacher to the child. Its confidence will not be misplaced. What matters it if each of a thousand pioneers in education takes a path of his own? If they are all animated by reverence for the indwelling Spirit of God, and therefore for the unfolding spirit of the child, they will all arrive, in the fullness of time, at the same goal.

For they will have taught their pupils, or rather helped them to learn of themselves, the great lesson of disinterested devotion, the great lesson of loyalty to the community—to an ever-widening community—in and through loyalty to one's own higher self. When this lesson has been widely learnt and practised, the reform of our social life will become something more than a politician's promise or an enthusiast's dream. It is through its action on the child, even more than on the adult, that the cult of the autocrat of the universe has corrupted man's nature and demoralised his life. The adult is what his upbringing has made him, and it is not easy for him to become anything else. But the child may become anything. The Kingdom of Heaven is as open to him as is the prison of self. We have hitherto gone out of our way to drive him into the prison of self; and the consequent selfishness of *his* child, " the man," is the chief obstacle to the desired reconstruction of society. Let us now help him to enrol himself as a citizen of God's kingdom. Then, in the next generation, we shall perhaps have a better and a happier world.

November 1919.

THE RELIGIOUS TRAINING OF
THE YOUNG

A PAPER READ AT MANCHESTER IN NOVEMBER 1919

I AM not going to sail under false colours; so I will begin by saying that I do not belong to any church or sect or other religious body. Some persons might say that I was a pantheist; others, an agnostic. But those who used those words as terms of reproach would mean by them something very different from what they mean for me. I am a pantheist in that I regard the order of things in which I find myself as a living whole, unified by its own indwelling soul-life—one world, one life, one God and Father of all, who is above all, and through all and in you all. And I am an agnostic in that my faith in the universal order is so complete and so unquestioning that it does not need to be formulated. I am quite content that it should remain fluid and indeterminate; dynamic, not static; a thing to be possessed by, not to possess. If I were to give myself any title I would say that, as an idealist and an optimist, I was, in spirit if not in practice, a follower of Christ.

The problem which we have met to consider is that of the religious training of the young. What do we mean by religion? If each of us were to write down an answer to this question we should get as many answers as there are persons in this room. Would those answers have anything, either actually or potentially, in common? Is there anything quintessential in the idea of religion on which we in this room can all agree? I think there is.

For I suppose we are all Christians, each in his own way. And I think that our Master, Christ, in the story or parable (I know not which to call it) of the Last Judgment, answered the question which I am asking, once and for all time. We know what evil fate has befallen that story; how it has been used to bribe and terrorise the believer; to debase and materialise his conception of salvation; to make him think of eternal life as a bare escape from hell-fire; to darken his days with the awful shadow of an approaching doom; to turn what should have been a trumpet-call to battle into the despairing cry of *sauve qui peut*. Was there ever such a tragedy? If there are any passages in our own or any other Scripture, in which the spirit is everything and the letter nothing, this is surely one of them. From first to last it is a glorification of unselfish love. For what happens at the Great Assize? Who are saved and who are lost? Those who have loved and served their fellow-men are saved. Those who have never loved or served their fellow-men are lost. If religion, whether implicit or explicit, is necessary to salvation, then it is certain that the quintessence of religion, as Christ conceived it, is *unselfish love*.

The word *unselfish* is all-important. The love which Christ had in mind was to be free from every taint of self. The words in which the Divine Judge pronounces judgment make this clear. " Then shall the King say unto them on his right hand, ' Come, ye blessed of my Father, inherit the Kingdom prepared for you from the foundation of the world; for I was an hungered, and ye gave me meat: I was thirsty and ye gave me drink: I was a stranger, and ye took me in: naked, and ye clothed me: I was sick and ye visited me: I was in prison and ye came unto me.' Then shall the righteous answer him, saying, 'Lord, when saw we thee an hungered and fed thee? or thirsty, and gave thee drink? When saw we thee a stranger, and took thee in? or naked, and clothed thee? Or when saw we thee sick, or in prison, and came unto thee?' And the King shall answer and say unto them, 'Verily, I say unto you, Inasmuch as ye have done it unto the least of these my brethren, ye have done it unto me.'" The righteous, those who loved and served their fellow-men, did so without any hope of reward. They did not even know that in serving their fellow-men they were serving God. They fed the hungry, they gave drink to the thirsty, they entertained the stranger, they clothed the naked, they ministered to the sick, they visited the prisoner, because they loved them, and for no other reason. Unselfish love, disinterested devotion, service which asks for no wages— this is the heart and soul of religion; and the subconscious knowledge of God which is implicit in such love and devotion and service is the only knowledge that really counts. I have high authority, the highest of all, for saying this.

That being so, the question arises, How shall we best teach religion to children? How shall we best initiate them into the knowledge of God? How do we teach religion? In nearly all our elementary schools—I speak of these because I know them best—religion is a kind of compulsory extra. Half an hour is set aside for it at the beginning of each morning session. When that half-hour is over, religion is done with for the day, and the real work of the school begins. In thus emphasising the distinction between the religious and the secular life, those who control the education of the young have made a fatal departure from the teaching of Christ. For in glorifying love as the fulfilling of the law and the only means of salvation, Christ taught us that what is the quintessential element in religion is also the quintessential in life. The "saved" in the story of the Last Judgment had all been religious without knowing it. In living for others they had gone to the heart of religion and also to the heart of life.

What goes on in the half-hour which is set apart for religious instruction? I wish those who talk and write and quarrel about religious instruction could see for themselves what form it usually takes. When I was a school inspector, an uncomfortably early train sometimes landed me at a school while the Scripture lesson (as it was usually called) was in progress. Having greeted the teacher and asked leave to wait in school till the lesson was over, I sat down and listened—and said nothing. But I thought a great deal. For the first thing that struck me was that all the glaring faults of method which the examination system had fostered in our schools, and which, since the abolition of that system, we inspectors had been fighting against, had found a safe asylum in the Scripture half-hour. Parrot-like repetition of what the teacher had said, collective recitation and reading, gabbling and mumbling, collective answering, irregular answering, scribbling on slates, and other objectionable practices were in full swing, and our efforts to extirpate them during the hours for secular instruction were to that extent being counteracted. There was no mistaking the significance of these sinister symptoms. The children were evidently being crammed for a formal examination on a prescribed syllabus. As usually happens in such cases, the victims of the cramming process took little or no interest in what they were doing, while their teachers were too much preoccupied with the work of preparing for the impending examination, to think about anything else.

This is a fairly accurate account of what went on in most of the Denominational (or "non-Provided")

Schools. In the Board (or Council, or " Provided ") Schools the Scripture lesson was somewhat shorter and was as a rule confined to instruction in the Bible, which in many cases was carried out according to a prescribed syllabus and tested by periodical examination.

Such were the methods by which nine-tenths of the children in this country were initiated into the knowledge of God. Have things changed since then? Not materially, as far as I can see. The Diocesan Inspector is still in evidence. Syllabuses of religious instruction are still prescribed. And yearly examinations are still held. Can we wonder that our country is relapsing, as religious people say it is, into paganism?

What is to be done? The first and most obvious thing to do is to cease to examine children in what we call religious knowledge. If by religious knowledge we mean knowledge of God, and if it is by losing himself in love and service that a man attains to knowledge of God, then the folly of pretending to examine in religious knowledge is self-evident, and some other method of gauging the spiritual vitality of a school must be found. How can you examine children in unselfishness, in singleness of heart, in brotherly love? You can, if you please, examine them in knowledge of hymns and texts and catechisms and Bible stories. But, in the first place, knowledge of these things no more constitutes religious knowledge than knowledge of the definitions of geographical terms or of the names of capes and bays constitutes knowledge of geography, or than knowledge of dates and battles and the names of kings and queens constitutes knowledge of history. Indeed, the difference between formal and real knowledge is far greater in the case of religion than of any secular subject. And, in the second place, if it is thought desirable that children should have some knowledge of hymns and texts and catechisms and Bible stories, why should not the teacher be trusted to give such knowledge? Why should he not be relieved from the hateful necessity of cramming children for an examination in it? He would then be free to approach the Scripture lesson in another spirit and from another point of view.

But if the Diocesan Inspector is to give up examining, what will be left for him to do? Well, let him become an inspector, in deed as well as in name. Let him go to a school unannounced, and spend a whole day in it. Let him be with the children in the class-room and the playground. Let him walk home with some of them and talk to them freely—about things in general, not about religion, in any narrow sense of that word. Let him discuss things with the head teacher and his staff. Let him get them to tell him of their experiences, their difficulties, their encouragements. Let him tell them what has been done in other schools, and in this and other ways give them help and guidance. He will then get to know far more about the tone and spirit of the school than will be possible if he does no more than examine it once a year on a prescribed syllabus. The real, the only, test of religious knowledge is life. Insight into the daily life of a school may give an inspector some idea of its spiritual vitality. Asking questions of drilled classes and listening to their answers will give him little or none. Let me add that the inspector who took this view of his work would soon realise the futility of writing formal reports on the schools that he visited and classifying them as *Excellent, Good* and *Fair*.

But what can the teacher do to give his pupils religious instruction, in the true sense of the phrase—initiation into the knowledge of God? If he can do nothing else, he can at least make it possible for them to learn the great lesson of disinterested devotion, of unselfish love.

Let me say again that the words *disinterested* and *un-selfish* are all-important. Devotion to a cause or a community does not necessarily take one to God. If it did, the robber who was loyal to his gang would be one of the children of light. Nor does love of a human being. Nor does religious zeal. The pre-war devotion of the German to his country was a noble sentiment as far as it went; but because it did not go far enough, because it stopped short with his country, because there was no love of humanity at the heart of it, there was a strain of selfishness in it which demoralised it and him, and led him to perpetrate various crimes and atrocities in the full belief that the end—the triumph of his country —justified whatever means might be taken to secure it. The mutual love of two human beings may be nothing better than an *égoïsme à deux*. And much of the devotion which has been given to God, to Christ, to the Church, to the Saints, has been fundamentally selfish, having been inspired by the fear of eternal punishment, by the hope of being numbered among the remnant of the elect, by the desire to secure temporal boons or even to compass immoral ends. Many a man who believed himself to be religious has prayed for vengeance on his enemies or for success in some nefarious scheme.

If love and devotion and service are to take us to God they must be purified of every taint of self. No profit-and-loss calculation must enter into them. They must be given because we cannot help giving them, because their objects draw us with irresistible force. How is this purification of the heart to be effected? How is the lesson of unselfish love to be learnt? There is an obvious answer to this question. Devotion to a cause or a community must always have at the heart of it devotion to a larger cause or a wider community, till we come at last to the largest of all causes and the widest of all communities, to the service of God, to membership of his kingdom. And this is the only pathway to God. There are no short cuts to salvation. " He that loveth not his brother whom he hath seen, how can he love God whom he hath not seen? " We must pass through all the stages in our pilgrimage and rest in none of them till we enter into the rest which transcends repose, the peace which passeth all understanding, rest in the Infinite and the Divine. Yet there is no community so small, no cause so humble, but, if we serve it unselfishly and uncalculatingly, it has the Infinite and the Divine at the heart of it. " Forasmuch as ye did it unto the least of these my brethren, ye did it unto me." It is this reaching on into the Infinite, in the endeavour to escape from self, which distinguishes religion from morality; or rather which moralises religion and spiritualises morality, and makes the two no longer two but one. The failure of the Positivists to develop the religion of humanity, the failure of the Ethical Societies to evangelise mankind, are easily accounted for. There can never be a religion of humanity; for though the service of humanity is a noble end of action, it is not an end in itself. There must needs be a nobler service at the heart of it, if it is not to degenerate into a mere effort to diffuse creature comforts, to raise wages all the world over and shorten the hours of work. The best service that we can render to humanity is to help it to realise its own ideal; and its ideal is something beyond itself.

Let us go back to our children. If they are to become religious, if they are to attain to knowledge of God, they must learn the lesson of disinterested devotion. They are ready to learn this lesson, readier than we are; for they are less given to making profit-and-loss calculations, to weighing the advantages and disadvantages to themselves of proposed courses of action. When a cause appeals to them they give their hearts to it, and ask for no reward. But they must learn the lesson for themselves. We cannot drill it into them. We cannot coerce them into unselfishness. We cannot bribe them to forget themselves. For coercion and bribery involve an appeal to selfish motives, to fear in the one case, to greed in the other; and to teach unselfishness through an appeal to selfish motives is to undermine the foundations which we are trying to lay. The best thing that we can do is to set children free to learn the greatest of all lessons for themselves. Here we come to the fundamental principle for which some at least of us stand. We believe in learning by doing, as opposed to learning by listening and memorising and obeying the word of command. This principle is applicable to education because it is applicable to life. It is therefore as applicable to religious as to secular education. Indeed it is through its action that the distinction between religious and secular education effaces itself, and the two merge into one. Experience has proved that if learning by doing is to answer its purpose, a generous measure of freedom must be given to children; for if, when they are trying to do things, you insist on holding their hands and directing all their movements, they will do little and learn less.

We must begin, then, by giving children freedom for self-development, and, with freedom, so much of sympathetic help and judicious guidance as they need and can turn to good account. In the atmosphere of freedom, interest in work and joy in working will take the place of the distaste for work, the unwilling obedience, the perfunctory discharge of duties, which the dogmatic, dictatorial, disciplinary type of education has always tended to produce. When work comes to be enjoyed for its own sake the need for rewards and punishments will cease. This will be a notable step in advance. The threat of punishment appeals to an unworthy motive. But the offer of rewards is even more demoralising, for it makes competition compulsory and thus involves the deliberate exploitation of ambition, vanity, envy, jealousy and other forms of self-love. With the passing of competition between child and child, the co-operative instinct will be free to assert itself and the spirit of comradeship will awake in the school.

The spirit of comradeship is not *necessarily* unselfish. On the contrary, it is compatible with collective selfishness in each of the many forms which the latter assumes. There is comradeship as well as honour among thieves. The miners and other workers who hold up the economic life of the country in order to enforce their demand for higher wages and shorter hours, are no doubt good comrades in their relations to one another. So were the Germans who devastated and terrorised invaded countries in the supposed interest of their Fatherland. But the spirit of comradeship is *essentially* unselfish; and when it first awakes among children, as the natural overflow of their joy and good-will, there is something spontaneous and uncalculating in it which keeps it free from the taint of self. Such a spirit is potentially religious, in the deepest sense of the word; there is no side of the child's life which it will not illumine and inspire; and if it develops itself under favourable conditions, there is no height of heroism or self-sacrifice to which it will not at last ascend.

I leave it to others to make suggestions as to worship and ceremonial, doctrinal instruction, the study of the Bible and, above all, the use of music to awake or quicken religious emotion. These, as it seems to me, are accessories of religion, accessories which are indispensable for some temperaments and some types of mind, but not for others. The life and soul of religion, the essential element in it which no one can dispense with, is disinterested devotion, unselfish love. Children will teach themselves this greatest of all lessons, if we will make it possible for them to do so. If they do not teach it to themselves, it will never be taught. When the Diocesan Inspector has made a radical change of method, the change from examining to inspecting, in the true sense of the latter word; when the yearly parade-day in religion has become a thing of the past; when the fatal distinction between religious and secular education has been effaced; when teachers have ceased to exploit the competitive instincts of their pupils; when faith in the natural goodness and intelligence of the child has taken the place of the deep-seated distrust of him which has hitherto dominated education; when children of all ages have been given such a measure of freedom as will enable them to work out their own salvation in all the spheres of their activity; when the spirit of co-operation, of good fellowship, of comradeship, which has so long been forcibly repressed, is given free play; then the religious instinct which is at the heart of human nature will begin to develop and express itself, and the problem of the religious training of the young, which seems to be insoluble, will begin to work itself out to its true solution.

Let me say, in conclusion, that the need for religion, the religious spirit, the spirit of disinterested devotion, has never been so urgent as it is to-day. The world is sick unto death, and the malady from which it is suffering is, in a word, selfishness. Individual selfishness is rampant. The profiteer, the slacker in mine or factory, the superfluous official who is firmly entrenched in a Government bureau, each of these is playing for his own hand, without any regard to the well-being of his country.

And collective or corporate selfishness is an even graver malady. The selfishness of this or that nation, or of this or that political party, is delaying—fatally delaying—the re-settlement of the disordered world. The selfishness of this or that ring of capitalists or of this or that trade union is strangling the economic life of mankind and threatening to disintegrate society. And collective selfishness is an insidious as well as a malignant malady, for it easily mistakes itself for unselfishness, the individual priding himself on his loyalty to the community and counting it as virtue, even while the community —the clique, the gang, the ring, the syndicate, the trade union, or whatever it may be—is working for essentially selfish ends.

There is but one remedy for this desperate disorder, the remedy which I have already indicated. Devotion to a community, if it is to purge itself of selfishness, must have at the heart of it devotion to a wider community, till we come at last to the widest of all communities, the Infinite, the Ideal, the kingdom of God. No service but that of God—not even the service of humanity— is to be regarded as an end in itself. In other words, in the awful crisis through which we are now passing religion, and religion alone, can save us. But though religion is still widely professed, it shows no sign of saving us. Why? Because profession is one thing and practice another, and because, if practice is to be real and effective, it must begin in the nursery and the schoolroom. Hitherto profession has preceded practice in religion as in all the branches of secular instruction. We have taught our children to profess religion. We have not taught them, or encouraged them, or even allowed them, to practise it. Over the whole field of education the tide is now turning in favour of practice. We are beginning to realise that practice must precede profession; that the subconscious knowledge which is implicit in practice must precede the conscious apprehension of facts, laws and principles if the latter is to have any meaning or purpose. What is true of education as such is true of religious education. Practice must come first, the practice of pure religion and undefiled. Children must learn the lesson of unselfish love, of uncalculating loyalty, of service which asks for no reward. They must learn the lesson with our help and our guidance, if indeed we are competent to give help and guidance, but they must learn it in the main for themselves. If it is too late for us adults to master that lesson, let us at least set our children free to learn it. When they have learnt it, they will be able to do what we are now dreaming of doing—to rebuild the ruined world.

THE PHILOSOPHY OF MY OLD AGE

IF I had to give a name to the philosophy in which my soul has found refuge—the refuge, not of a safe harbour, but of the open sea—I would call it the philosophy of *wholeness*. When I made my choice between materialism and idealism, I committed myself to the assumption that what is ultimate in synthesis, not in analysis, is real. What is ultimate in synthesis is the universe itself, the totality of things regarded as an organic whole. This is real—supremely real, absolutely real, alone real. The things that surround me are real in varying degrees; but they are real with, and in, and through, the reality of the all-embracing whole. The unifying principle in things is life. Whenever we have the one in the many, unity in complexity, we have either life, or—as in the case of man's handiwork, whether artistic or mechanical—the expression and embodiment of life. The greater the complexity the higher is the unity, and the higher the life to which it bears witness.

As life gains in complexity and unity it begins to transform itself into soul-life. It may indeed be contended that all life is soul-life, that even in the humblest beginnings of life the germs of soul-life are discernible. Perhaps they are. What is certain is that the higher the life the more worthy is the organism, the thing that lives, to bear the title of living soul. If this is so, then the life of the whole is soul-life, pure and simple. In other words, the soul of the universe (God, as we call it) is what is ultimately real in the universe; real in a

sense which it is difficult to define, but which is implicit
in Emily Brontë's sublime apostrophe of the Eternal:

> Though earth and man were gone,
> And suns and universes ceased to be,
> And Thou wert left alone,
> Every existence would exist in Thee—

real in the sense of being the fountain-head of reality,
the ocean which is at once the source and the goal of
all its own affluent and refluent streams, and which is
also *in* each of these, from the trickling rivulet to the
great river which is widening out into the sea.

In what relation do I, the individual, stand to the
universal soul? The answer to this question is to be
lived rather than spoken. My bias towards wholeness
is practical as well as theoretical. In the very act of
recognising the supreme reality of wholeness, I recognise self-integration, or the achievement of wholeness,
as the end and purpose of my life. The transition from
the one position to the other is real rather than notional,
vital rather than logical.

But what is self-integration, and how is it to be
achieved? It is obviously the goal, the unattainable goal,
of the process of self-realisation or soul-growth. If I am
to achieve wholeness, I must realise all my potentialities,
I must grow to the fullness of my predestined stature.
The law of growth is the master law of my being, and
the essence of growth is the realisation of the ideal which
is at the heart of the actual. What is the ideal self which
is at the heart of my actual self? And in what relation
does it stand to the ideal self or soul of the universe?

This is the question of questions. Can I integrate
myself independently of the supreme integer, the living
whole? Surely not. If the universe is a living whole,
I live in its life, and apart from its life I am nothing.
In a perfectly-organised organism each part and each
particle functions for the good of the whole, and finds

its own *raison d'être* in doing so. When the part or the
particle is itself a living being, it finds the well-spring
of its own life in living for the whole. We, as conscious
intelligent beings, are free within varying limits to make
our choice between living for the whole and living for
self. We can, if we please, try to integrate self apart
from the supreme integer. In other words, we can, if
we please, try to achieve wholeness by living for self.
But the attempt is foredoomed to ruinous failure. For
either it takes the form of undue specialisation, as when
the artist lives for art, the fanatic for religion, the voluptuary for pleasure. Or it takes the more familiar form
of accepting the actual self as adequate and final, of
idealising it, of ministering or trying to minister to all
its desires and demands. Undue specialisation is obviously the negation of self-realisation. The specialist
deliberately sacrifices the whole to the part; and his
punishment is that the special end at which he aims
eludes his pursuit owing to his failure to relate it to the
meaning and purpose of the whole. The artist who
lives for art and art only, misinterprets the function of
art as surely and as profoundly as the fanatic misinterprets the function of religion, or the voluptuary
the function of pleasure. It is the same with the man
who idealises his actual self and tries to live for it. He,
too, is doomed to stultify his own efforts, to " baffle his
own prayers." For the more assiduously he ministers
to the desires and demands of self, the more insatiable
do these become; so that, instead of integrating self, he
finds, sooner or later, that he has been working for its
— and his — disintegration, contracting its range and
lowering its level by his life of self-indulgence and self-
absorption, till at last, with the ever-narrowing circles and
ever-accelerating velocity of a whirlpool, it begins to lose
itself in, and draw him down into, its own deadly depths.

Selfishness is universally reprobated, and unselfishness is universally honoured. We realise, subconsciously, if not consciously, that these are the left-hand and the right-hand paths respectively, between which each of us must make his choice. But we do not sufficiently realise that the choice between the two resolves itself in the last resort into the choice between the individual and the universal self, between bondage to the actual and the finite, and devotion to the ideal and the whole. In the sphere of conduct the choice between un-self and self is the choice between right and wrong. There is no kind of right-doing which is not ultimately resolvable either into self-control or into self-surrender; no kind of wrong-doing which is not ultimately resolvable either into self-indulgence or into self-assertion.

But in neither case does our analysis go deep enough. We do not realise either the purpose or the scope of either of these ways of life. Hence the confusion, the demoralising confusion, of our views about morality. Hence our inability to come to an understanding with ourselves as to the relation between morality and religion. Matthew Arnold defined religion as morality touched with emotion. This definition is, I think, wholly inadequate. Would it not be nearer to truth to say that religion is morality transformed and even transfigured by " the intuition of totality " and the consequent sense of obligation to the whole? The essence of religion is disinterested devotion, devotion to an end so large that the service of it must needs exclude every thought of self. And it is the capacity for disinterested devotion which distinguishes the dwellers on the higher from those on the lower levels of morality,—the saint and the hero from the man who is content to do his duty to his neighbour and obey the law.

If the religious sense, the sense of obligation to the

whole, is the ideal basis of man's moral life, it is also, and in no less a degree, the ideal basis of his social life. The distinction between the moral and the social life is a more or less artificial one, and will not (one may safely predict) be permanently maintained. The social life is the life of obligation to one's neighbour as a fellow-citizen; the moral life the life of obligation to him as a fellow-man. When the tribe was the only political unit, the two lives were one, or rather the moral life had not yet begun to disengage itself from the social. With the gradual supersession of tribalism, first by civicism (if there is such a word) and then by nationalism, the separation between the two lives began. This was a necessary stage in man's development, but it was also a misfortune for each of the diverging lives. While the two were still one their union was blest by religion, but it was a narrow religion, the cult of a tribal deity, a god whose hand was (or might be) against other gods. When the two become one again, religion will again bless their union. But it will be a religion as wide as the tribal religion was narrow. Christianity tried to fuse the two lives into one, but it failed disastrously because, in defiance of the teaching of its Founder, it worshipped a glorified tribal deity, a god who was supposed to be pan-cosmic, and who yet was jealous and had favourites and took sides. If the two lives are indeed to become one, their fusion will have to be effected through the worship of the All-Father, the living Whole.

The separation of the moral from the social life has thrown both lives into dire confusion. When the well-being of the tribe was the final end of moral action, the path of duty was direct and clear. To-day, in the labyrinthine maze of our complex life, the path is hard to find and easy to lose. Selfishness mistakes itself in all sincerity for unselfishness, and a hideous crime may even pose as a heroic act. That Germany should have sought to justify her treacherous invasion of Belgium, and prided herself on the sinking of the *Lusitania* and other atrocities, shows what urgent need there is for a paramount principle, for a High Court of Appeal, to adjust the respective claims of the two lives. Such a principle, such a Court of Appeal, is at our service if we will but invoke its aid. We have seen that the supreme choice for each of us, whether our outlook on life be wide or narrow, is that between selfishness and unselfishness. Let us take care then, when we devote ourselves to a community or a cause, that there are no dregs of selfishness in our seemingly disinterested devotion. Collective or corporate selfishness is as real and as immoral as individual selfishness, and has the advantage (from its own point of view) over the latter of wearing a mask of disinterestedness which hides its real nature even from the conscience of those who indulge in it. The Great War has been followed by wide-spread social chaos; and one of the chief causes of this state of things is that corporate selfishness is everywhere masquerading as virtue. The worker prides himself on his loyalty to his union, and is animated by the spirit of comradeship when he goes on strike. But when his union threatens to strangle the economic life of the nation in order to secure material benefits for its members, he becomes a partner in its corporate selfishness, and his very virtue begins to savour of vice. And his case is typical of what is going on in all parts of the world and in all social grades.

There is one way, and one way only, in which this sinister tendency can be corrected and the disorder of our social life cured. Devotion to a community or a cause must always have at the heart of it devotion to a wider community or a larger cause, and the claims

of the latter must, in the event of a conflict, take precedence of those of the former. This is the golden rule.[1]
Wherever it is recognised and obeyed, ethics, civics and
economics lose themselves in religion and become one.
For the wider community must have a still wider, the
larger cause must have a still larger, at the heart of it,
until we come at last to the widest and the largest of all.
Some of us seem to think that pan-humanism is the cure
for all our social ills. I doubt if it is. The failure of
Positivism, the religion of humanity, to evangelise more
than a handful of theorists and enthusiasts is significant.
If the service of humanity were regarded as an end in
itself, a too materialistic view of the needs and desires
of humanity would almost certainly be taken; and this
would react sooner or later on all our lesser loyalties
and humbler services. The universal diffusion of comfort
and leisure would become the highest end of human
endeavour; and one result of this would be that each
nation, each class, each trade would claim for itself its
share, or more than its share, of comfort and leisure,
and the old jealousies and quarrels would re-appear. If
we would serve humanity aright we must help it to
realise its own perfection, to fulfil the end of its own
being; and that perfection is unattainable, and that end lies
beyond itself. Therefore, if pan-humanism is to give us
order and peace in the place of chaos and strife, it too
must have at the heart of it devotion to a wider community, to the widest of all communities, the kingdom of God.

And the lesser loyalty will not suffer because the
larger loyalty takes precedence of it in our hearts. On
the contrary, being to that extent purged of selfishness,
it will be purer and stronger than it would otherwise

[1] I ought perhaps to apologise for my frequent repetition of this
formula. But it is in very truth the golden rule of man's political,
social, moral and spiritual life; and in my heart I can only reproach
myself for having done less than justice to its claims.

have been. The member of the sectional trade union will serve it more effectively if he recognises that the union as a whole has the prior claim to his allegiance. As a member of the larger union he will best prove his loyalty to it by being ready on occasion to subordinate its interests—its apparent interests—to the welfare of his country. The patriot will be the better patriot if he serves his country, not for its own sake only but also because it is a province in the human commonwealth. And the humanist will be the better humanist if he interprets the claims and needs of humanity through his vision of the Ideal and the Divine. " Seek ye first the Kingdom of Heaven and its righteousness, and then all these things will be added unto you."

Devotion to the whole, then, is the only effectual antidote to the selfishness of the individual and the separatism, or corporate selfishness, of the community. In other words, it and it alone can moralise and socialise our lives.

This is one aspect of the philosophy of wholeness. But it is not the only aspect. There are three ideal ends of man's being—Truth, Beauty and Love. And the reason why these ends are lodestars in our lives is that devotion to each of them, if it is pure and disinterested, readily and of inner necessity transforms itself into devotion to the whole. Love indeed stands apart from the rest in that love of Love *is* love of the whole; and that it is therefore the medium through which the quest of Truth and the quest of Beauty lose themselves in the quest of the Divine. But Truth and Beauty are of the same sublime brotherhood; and if Love is greater than they are, it is only " first among its peers."

The distinction between Truth and Beauty is inherent in the distinction between reason and intuition, between conscious thought and subconscious vision. It will hold good as long as that distinction holds good. It will be transcended when, if ever, that distinction is transcended. Truth is the objective side of knowledge, the subjective side of reality. Ideal truth is therefore the subjective side of ultimate reality. The pursuit of truth is the attempt to discover the real in the phenomenal, the one in the many, the laws which are behind facts, the principles which are behind laws. When order, inward harmony, is discovered by reason we have truth. When it is discerned by intuition we have beauty. The greater the complexity, the higher is the underlying unity, and the nearer we are, if reason can discover that unity, to ideal truth. In the whole the complexity is infinite, and the underlying unity is infinite. In other words, the cosmic order, the inward harmony of the whole, is perfect. In the unravelling by reason of the cosmic order we have the pursuit of ideal truth. In the revelation to reason of the inward harmony of the universe we have the attainment of ideal truth. But the goal is unattainable. The pursuit of ideal truth is an adventure into the infinite. As such it is its own reward. The dogmatic spirit, which seeks to find rest in a formula, is the negation of the scientific. Reason will never succeed in unravelling the order which underlies the complexity of things; but it will never weary of trying to do so.

For the adventurous mind, then, the universe is ideal truth. For imaginative insight, for inward vision, the universe is ideal beauty. The direct perception of wholeness is of the essence of the æsthetic sense. Where ordinary men see only a chaos of details, many of which are sordid and even repulsive, the artist sees a whole; and that whole is a thing of beauty. There is no need for him to unravel by force of reason the order which unifies the multiplicity of details. The one in the many, the inward harmony of things, is for him the object, not of thought, but of vision. In other words, it is " the intuition of totality " which distinguishes the artist from other men. It follows that the goal of artistic aspiration is the vision of the universe, the immediate perception of the sum of things as an indivisible, unanalysable whole. This would be the revelation of absolute beauty, the beatific vision, the fulfilment of all dreams. But here too the goal is unattainable. The part can no more see the whole than it can understand the whole. Or, if it can come nearer to vision than to understanding, it can never attain to it. There may be less of self, less of the desire for possession, in the thirst for beauty than in the thirst for truth. But there is enough, and more than enough.

What then? Will the part never understand, will it never see the whole? Yes, it will; but not until it has lost itself in the whole. Not until the desire to possess has been submerged by the desire to be possessed. Not until the thirst for truth and the thirst for beauty have slaked themselves at the fountain of love. For in love you become one with what is loved, and being one with it you understand it with an intimacy and a subtlety which transcend the range of vision; and you see it with a transfiguring vision which transcends the range of the artist's creative eye. This is so when the beloved is a kindred soul, a man or a woman like oneself. How much more would it be so if the beloved were the Divine Lover, the living Whole! The ideal end of love is the whole and nothing less than the whole. For the essence of love is complete self-loss. While the passion of love lasts the whole of self is wholly surrendered. But the passion is as a rule as transient as it is intense. If it is to endure for ever its object must be worthy of it. And what object is worthy of so great a passion but the Divine Lover, who is himself the Soul of Love? " My son, give me thy heart! " This is what the soul of all things is ever saying to each of us, as it speaks to us through all the voices of earth and sky, of land and sea, of day and night, through the pageant of history, through the work of the artist, through the song of the poet, through the deeds of the hero, through the eyes and the lips of all who are near and dear to us. " My son, give me thy heart! " If Truth, Beauty and Love are indeed the supreme ends of one's being, there can be but one response to this appeal. Give your heart to the Divine Lover; and you will become one with supreme reality and therefore with ideal Truth. Give your heart to the Divine Lover; and you will become one with the inward harmony of the universe and therefore with ideal Beauty. Give your heart to the Divine Lover; and you will become one with Love.

I think I can now see what self-integration really means. It means that the whole is realising itself in each individual life. Self-integration apart from the whole is spiritual suicide. Self-integration through oneness with the whole is eternal life. This is the mystery of mysteries, that the whole can hide itself, as it were, in each human heart, as a tree hides itself in each of the seeds which it bears, and can realise itself in each heart in all the infinitude of its wholeness.

> They tell us that the mighty banyan-tree,
> Itself a forest, has a speck-like seed,
> In which it hides its life's totality,
> A spell-bound prisoner, waiting to be freed.
> So do you hide your Self—the One, the All—
> In this my heart, this seed which you have sown;
> Waiting to wake from slumber at my call,
> Waiting for me to claim you as my own.
> Patient you wait. Shall I with stubborn will
> Rest in myself, content with what is mine?
> Or, with high purpose, labour to fulfil,
> Dying to self, my fate and your design?
> Nay, but who dies to self doth self renew;
> For I am I only when one with you.

January 1920.

THE PSYCHOLOGY OF SANITY

I HAD heard so much about the new science or would-be science of psycho-analysis that at last I determined to study it for myself. I began by reading a little book called *The Psychology of Insanity*, by Dr. Bernard Hart. I found this book so interesting and suggestive, and even (within limits) convincing, that I read and re-read it. And the more carefully I read it, the more it set me thinking.

Psycho-analysts claim that the science which they are elaborating will be useful for the treatment of mental disease. They might, I think, make a bolder claim for it than this. To cure disease is a good thing. To prevent disease is better. To secure good health is better still. If the psycho-analytic method can cure insanity, why should it not also be used for the higher purpose of securing sanity, in the more positive sense of that word? If it makes for psychiatry, for soul-healing, why should it not also make for psychotrophy, for soul-culture and soul-growth? Why should not the psychology of insanity form the basis of the psychology of sanity, the psychology of mental, moral, and spiritual health?

The latter science would have to be based, in part at least, on the former. If we would know what is normal, we must study departures from the norm. And the more flagrant the departure from the norm, the more deeply will it initiate us into the secret of normality. Such flagrant departures from the norm of mental health

are offered by the phenomena of insanity, in the medico-
legal sense of the word.

Insanity takes many forms. One of the commonest
of these, and from the point of view of psychology
the most significant, is what is known as " dissociation
of consciousness." " A vast number of abnormal phenomena," says Dr. Hart, " ranging from hallucination and
delusion to . . . complicated phantasy production . . .
are to be regarded as examples of dissociation." What
do we mean by dissociation of consciousness? " We
mean," says Dr. Hart, that " the mind has lost that
homogeneity which is the ideal of the normal personality,
and has become disintegrated into more or less independent portions, each pursuing its own course and development without reference to the welfare of the whole."
" This disintegration," continues our author, " invari-
ably owes its existence to the presence of a conflict."
By a conflict he means an internal conflict, a civil war
in the kingdom of the mind. The parties to this internal
conflict are, on the one hand, the personality as a whole;
on the other hand, what is known to psychology as
a *complex*.

What is a complex? Dr. Hart defines it as " a system
of connected ideas with a strong emotional tone and a
tendency to produce action of a definite character." Dr.
Maurice Nicoli, in his book on *Dream Psychology*, says
that " when a mass of ideas and emotions collect round
a nucleus in the mind, a system is formed which will
react in a particular way to incoming stimuli," and adds,
" This system is called a complex."

A complex is not a thing to be ashamed of. If we
had not, each of us, many complexes, we should be less
than human; or rather, we should fall below the level
of organic life. A complex is nothing more nor less than
a sub-centre of the soul's life, analogous (within limits)

to a nerve-centre in the body, or to a centre of local
government in a well-organised state. A hobby, as Dr.
Hart points out, is a particular variety of complex. So
is each of the many sub-selves which each of us is aware
of in himself—the domestic self, the social self, the
professional self, the commercial self, the artistic self,
the religious self, and so on. If a man is deeply interested
in a subject of study, a corresponding complex is formed
in his mind. If he takes up a cause with energy and
enthusiasm, such as the emancipation of woman, social
reform, educational reform, the remedying of an evil or
an injustice, a mass of ideas and emotions will collect
round this centre of interest, and a complex will be
formed. Different men take up different hobbies, different subjects of study, and different causes, and the
corresponding complexes are therefore not strictly analogous to the nerve-centres of the body, which are common
to all men. This differentiation is due to the fact that the
constitution of the soul is far more complicated and much
further removed from finality than that of the body, and
that consciousness extends indefinitely the environment
of the race, whereas circumstances limit the environment of the individual, with the result that no two
individuals have exactly the same environment or the
same opportunities for the formation of complexes. But
however great may be the diversity of complexes, however much they may vary from man to man, the fact
remains that complexes are sub-centres of the soul's life.

How then does a complex cause insanity? By drawing
to itself more than its share of the man's thoughts and
emotions, and so impairing the inward harmony of his
soul. More especially is this the case when the complex
has a morbid origin, when it has no right to be a sub-
centre, as, for example, when a man broods over a wrong
which has been done to him, or feels remorse for a

crime which he has committed.[1] The loss of inward harmony need not amount to insanity. There are few men whose inward harmony is even approximately perfect. Hypertrophy of a complex is a very common phenomenon. A man may easily ride a harmless hobby to death. His devotion to a worthy cause may amount to fanaticism. He may overdo a good habit (such as economy) till it becomes a bad habit (such as stinginess). He may become a monomaniac, a man of one idea, of one absorbing interest, of one cankering grievance. And yet he may be far removed from the insanity which necessitates confinement and restraint. He is, however, on the road to that goal; and if he does not keep himself in hand, he may possibly arrive at it. When hypertrophy of a complex is carried so far that what ought to be (at most) a mere sub-centre of a man's life becomes, whether permanently or temporarily, *the* centre, or, in its attempt to become *the* centre, disintegrates the man's personality, then we have insanity, in the strict sense of the word. In other words, when a complex becomes a centre of rebellious, and therefore disruptive, tendency, when it provokes a civil war which will lead to its dividing with the ruling self the kingdom of the man's life, and may even, in extreme cases, end in its forcibly usurping the throne, then its victim is said to be insane; and for his own sake, as well as for the sake of his neighbours, he has to be interned.

According to Dr. Hart, the conflict which produces insanity is, as a rule, one between " primitive instinct " and " herd instinct." Dr. Freud, the founder of psychoanalysis, resolves all primitive instinct into sex-instinct;

[1] Complexes may perhaps be classified as *essential, desirable, useful, harmless,* and *morbid.* A morbid complex, if not duly controlled, may easily become malignant. But there is no complex which will not, if hypertrophied beyond measure, become first morbid and then malignant, and therefore a menace to the sanity of the soul.

but few of his followers go as far as this. I doubt if the problem of conflict is quite so simple as Dr. Hart seems to think. The soul is a complex of many complexes; and the civil war which sometimes afflicts it may be expected to have many causes and take many forms. It is not easy to say where primitive instinct ends and herd instinct begins. And it is possible to exaggerate the importance of the part that herd instinct plays in man's life. Dr. Hart says that " from it (herd instinct) the tendencies generally ascribed to tradition and education derive most of their power." It would, I think, be equally correct to say that from tradition and education the tendencies sometimes ascribed to herd instinct derive much of their power. In any case, it is well to remember that in our complicated modern society each of us belongs to many herds. There is the family herd, for example, the class herd, the clan herd, the professional herd, the national herd, the human herd. And any one of these, if its claims are unduly insistent, may give rise to a complex which will upset the balance of one's life.

On the whole, then, it is safer to say, in general terms, that the normal cause of insanity is a conflict between a usurping, self-assertive sub-self, and the self which ought to rule. Even the enthusiasm of humanity, if the enthusiast brings too much self into it—if, for example, he insists on reforming the world in his own particular way,—may become a rebellious and dissociative complex, and may even in the last resort give rise to actual insanity. So may devotion to God, if it is allowed to degenerate into religious fanaticism, or into undue concern for one's own individual salvation. Selfishness, in the sense of absorption in a narrow and ever-narrowing self, is of the essence of insanity. The rebellious complex, if we may for the moment personify it, thinks only of itself and subordinates to its own imagined interests the well-being of the whole personality. And this inward selfishness, this claim of the subordinate part to dominate the whole of the man's life, has its counterpart in outward selfishness, in callous indifference to the claims and interests of others and to the demands of social life. Speaking of those who have become insane, Dr. Hart says:

The patients have lost the gregarious instincts of the normal man, and the sanctions of traditional conduct have no longer any significance for them. In the milder cases this shows itself as a loss of interest in the affairs of their fellows, a tendency to be solitary and unsociable, an atrophy of their affections for friends and relations, and an indifference to the ordinary conventions of society. In the advanced cases the change is much more marked, and the mind is completely withdrawn from participation in the life of the herd. The code of conduct imposed by convention and tradition no longer regulates the patient's behaviour, and he becomes slovenly, filthy, degraded, and shameless.

The conflict between the rebellious complex or sub-self and the self which ought to rule does not always, or even often, lead to actual insanity. When that is the issue of the conflict, what has happened? The ruling self has not been strong enough to enforce its authority. This is the answer which common sense and psycho-analysis unite in giving. Psycho-analysis sets forth the answer in its own peculiar notation. " In cases of insanity," says Dr. Hart, " homogeneity ['which is the ideal of normal personality '] has disappeared because the mind contains elements which are incompatible with each other, and dissociation has arisen as a means of avoiding the storm and stress which the warring of these mutually hostile elements would otherwise inevitably produce." Is not this equivalent to saying that the ruling self has so far yielded to the pressure of the rebellious sub-self as to consent to divide the kingdom with it, just as in history we sometimes read of a monarch who ended a rebellion by allowing the rebel leader either to share the central authority with him or to become ruler of part of his realm? The monarch who could do this was a weak ruler who had never been firmly seated on the throne; and the ruling self which allows a rebellious sub-self to usurp its authority, either in part, as in cases of dissociation, or, as sometimes happens, in full, proves its incapacity by its failure to put down the rebellion against its lawful rule.

The antidote to civil strife in a community is twofold —to remove legitimate grievances, and to strengthen the central authority. Should it not be the same in the soul? Should not our aim be to relax the pressure of tradition and convention on primitive instinct or on any other natural instinct so far as that pressure is injurious and provocative, and at the same time to strengthen the authority of the ruling self? Psycho-analysts, if I may judge from Dr. Hart's book, are more concerned with relaxing pressure than with strengthening authority.

It is possible [says Dr. Hart] that the future may demonstrate the fault to be, not in the tendency to dissociation, but in the nature of the conflict which has provoked it. The only remedy would then lie in altering one or another of the antagonists so that incompatibility no longer existed. The primitive instincts cannot presumably be altered, and the attack would therefore have to be directed against the traditions and codes which obtain their force from the operation of herd instinct. . . . It is at least conceivable that our present complacent assurance that every individual must live and act within the arbitrary limits assigned by conventional and purely artificial standards of conduct, or else be segregated from society, may be fallacious and inimical to the best development of the race. It is possible that insanity, or a part of insanity, will prove to be less dependent upon intrinsic defects of the individual than on the conditions in which he has to live, and the future may determine that it is not the individual who must be eliminated but the conditions which must be modified.

Here our author goes perilously near to suggesting that

the only way to prevent insanity is to make concessions to primitive instinct. Not a word is said about the need for strengthening the central authority, the ruling self. Yet, unless this is done, the policy of indulging primitive instinct, by relaxing the pressure to which traditions and codes have subjected it, can lead to nothing but general demoralisation.

The truth is that when we are dealing with problems of insanity we are too ready to assume that what is not actually or approximately insane is sane, and that, if dissociation of personality can be avoided, all is well. I doubt if we shall ever really master the psychology of insanity until we have materially widened the scope of the idea of sanity; until we have risen to the conception of perfect or ideal, as distinguished from normal, sanity; or rather, until we have realised that in the world of life and growth the ideal is the norm. Between actual insanity and perfect sanity, between disintegration of personality and perfect homogeneity or inward harmony, there are many intervening stages, which partake in varying degrees of disharmony, of want of sanity. If we could find a remedy for these shortcomings we should have made the best possible provision against the outbreak of insanity, which is the natural goal of mental and spiritual disharmony—a goal which the latter may never reach, but towards which it necessarily tends. The problem of securing sanity covers and far overlaps the problem of preventing (and curing) insanity; and it is to the former problem that the psychologist should give his closest attention and his deepest thought. Let him by all means continue to study what is morbid and abnormal—it will have much to teach him,—but let him add to this the study of the conditions under which sanity, in the fullest sense of the word, is attainable— the sanity of inward harmony, of radiant health.

I have said that for the cure of the civil strife which
we call insanity two things are needed—the redress of
grievances by the removal of injurious pressure, and the
strengthening of the central authority. The two remedies
are really one. To redress grievances is to strengthen
the central authority. What causes the growth of a
morbid complex is, as a rule, either illegitimate pressure,
or legitimate pressure carried too far. In the latter case,
which is the more common, the source of the pressure
is undue regard for tradition and convention, the authority of which is accepted as full and final instead of as
partial and provisional. In other words, the source of
the pressure is the weakness of the ruling self, which,
led astray by the desire for finality, leans exclusively on
tradition and convention, instead of trying to walk, in
part at least, by its own inward light. And the effect
of the pressure which it exerts is to increase its own
weakness. For repression, when carried too far, starves
and stunts natural tendency, with the result that, if the
pressure is evenly distributed, growth is arrested, and
if it is unevenly distributed, certain tendencies only being
selected for repression, growth becomes inharmonious
and one-sided, and balance and symmetry are lost.
But whatever tends to arrest or distort the growth of
the soul must needs weaken the central authority; for
the ruling self is the whole personality, just as in a
well - ordered commonwealth the whole community,
acting through a hierarchy of administrative nerve-
centres, is the state.

If, then, the relaxing of injurious pressure is to be
accompanied by the strengthening of the central authority, our aim must be, not so much to cure this or that
morbid complex, as to secure the well-being of the
whole personality by fostering mental and spiritual
growth. It is when an organism is making vigorous

growth that the inward harmony of its various vital parts is most nearly perfect; for then all the parts are functioning with one end in view, that of furthering the growth of the whole organism; and as they draw to themselves all the rising sap of the organism's life, there is no opportunity for morbid sub-centres to establish themselves at the expense of the health and harmony of the community. It is to the organism as a whole that the various parts owe allegiance. But what is the organism? The process of growth alone can answer this question. What the organism will be when its process of growth (if healthy and unimpeded) is complete, that it really is. Therefore the parts owe allegiance to the organism, not as it is at the passing moment, but as it will be when it has reached its maturity. In other words, they are sustained and animated and kept in harmony with one another by devotion to a common ideal.

It is the same with the human soul. But there is a difference between the growth of the soul and the growth of any physical organism. The organism does arrive at maturity. It has its moment of consummation. But the growth of the soul goes on, or should go on, for ever. The potentialities of the soul are limitless, and the process of realising them is a veritable adventure into the infinite. If we would attain to sanity, the sanity of spiritual health, we must pursue that adventure to its limitless limit. We must always, and at all costs, resist the lure of finality. Devotion to an unattainable ideal alone can keep us sane. If we forswear the service of the ideal and try to content ourselves with finite ends, the worse type of dissociation, dissociation of the actual from the ideal self, may be our doom.

Let us take the case of a man who is neither a criminal nor a lunatic, but who leads a sordid, selfish, self-indulgent, immoral life — an unfaithful husband, an unkind father, a churlish neighbour, a grasping and exacting creditor, a shifty and evasive debtor, unsympathetic, uncharitable, recognising no obligation which is not legally defined, taking no interest whatever in the deeper issues of life. Such a man is sane enough, as the lunacy laws measure sanity. But he is not sane in the deeper sense of the word. He has not attained to spiritual health. What is wrong with him? No civil strife mars the harmony of his mean, narrow, ill-spent life. His being, such as it is, is all of a piece. But his very harmony is disharmony. His very sanity is insanity. He has no more attained to wholeness than has a stunted, diseased, misshapen tree. It is true that there is no rebellious, dissociative complex to upset his inward balance. Yet that balance has been completely and, as it seems, irretrievably upset. For his whole personality, or what passes for such, has degenerated into a rebellious, dissociative complex; and what it is in rebellion against, what it is dissociating itself from, is his own real or ideal self.

Or let us take the case of the miser, a familiar figure in the annals of the human race. Here we have a typical example, not of a personality degenerating into a morbid complex so much as of a morbid complex overrunning the entire field of consciousness and becoming, apparently, the whole man. The miser is a monomaniac, a man of one ignoble but all-absorbing interest. Yet he seldom qualifies for the madhouse. The explanation of this is that, owing to the completeness of the victory won by the complex over the personality, the former is able to annex and use for its own purposes all the psychical machinery of the latter, including its power of reacting to a social environment. In other words, the sub-self has compelled the man, the ruling self, to identify himself with it and devote himself to its service. Hence his apparent sanity. Yet, in the deeper sense of the word, he is insane, and insane in the highest degree. For, in the act of absorbing into itself the whole of his normal personality, the miser in him has dissociated itself, and therefore dissociated him, from his real or ideal self. It has seated itself, a lawless usurper, on the throne of his spirit; and its reign, though orderly to outward view, is really a prolonged riot of insanity. For sanity is health; and health comes with vigorous and harmonious growth. But the triumph of a rebellious complex means that all the forces which make for the growth of the soul are diverted into one narrow channel, with the result that the process of growth—which is nothing if not harmonious and many-sided—is forcibly arrested, and degenerative insanity takes its place.

These are extreme cases. Yet something akin to this is happening to each of us when and so far as we succumb to the lure of finality, and give up that adventure into the infinite which is of the essence of spiritual growth. Self-integration, which is the true antidote to insanity, in every sense of that word, is to be achieved only by realising the limitless possibilities that are wrapped up in the human embryo, by growing into oneness with that soul of all things which is the true self of each of us. The goal is unattainable. Yet to pause in the pursuit of it is to bring disharmony, or the menace of disharmony, into one's life. The infinite in man is the lawful ruler of all his parts and powers and passions; and it is rebellion against that ruler, it is dissociation of personality, to accept any actual self as the true man.

In conclusion: the secret of sanity is devotion to the infinite and the ideal. This is the lesson which psychoanalysis, so far as I have studied it, has taught me. Dissociation—disintegration of personality—makes for insanity. If we would be sane, then, we must take the opposite path, the path of self-integration, the path which leads to wholeness of spirit, to inward harmony. If inward harmony is to be achieved, the whole personality must assert its supremacy over each of the subordinate centres, and so prevent the hypertrophy of any of these, as well as the outgrowth of morbid sub-centres, which cannot establish themselves as long as the legitimate sub-centres are energising vigorously under the direction and in the service of the whole. By the whole personality we mean, not the actual average man, "the finished and finite clod," but "the light that lighteth every man," the ideal or universal self. The ideal self asserts its supremacy by becoming the goal of an eternal process of growth, the end of an endless quest. So long as that quest continues, so long as the soul continues to grow, so long as the man lives in the infinite, the subordinate centres of his being will fulfil their several functions in obedience to the will of the self-evolving, self-revealing whole, and therefore in perfect harmony with one another. This is sanity, in the fullest sense of the word, the sanity of organic wholeness, of immortal youth.

April 1920.

THE SPIRIT OF THE QUEST

WHAT does our society stand for? This is the question
which suggested itself to me when you did me the great
honour of making me your president for the year which
has just begun. The title of our society is a provisional
answer to this question. We are embarked on a quest,
not on a missionary enterprise. We do not stand for
proselytism, or propagandism of any kind. We want
our recruits to have the spirit of adventure, not of
discipleship. We have no secret to confide to them,
no theory to explain to them, no catechism to drill into
them, no creed to present to them for acceptance. Or
if we have a creed—and I think we have—it is not a
form of words, but a living conviction, the conviction
which has started us on our great adventure, the conviction which is implicit in the idea of the quest.

What is the object of our quest? Is it not ideal truth?
On this point we are, I think, all agreed. But why have
we thought it necessary to seek for ideal truth? Was
not the truth of things authoritatively taught to us in
our childhood? Was not the will of God revealed to
us, and a scheme of life, based on that revelation, set
before us? Yes, it was; and that was why we had to
embark on our quest. For we found, as we grew up,
that there were many religions and that each of these
had its own theory of things, its own interpretation of
the will of God, its own scheme of life. We realised

227

that these could not all be—what they all pretended to be—divinely true. We realised that the religious faith which a man professes is in the main determined by the accident of his birth. We realised that creeds are many, but that ideal truth is one.

Πολλαὶ μὲν θνητοῖς γλῶσσαι, μία δ'ἀθανάτοισι.

Mortals have many tongues—and therefore many creeds. The immortal gods have one.

There is a passage in one of the prose works of Lessing, the poet and critic, which our society might, I think, adopt as its motto:

If God held enclosed in His right hand all truth and in His left hand simply the ever-moving impulse towards truth, although with the condition that I should eternally err, and said to me " Choose," I should humbly bend before His left hand and say, " Father, give. Pure truth is for Thee alone."

Pure truth is for God alone. For pure truth is the subjective side, so to speak, of absolute reality, and God alone is absolutely real. And what the real is in itself is known to the real and to it alone. If man would attain to ideal truth he must try to rise to its level. He must cease to be phantasmal and must become more and more real. In other words, he must try to find his true self. But this is a process to which there is no imaginable goal. It is an adventure into the infinite. It is an ascending " series " in which there is no final term.

And though thy soul sail leagues and leagues beyond,
Still leagues beyond those leagues there is more sea.

The effort to become one with the real, and in doing so to attain to ideal truth, will be its own reward, but it will never compass its own apparent aim. The certainty of its failure is indeed the very measure of its success. " Give it the glory of going on and still to be." " You will enter the light but you will never touch the Flame."

" Pure truth is for God alone." Does it follow that
we who believe this are a band of agnostics? Our
orthodox friends will no doubt label us with this title
and use it as a term of reproach. Have they the right
to do so? Before we can answer this question we must
come to an understanding with ourselves as to the
meaning of the word " agnostic." For few words are
more loosely used. There are at least four distinct brands
of agnosticism. The *first* ought more properly to be
called indifferentism. It is the mental, or rather temperamental, attitude of the worldling, the Gallio, the man who
cares for none of these things. Agnostics of this brand
are to be reckoned by millions, but there are few of them
who take the trouble to call themselves agnostics. For
the word " agnostic " is suggestive of some sort of an
interest in great matters; and it is characteristic of the
true worldling that such matters do not interest him in
the slightest degree. The *second* brand is the agnosticism
of the man who takes an interest in great matters and
yet contrives to keep his judgment about them in a
state of complete suspense. Agnostics of this type are
as rare as the proverbial snakes in Iceland. For though
a man may profess entire neutrality in the sphere of
high thinking and may even succeed in persuading himself that he is entirely neutral, it is certain that if he
has ever seriously interested himself in the greatest of
all problems, he inclines in his heart of hearts either
towards the positive or the negative solution of it. This
leads me to speak of the *third* brand of agnosticism.
My own experience is that nine-tenths of those who
call themselves agnostics are really negative dogmatists,
men who, though professing entire neutrality, have really
committed themselves, half consciously, half unconsciously, to the negative solution of the supreme problem.
When such persons call themselves agnostics they usurp

a title to which they have no just claim. The *fourth* brand is the agnosticism of unformulated faith. It is the attitude of the man who proves his faith in the real by his unceasing quest of the ideal; the man whose faith is so secure of itself that it does not ask for any sanction or guarantee, so strong that it breaks all the barrages and bursts all the dams in which dogmatism seeks to imprison it; the man who regards the pursuit of truth as its own goal and its own reward; the man who

> Finds life's treasure in this endless quest,
> And peace of mind in infinite unrest.

This is, I think, the only genuine brand of agnosticism. All the other brands are spurious. I will ask those who challenge this statement to go back with me to the root-meaning of the word " agnostic." The word was coined by the late Professor Huxley. It is compounded of the privative prefix *a* and the word *gnosticism*. The Gnostics seem to have been masters of the art of defining the undefinable, formulating the unformulable, and pretending to know the unknowable. Such at least has been their reputation. It is probable that their enemies and detractors have done them less than justice. But that is a matter with which we need not concern ourselves. What is certain is that when Huxley coined the word " agnostic " he regarded the Gnostics as the ultra-dogmatic exponents of religio-philosophical doctrines; and one may infer from this that the essence of agnosticism, as he conceived it, is antipathy to dogmatism and the dogmatic spirit, especially in the region of religious belief and speculative thought.

Why, then, it will be asked, are so many self-styled agnostics negative dogmatists? I think I can work out an answer to this question. I have said that no one who is interested in great matters can remain for more than

a moment—a timeless moment—at the point of entire
neutrality. From that point one must incline either
towards the positive or the negative solution of the
great problem. One must either take the path of submission, of trust, of aspiration, of hope—the path which
leads at last to the "everlasting yea"; or take the path
of revolt, of mistrust, of cynicism, of despair—the path
which leads at last to the "everlasting no." Which path
a man shall take will probably be decided for him by
what I may call temperamental bias; but he is not the
helpless victim of his own temperament; for when he
realises in what direction the chosen path is taking him,
it will always be open to him to retrace his steps.

Has not the man who inclines towards the "everlasting
no" as good a right to call himself an agnostic as the man
who inclines towards the "everlasting yea"? In theory,
yes. In practice he seldom establishes his right. In
theory Achilles never overtakes the tortoise. In practice
he catches him in a few strides. If you make unity your
starting-point you can do one of two things. You can
take the downward path of progressive division—by 2,
let us say—($\frac{1}{2}$, $\frac{1}{4}$, $\frac{1}{8}$, $\frac{1}{16}$, etc.). Or you can take the upward
path of progressive multiplication (2, 4, 8, 16, etc.). In
the former case, the descent into the infinitesimal will
in theory go on for ever, and its ideal goal, which we
call *zero*, will never be reached. But all the time, zero
is the next-door neighbour to unity, as near to it as 2 is,
and it can be reached in practice, on the principle of
solvitur ambulando, in a single step. If, on the other
hand, you take the upward path, you may go on for
ever and ever and yet never approach your goal; and
since there is no short cut to infinity, as there is to
zero, you must resign yourself, in practice as well as in
theory, to an endless task. In like manner, if, having
started from the point of mental neutrality, you take

the path of ultra-sceptical disbelief and denial, your
root assumption being that only what is ultimate in
analysis is real, you will speedily arrive at the zero
of dogmatic negation; and your agnosticism, if you
continue to call yourself an agnostic, will be purely
theoretical. In practice, you will be more narrowly
and rigidly dogmatic than you were before you abjured
the dogmatism of orthodoxy. But if, on the other hand,
starting from the same point, you take the path of trust
and hope and imaginative desire, your root-assumption
being that only what is ultimate in synthesis is real, you
will find that your goal—the "everlasting yea"—recedes
from you for ever and for ever, that you have committed
yourself to a veritable adventure into the infinite, and
that you will remain agnostic to the very end.

How short is the journey from the imaginary point
of mental neutrality to the goal of dogmatic negation,
a simple experiment will suffice to prove. Ask the
average self-styled agnostic what he thinks about such
matters as immortality, spiritualism, re-incarnation, the
reality of the spiritual plane, the problem of the soul,
the idea of the Divine, the moral government of the
world, and the like—and you will probably find that,
far from having the tolerance and open-mindedness of
genuine agnosticism, your agnostic's attitude is one of
comprehensive denial, based on the prepossessions of
commonplace materialism. You will find, in other
words, that, with or without the consent of his consciousness, he has taken the short cut to the zero of
dogmatic negation.

The truth is that the average sensuous, healthy, well-
balanced man, though he may well be an idealist on the
emotional plane, is a materialist and therefore a dog-
matist on the mental plane of his life. "The solidarity,"
says a French psychologist, "of his superior psychism

with his cerebral psychism being absolute, all the activities of the former are limited by the extent of the latter and restrained within its conditions." One result of this is that he instinctively takes for granted the self-existence of the world of appearances which surrounds him. The air of intrinsic reality which this outward and visible world wears overpowers him. He cannot resist it; and if he takes any interest in ultimate problems, it must needs control the whole current of his speculative thought. But his primary postulate that the world of appearances is self-existent and intrinsically real is the central dogma in what is not so much a system of philosophy as a rigidly-formulated but mainly negative creed. For denial of reality to whatever does not belong to the world of appearances is of the essence of materialism; and as such denial, being instinctive and irrational, is absolute and final, the passage from materialism to dogmatism takes less than a single step.

The man whose mind is in bondage to his brain may accept without question or misgiving the dogmatism of supernatural religion, with which tradition, habit and formal teaching have familiarised him; but if he should find reason to reject that dogmatism, it is not agnosticism but the dogmatism of what is miscalled naturalism that would take its place. For men of this type of mind need fixed and definite ideas even about things with regard to which, as Joubert has well said, " toute précision est erreur." They have no wings; they cannot sustain themselves in the air; they must always feel solid ground beneath their feet. Joubert would have us " lie to them " as the only alternative to " deceiving them," fearing, I presume, lest, if the dogmatism of religion were discredited in their eyes, they should pass on to the dogmatism of denial and revolt. His fear is well-grounded; but the time for following his advice is past.

Such persons, though they may call themselves agnostics—for the word, as they interpret it, means nothing more than departure from " orthodoxy "—are, I repeat, temperamentally averse from agnosticism. The mental unrest of the genuine agnostic, the unrest which is the counterpart of mobility of thought, is a state of mind which they do not understand. There is no need for them to keep their judgment in suspense with regard to the ultimate mysteries of existence. For, if the truth must be told, they doubt if there are such mysteries. What is ultimate, as it seems to them, is not particularly mysterious. In their orthodox days the supernaturalistic explanation of the universe seemed quite reasonable. Now that those days are over, the mechanistic explanation, which is a comparatively simple affair, contents them, and they do not care to look beyond it. In the words of the French psychologist whom I have already quoted, " to them everything is relatively simple because they avoid going to the bottom of anything."

The quest on which our society has embarked appeals to minds of a different type from this. The true seeker is, as I have already suggested, the only genuine agnostic. For he realises, as no one else does, that one of the first qualifications for the quest of ideal truth is freedom from bondage to those religious and quasi-philosophical dogmas which block the windows of the soul and shut out the rays of divine light. To realise this is to clear the way for the greatest of all adventures. The genuine agnostic is the only true seeker, the only duly chartered adventurer into the mysterious and the unknown. For the words of the Kêna Upanishad are eternally true; God, who is supreme reality and therefore ideal truth,

> Is unknown to whoso think they know,
> But known to whoso know they know him not.

And so, when our orthodox friends reproach us with our

agnosticism, let us tell them that we admit the impeach-
ment, but that we glory in what they regard as our shame.

I have said that when a man quits the imaginary point
of mental neutrality, he must incline (if he does not
relapse into pure indifferentism) towards either the positive or the negative solution of the great problem. That
we incline towards the positive solution goes without
saying. We have taken the path of faith, of hope, of
spiritual desire. In doing so we have in a sense prejudged
the issue of our quest,—prejudged it in the sense hinted
at by Pascal when he said, " You would not have sought
me if you had not already found me." For we know
beforehand that there will be no issue to the quest. We
know that in pursuing it we shall lose ourselves in the
infinite and the ideal. We cannot help that. We must
be true to the vital impulse that has set us seeking. For
why have we embarked on this high adventure? What
is our ultimate motive? It is not the desire for success,
for achievement. We know at the outset that we shall
never reach our goal. Still less is it the desire for possession. We know that we shall never be able to imprison
ideal truth in a system or a creed. What is it then? Is
it not the desire for expansion, for growth, for self-
transcendence, for freedom in the true sense of the word,
for escape from the prison-house of self?

Why did dogmatism, whether positive or negative,
content us in the days when we were in bondage to it?
What is the strength of dogmatism? Why is negative
dogmatism so ready to claim us as its votaries when
positive dogmatism has been discredited by the advance
of knowledge and critical thought? I have given the
psychological—or shall I say the psycho-physiological?
—answer to the latter question. I will now give the
ethical answer to the larger question. The strength of
dogmatism lies in this: that it ministers to two desires

which are common to all of us, but which it is our mission to transmute or otherwise outgrow—the desire for possession and the desire for repose.

The secret desire of the average man is to become the possessor of a cut-and-dried theory of things, including a solution of the problem of his own meaning and destiny and an explanation of the origin and purpose of the universe,—a theory, set forth in doctrinal form, which he can accept as authoritative and final, and can then lock away, so to speak, in a place of safety, feeling free thenceforth to devote himself, without any mental misgiving or *arrière pensée*, to secular pursuits. The various churches minister to this desire by providing their votaries with formulated creeds. A price has to be paid for this service. The authority of the church must be duly recognised, its teaching must be accepted without question and its commands must be obeyed. But the price will be gladly paid by one who desires to be put in possession of ultimate truth instead of having to win it, or try to win it, for himself—one who shrinks from the strenuous labour of high thinking and the wear and tear of mental unrest.

The desire for possession is, however, insatiable. It is not enough for the believer to have proprietary rights in ultimate truth. He must also have proprietary rights in the fountain-head of ultimate truth, in the supernatural God, whose revelation of his will has determined the boundaries of truth and error, of right and wrong. He must feel that he belongs to a community which enjoys the special favour and grace of God—to a chosen people, a chosen church, a chosen sect, or even a chosen remnant of the elect. He must feel that God is on his side, that God's enemies are his enemies, or rather— for this proposition is all too easily " converted "—that his enemies are God's enemies, and in particular that whoever would deny or even cast doubt upon his creed is not only a robber who seeks to deprive him of his most cherished possession and his peace of mind, but is also a rebel against God. When he has persuaded himself of this he will be ready to take his base desires and his evil passions—his selfishness, his self-will, his ambition, his greed, his love of power, his envy, his hatred, his intolerance — and solemnly dedicate these to the service of God.

For in truth the desire for certitude in the sphere of high thinking, the desire for the immediate possession of ideal truth instead of for the eternal pursuit of it, the desire for a repose which shall never be broken instead of for the toil of an ascent which shall never end,—though it may disguise itself behind such names as obedience, humility, faith, piety, religious devotion, and the like—is all the time a prompting of the old Adam, the lower self. At the root of it is the besetting weakness of our undeveloped nature, egoism, in a word, —the desire to rest in self for good and all; to avoid at whatever cost the " growing pains " of self-transcendence; to press all things, to press God himself, into the service of self; to make the individual life co-terminous with the universal, not by expanding the former but by contracting the latter; to silence the ideal, with its insistent demand for devotion and service, by confining it within the limits of the actual; in fine, to achieve salvation by any method but that of outgrowing and transforming self.

It is the desire to rest in self—the ordinary, familiar, superficial self — that generates the fierce antipathy to the psychic and the occult, the haunting dread of the infinite and the ideal, which are characteristic of the average, hard-headed, common-sensical man, who shrinks with terror, one might almost say, from whatever is mysterious and inexplicable, fearing in some secret recess of his consciousness lest it should enlarge the horizon of his thought, break in upon the slumber of his soul, and force him to reconsider his whole outlook on life.

It is a reproach to supernatural religion that, through the definite dogmatic teaching on which it prides itself, it has ministered in all times and places to the spiritual indolence of the average man, to his demand for certitude about great matters, a demand which is the outcome, as we have seen, of two ignobly selfish desires—for possession, and for repose. In ministering to this demand, in pandering to the love of finality, in discouraging the spirit of high adventure, supernaturalism has done much to retard and even arrest the development of man's higher nature; so much indeed that it may be doubted if this one disservice does not outweigh all the services that it has rendered to the cause of human progress. Let physical science, with its quasi-professional prejudice in favour of exact knowledge, and its leaning (in the sphere of philosophy) to negative dogmatism, take care that it does not pander to the same human weakness and incur the same reproach.

To find an antidote to the subtle poison of dogmatism is the purpose of the quest. For what does the quest of ideal truth demand of its votaries? In the first place, strenuous and many-sided mental endeavour. In this sentence the word "many-sided" is all-important. To entrust the treatment of the supreme problem to reason alone, in the narrower sense of the word, would be equivalent to asking for a materialistic solution of it. For reason functions best when it is dealing with the data of the bodily senses, in other words when it is investigating the phenomena and determining the laws of the material world. Therefore to assume that reason

is competent to solve the problem of ultimate reality
implies the further assumption that the material world
is all in all. But if the material world were all in all the
quest would have ended before it had begun, ended
where the rationalistic free-thinker so often ends—in
the zero of dogmatic negation. The higher reason is
not wholly rational. Or rather it is not wholly intellectual. Hard thinking, as we call it, may enable us to
explore the mysteries of mathematics, of physics, of
chemistry, of physiology. But when larger and deeper
problems challenge us, and when the verification by
observation and experiment which physical science demands becomes impossible, conscious thought needs for
its own sake to be supplemented by subconscious vision;
and the name for this is intuition.

The estrangement of reason from intuition is one of
the greatest calamities that have befallen the human
spirit. And it is a calamity for which religious dogmatism,
by its virtual proscription of reason and its demand for
blind and literal obedience, has been largely responsible.
We owe it to this unhappy estrangement that rationalism
is so often indistinguishable from materialism, that the
pursuit of truth is so often a mere formality, and the
issue of it so often a foregone conclusion. This on the
one hand; and on the other hand that mysticism is so
often irrational and unconvincing, an upsurging from
the depths of the unconscious, which does not submit
itself to the control of reason, and therefore cannot
transmute itself, or even begin to transmute itself, into
conscious thought.

It is not by retiring into seclusion—the seclusion of
a laboratory, or a study, or a cell—that we shall be able
to solve the insoluble problem of ultimate reality. It is
by living our lives in the outward as well as in the
inward world. Intuition is a moral as well as a mental

faculty. It reflects one's character and is continuously modified by one's manner of living. A French moralist has well said that "our taste declines with our merit." The range of taste, as the word is used in this sentence, is unlimited; and as judgment—the power of discriminating between the real and the unreal, the true and the false—is an essential element in taste, it behoves us, if we would train our judgment aright, and so purify our taste and clarify our vision, to try to live wisely and well. "You will fail least in your judgments," says Epictetus, "if you yourself fail least in your life." In nine cases out of ten a man's philosophy is the quasi-rational expression of a temperamental bias. If this is so, and if conduct reacts, as it certainly does on temperament, it may well be that a man's way of living, though from one point of view the outcome of his way of thinking, is from another the main factor in the evolution of his speculative thought.

It will need but a moment's reflection to convince us that the quest of ideal truth is a moral and a spiritual even more than an intellectual effort. The seeker must bring an open mind to his task, or he will have prejudged the issue of it in his manner of approaching it. We know from experience how fatally the advancement of knowledge in all fields and in all ages has been hindered by the blind prejudice which has its roots in self-love. And what is true of knowledge in general is still truer of that knowledge of ultimate reality which is the goal of our quest. The seeker must think of ideal truth, not as a treasure to be discovered and appropriated and paraded, but as a far-off orb of light to which there are as many paths as there are rays that emanate from it, paths that are ever tending to come together and melt into one another, in proportion as those who follow them, having learnt the great lesson of mutual tolerance, come nearer and nearer to the central flame. For open-mindedness has tolerance as its other self; and tolerance is a great virtue in which a score of other virtues are potentially present. Much of what St. Paul says in praise of charity might with almost equal fitness be predicated of tolerance. Tolerance " suffereth long and is kind "; tolerance " envieth not "; tolerance " vaunteth not itself, is not puffed up. Doth not behave itself unseemly, seeketh not its own, is not easily provoked, thinketh no evil; rejoiceth not in iniquity, but rejoiceth in the truth; beareth all things, believeth all things, hopeth all things, endureth all things." Tolerance " never faileth." I am thinking, I need hardly say, of the positive, the active tolerance of the lover of truth, not of the merely negative tolerance of the Gallio. The word tolerance may seem to savour of negativeness and passivity; but when we remind ourselves how terrible a power for evil is intolerance, how fiercely egoistic it is, how ruthlessly cruel, for what horrors it has been responsible, how active a principle it has been of division and strife, we shall realise that its opposite is, in potency if not in actual achievement, a mighty power for good. Tolerance, sympathy, love—these are the three chief stages in the ascent of the soul to the throne of God. And tolerance is, I repeat, the other self of open-mindedness, being indeed the openness of heart, without which openness of mind cannot sustain itself for more than a passing season. It follows that to keep the open mind, which the quest of ideal truth imperatively demands, if the quest is not to abort owing to the seeker caring more for himself than for truth, involves an arduous moral effort which must never be relaxed.

The truth is that the movement towards the ideal is a movement, not of the mind only, but of the whole higher nature of man. This is a truth on which mystics and occultists have always laid the utmost stress. The mystic will tell you that knowledge of ultimate truth is not to be achieved except through consciousness of God, and that consciousness of God is the reward of absolute purity of heart. And the occultist will tell you that only by systematic self-discipline and self-culture can a man realise his latent capacity for reading the memory of Nature and so penetrating the deeper mysteries of his being. In principle, the mystic and the occultist are surely right. " La Verité," says Joubert, " Dieu seul la voit. C'est en cela que consiste la verité. Elle consiste à conçevoir ou à imaginer les personnes et les choses comme Dieu les voit." To see things as they are is to see them as God sees them, to see them, as it were, through the eyes of God. This is ideal truth. This and nothing less than this is the goal of our quest. The goal is unapproachable and unimaginable. Yet the way to it cannot be mistaken. It is the way of never-ending self-development, of the never-ending expansion and illumination of consciousness, of the never-ending endeavour to become one with God.

The social aspect of the quest is a theme on which there is much to be said. I cannot do more than briefly indicate its importance. When our society was formed we realised that we, its members, had different ways of thinking about the problems that attracted us, and therefore, if the society was to prosper or even endure, that we must learn the lesson of mutual tolerance. As we learned this lesson we realised further that the spirit of tolerance is an active principle of unity in diversity, and therefore a potent bond of social union and cohesion. We realised the truth of the saying that " Each man is to himself absolutely the way, the truth and the life." But we also realised the truth of the counter-saying that " The united spirit of life is one's only true self." If the

whole human race could become a Quest Society, I
think we might at last begin to hope for the advent of
the kingdom of Heaven on earth. Ever since the world
began, intolerance in matters of opinion has been one
of the chief hindrances to our social evolution, one of
the most fruitful sources of disharmony, disunion and
open strife. And ever since the Jews took it into their
heads that they were God's chosen people, religious
intolerance has been the curse and scourge of the whole
Western and near Eastern world. Think of the Catholic
Church claiming a monopoly of God's grace and favour
and virtually excommunicating the rest of mankind.
Think of the Arab conquerors of Western Asia and
Northern Africa giving the conquered peoples their
choice between the Koran and the sword. Think of
the thousand years' war between the Crescent and the
Cross. Think of the hideous massacres of the Albigenses.
Think of the horrors of the Inquisition in Spain. Think
of the wholesale burning of heretics being counted an
"act of faith." Think of what the religious wars did
to France in the sixteenth century. Think of what the
Thirty Years' War did to Germany in the seventeenth.
Think of the Moslems in all ages massacring their
enemies, as the Turk to-day massacres the Armenian,
to the honour and glory of God. And the worst of
religious intolerance is that it affects the whole character,
that it generates an intolerant disposition, that it makes
men dogmatic, self-assertive and self-centred, that it
raises to a high power the selfishness of the natural
man, and that it easily overflows into the channels of
politics and social and economic life. What hope is
there of peace on earth and goodwill among men until
men can teach themselves the lesson of mutual tolerance
—not the tolerance of indifference, but the tolerance of
sympathy and understanding—in the various spheres of

opinion, and above all in the sphere of ultimate belief? And what chance is there of their mastering this lesson until they have learned to subordinate devotion to their own creeds and churches and war-cries and parties to devotion to ideal truth?

Let us, in conclusion, ask ourselves one searching question. What will be the reward of the seeker? Not the possession of ideal truth. He left that unworthy desire behind him when he embarked on the quest. Not to possess, but to be possessed; to be lost in the infinitude of the Ideal; to be lost in the light of the Divine. Not repose; for that dream too he left behind him at the outset. Not repose, but in its stead the peace which passeth all understanding, the peace of unending movement, of infinite unrest. The path of the quest is the path of eternal failure; but eternal failure, just because it never accepts defeat, is the only real success, the only success that can never pall.

Things won are done; joy's soul lies in the doing.

If our joy is to endure our doing must always fall short of achievement. The path of the quest is the path of unending self-development, of unending growth, of an unending ascent of the arch of life, an ascent which never reaches its meridian. It is the path, in fine, of immortal youth. For all these reasons, which readily merge into one, the quest of ideal truth is, and will always be, its own reward.

May 1921.

DOES CONTEMPORARY SCHOLARSHIP DO JUSTICE TO THE TEACHING OF JESUS?

I HAVE lately read, with deep interest and with warm appreciation of its many merits, the first volume of *The Beginnings of Christianity*, edited by Drs. Foakes Jackson and Kirsopp Lake. The book is obviously a monument of sound scholarship and patient research. I would say more on this point did I not feel that it ill becomes one who knows little to praise the industry and the learning of those who know much. The book is also to be commended for its transparent candour and its earnest attempt to be strictly impartial. I use the word "attempt" advisedly. I do not think the attempt has succeeded, and I doubt if such attempts can ever be wholly successful. "He that is not with me is against me." It is impossible to be absolutely impartial when the question to be answered is one in which one happens to be interested. In matters of sentiment, as of opinion, one has one's choice between *for* and *against*, but one cannot remain for more than an instant at the point of complete neutrality. The citizen who is not prejudiced, however slightly, in favour of his own country, is pretty sure to be prejudiced, subconsciously perhaps, but not the less really, against it. It is the same with the religion which one has inherited. Indifference may sometimes pose as impartiality, but genuine impartiality in the sphere of religious sentiment and thought is beyond one's reach. This leads me to say that the only criticism which I will allow myself to pass on this book is that the editors, in their laudable desire to do full justice to Judaism in general and Pharisaism in particular, and to free themselves from any suspicion of pro-Christian bias, have overstepped the line of strict impartiality and done less than justice to the originality of the thought of Jesus and the revolutionary character of his teaching.

Having no learning I will accept without demur every statement and every conjecture in this book which belongs to the region of scholarship proper, the region of textual criticism and historical research. The boundary of that region is of course indefinable. Indeed, it partakes of the nature of a borderland rather than of a boundary line. While passing through that borderland, the reader, even if he has hitherto been the most docile of pupils, may be pardoned if he occasionally adopts an attitude of reserve. Beyond the borderland he enters a region in which scholarship proper counts for less than criticism, in the larger sense of the word, the criticism which is the outcome of imaginative sympathy, of spiritual insight, of psychological experience, these having as their background the intuitive judgment and the common sense of the plain unsophisticated man. Here the reader instinctively begins to think for himself. And it is right that he should do so. A great scholar is not necessarily a great critic. It is one thing to interpret a text or other historical document, and another thing to interpret the sayings of a great teacher, to follow them out into their consequences, logical and practical, to determine their lateral bearings, and to trace them back towards their source in the teacher's subconscious self. The gifts and aptitudes which go to the making of the scholar do not coincide, and do not necessarily coexist, with the gifts and aptitudes which go to the making of the critic; and the course of study which fosters the former may possibly tend, in some slight measure, to atrophy the latter. For these reasons, while gratefully accepting the information

with which the editors of this book have provided me,
I hold myself free, within certain limits, to interpret
that information for myself.

There is one momentous judgment which the editors
have delivered with an air of authority, I might almost
say of finality, which may well impose upon their readers,
but which is not justified by the reason that they give
for their decision:

> In what way did the teaching of Jesus differ from that
> of his contemporaries? . . . Not—and the nature of much
> modern writing makes it desirable to emphasise the nega-
> tion—not by teaching anything about God essentially new
> to Jewish ears. The God of Jesus is the God of the Jews,
> about whom he says nothing which cannot be paralleled in
> Jewish literature.

From the tone which our authors adopt one would
imagine that there could be no appeal against this judgment. Here I must join issue with them. No amount
of learning can justify them in taking up a dogmatic
attitude towards one of the most intractable of all problems,—for what is more difficult than to determine what
a great teacher believed in his heart of hearts? When
scholars lay down the law on matters of general interest,
they should remind themselves that theirs is a Court
of First Instance only, and that their judgments are
therefore liable to be revised and perhaps reversed. So
highly do I value the right of appeal in these matters,
and so little am I impressed by the argument with which
these learned judges support their ruling as to the
identity of the God of the Jews with the God of Jesus,
that, though I am a " layman " and an outsider, I
propose to carry this particular case to a higher Court.

" The God of Jesus is the God of the Jews, about
whom he said nothing which cannot be paralleled in
Jewish literature." The second statement in this sentence may be true; but even if it is, it does not prove

the truth of the first. What Jesus said about God is not the only indication of what he believed about him. Other sources of evidence are at our service—the attitude of Jesus towards the Jewish Law being one of them—and it may well be that when these have been studied with a view to determining the " sovereign dogmas " of the creed of Jesus, they will throw light on the words that he used about God, and help us to discover turns and shades and depths of meaning in these, to which we might otherwise have been blind. Let scholars tell us, if they can, what Jesus said; but let them allow us " laymen " to join with them in the attempt to interpret his sayings. If Christendom were to-day to give birth to a great reformer, who would re-interpret for us the teaching of Christ, transfigure our vision of God, enlarge and spiritualise our conceptions of life, and destiny and duty, and in general re-illuminate our bewildered thought and re-vivify our flagging faith, it would probably be possible for a band of scholars to find parallels to all that he said in the vast literature of Christianity, especially in the non-theological part of it—in the writings of its devotees, its poets, its mystics, and its saints. But it would be a mistake to regard those more or less isolated utterances, or, in the case of the mystics, that more or less isolated literature, as belonging to the main current of Christian belief and thought. And it would be a mistake to argue that because our reformer said nothing about God which could not be paralleled in Christian literature, the God whom he worshipped was therefore no other than the God of Christendom, that hybrid deity, half tribal and half cosmic, or again half human, half supernatural, who has been worshipped, with much confusion of thought, by the plain, unlearned, unreflecting believer, in all lands and in all ages.

Let us go back from the present day to the beginnings

of Christianity. There is a strain of poetry in the Jewish soul, narrow perhaps but fervent and deep, which has always been liable to break out in unexpected places, and which may well have broken out, here and there, in the writings of the more large-hearted rabbis. And there is something spontaneous and upsurging in poetry which is ever tending to liberate one from bondage to tradition, convention and custom—in the name, on the one hand, of what is primitive, on the other hand, of what is ideal. Under its influence, which is as a rule short-lived, a man will subconsciously repudiate theories which he consciously holds and rules of life which he consciously obeys or professes to obey. In dealing with the semi-poetical, and therefore emancipative and " un-orthodox," sayings of the rabbis, it is well to bear this characteristic feature of poetry in mind. One feels that those sayings were the products of something akin to inspiration, sayings which had broken loose, as it were, from the control of those who uttered them, rather than aphorisms which had been deliberately charged by their authors with a new philosophy of life. They stand apart from the main body of rabbinical teaching, and there is no place for them in the general scheme of things which those who uttered them, in common with their less inspired and more conventionally-minded brethren, held to be divinely true. To assume that these exceptional utterances were typically Jewish, is to take too much for granted.[1] As well might it be said that the more

---

[1] The charge is sometimes brought against the Jews that their religion and their morality began and ended in legalism; that they worshipped God as the Lawgiver, and that obedience to the Law was for them the sum total of morality. This charge may be too sweeping. Mr. C. Montefiore, in the chapter which he has contributed on " The Jewish Spirit," thinks to rebut it by telling stories of rabbis who had freed themselves from some of the fetters of legalism. In all the stories—there are three—the limitations of legalism are discernible; but it is the more spiritual and

daringly mystical writings of Tauler, Eckhardt and Ruys-broek were representative of the central current of religious belief and sentiment in mediæval Christendom, and that the ultra-mystical conception of God coincided with the orthodox conception.

What was the Jewish conception of God? In a sense it was unique. Alone among the peoples of the earth, the Jews worshipped a deity who was at once cosmic and tribal, or at best national. Their God was the God of the Universe, and yet he was in a very special sense the God of Israel. And the narrow aspect of his being was ever tending to obscure and even obliterate the wider. How the Jews conceived of their own relation to this curiously hybrid deity, the editors of this book have set forth in the following words:

That God reigns over all, but in a special sense over those who recognise his rule, is one of the favourite themes of the

less formal side of legalism which is presented to us. This, how-ever, is by the way. The answer to Mr. Montefiore's argument is that one swallow does not make a summer. Nor, for the matter of that, do two or even three. No doubt there were individual rabbis and individual "lay" Jews, who rose superior to the narrow limitations of their creed. But what of the Jewish people as a whole? Were they not legalist to the core in the days which preceded the final Dispersal? And are they not still legalist to the core so far as they have kept the faith of their forefathers? On the latter point the testimony of such a book as *The Promised Land*, which describes the daily life of a Jewish family in Poland, seems to be conclusive.

There is one important matter in regard to which the editors and Mr. Montefiore seem to hold conflicting views. Mr. Monte-fiore alludes to writings by "Rabbis of the first century." But the editors say that "the Rabbinical writings are none of them earlier than about 200 A.D." Which of these statements is correct? If the latter, there would surely have been time for rabbinical thought to have been affected in some degree by the leaven of Judaeo-Christian teaching. Mr. Montefiore says that "the general tendency of the 300 years between 50 B.C. and 250 A.D. is un-questionably in the direction of conceiving God as more merciful, fatherly and gracious." May not this change have been due in part to the unacknowledged influence of Jesus?

Psalms. This point was taken also by the later Jews, and is
often emphasised by the Rabbis.   God's pre-eminence does
not depend on the attitude of his own creatures, but it cannot be considered perfect till it is recognised by men. Thus,
down to Abraham, it might be said, God reigns in Heaven
only.   By his faith Abraham made him King of the earth,
too, for in him God had one subject; so also did Jacob at
Bethel when he declared that Jehovah should be his God.
But the reign of God was thus far confined to individuals,
until at Sinai the Israelites said, "All that the Lord hath
spoken will we do and obey" and became a nation in which
God reigned. The reign of God is thus in the Old Testament,
the Apocalyptic books, and the rabbinical literature, a present
reality, so far as he is owned and obeyed by individuals and
by the people as a whole.   The Jews not only hoped and
prayed for this reign, but they lived under it, for its nature
is not political but religious.   They held that at the present
time the sovereignty of God is recognised only by Israel,
imperfectly by it and in different degrees by different individuals; but think in the future there will be a "good time"
in which the universal and complete sovereignty of God
will be acknowledged by all mankind and his revealed will
obeyed perfectly.

In this conception of God national pride and egoism
reach, as it seems to me, their high-water mark.   God
is conceived of as dependent, *de facto*, if not *de jure*,
first on one person, then on one family, then on one
small nation, for his *locus standi*, so to speak, on earth.
Through the codified law which he gave to the Chosen
People he declared his will to mankind. Where that
Law was accepted and practised he reigned on earth.
Where it was not accepted his writ did not run. But
99 per cent. of mankind had never heard of the Jewish
Law, and could not therefore be expected to practise it.
Yet because they did not practise it they and the lands
which they inhabited were outside the kingdom of God.
It might have been expected that when the Law was
delivered to the Chosen People, they would have been
directed to make it and its Divine Author known in all
parts of the world. But no such direction was given to

them, and they were not conscious of any obligation to evangelise the Gentiles. They kept the Law, and with it God's grace and favour, to themselves, and they seem to have had little or no desire to share their privileges with the rest of their fellow-men. It is true that, as the editors remind us, they, or at least some of their rabbis, looked forward to the " good time " in which the universal and complete sovereignty of God would be acknowledged by mankind. But in the first place " the realisation of the Sovereignty of God was not expected to be the result of missionary enterprise but of the self-determined will of God." And in the second place there was a strong strain of selfishness in this anticipation of the " good time." In the words of Mr. C. Montefiore " there was a desire and a hope that all men should recognise and worship the God of Israel, and this not only, or even not so much, for their own sakes as for the glory of God and the glory of Israel." Nor was this desire felt to be incompatible with another which was openly selfish, the desire " that vengeance and condign punishment should befall the idolater and the oppressor " of Israel.

Was this the God whom Jesus worshipped? I doubt it. I cannot think that either the restriction of the sovereignty of God or the exclusion of the greater part of mankind from God's favour was in keeping with his own profound faith in the goodness of his Heavenly Father. In the Sermon on the Mount, when he tells his audience not to be anxious for the morrow as regards either food or raiment, he gives the following reason for their trusting themselves to God's loving care:

Behold the birds of the heaven that they sow not, neither do they reap, nor gather into barns; and your heavenly Father feedeth them. Are not ye of much more value than they? And why are ye anxious concerning raiment? Con-

sider the lilies of the field how they grow; they toil not,
neither do they spin: and yet I say unto you that even
Solomon in all his glory was not arrayed like one of these.
But if God doth so clothe the grass of the field, which to-day
is and to-morrow is cast into the oven, shall he not much
more clothe you, O ye of little faith?

Elsewhere he says to his disciples:

Are not two sparrows sold for a farthing? And not one of
them shall fall on the ground without your Father; but the
very hairs of your head are all numbered. Fear not therefore;
ye are of more value than many sparrows.

Are we to suppose that God feeds the birds of the
heaven, clothes the lilies of the field and directs the
movements of sparrows in Palestine only? Surely not?
God's loving care of his creatures extends to all parts
of the world. Are we then to suppose that God feeds the
birds, clothes the lilies and cares for the sparrows in
Gentile lands, but has no care or thought for the human
inhabitants of those lands? Are we to suppose that he
numbers the hairs of Jews only? To ask such questions
is to answer them. If they mean anything these sayings
mean that God is in close and intimate relation with all
living things, at all times and in all parts of the world;
that he is the breath of all their beings, the life of all
their lives. Such a conception of God is nearer in
spirit to the higher pantheism of India than to the rigid
monotheism of the Jews.

But we need not concern ourselves exclusively or even
mainly with what Jesus said about God. It is the subconscious faith of his heart, the faith which he did not
formulate but which determined his general outlook on
life and his general attitude towards its practical problems—it is this obscure region of his inner life which
there is most need for us to explore. And there is, as
it happens, one source of evidence which throws light
on its semi-darkness. I refer to the feud between Jesus

and the Pharisees. This feud is one of the central features of the Gospel story. I am not sure that it is not the central feature. Whatever may be uncertain about Jesus, it is certain that he hated Pharisaism, and it is certain that he was hated by the Pharisees.

Let us see what this has to tell us as to the inner faith of Jesus. Of all the Jewish sects or parties in the time of Jesus, the Pharisees were the truest exponents of the main tradition of Judaism and were in closest touch with its essential spirit. That this was so is proved by the part that they played when the final Diaspora or dispersal of the Jewish people came. " In their hands," say the editors of this work, " lay the future of Judaism." In the year 135 A.D. the political nationality of the Jews was finally annihilated. The Pharisees then took the leading part in reorganising the Jewish people, as a non-political people, by means of the Mishnah, or code of rabbinic law. That they were able to do this shows that they were and had always been Jews of the Jews. For he alone can save a nation, when its nationality is in danger of extinction, who can tell it what it stands for, who can interpret it to itself.

That being so, we may safely assume that the God of the Pharisees was the God of the Jews. But was the God of the Pharisees also the God of Jesus? I am very sure that he was not. In all the weighty matters of life, and especially in what to a Jew was the weightiest of all—the practice of the Law, Jesus was in open conflict with the Pharisees. Is it conceivable, then, that his conception of God should have exactly coincided with theirs? What is the value of one's conception of God if it does not (to repeat my own words) determine one's general outlook on life and one's general attitude towards its practical problems? And if it does determine these, and if we find that A and B take opposite views of life

and conduct, we may surely argue that there is at least
a divergence between their respective conceptions of
God. But if the God of the Pharisees was not the God
of Jesus, it stands to reason that the God of Jesus was
not the God of the Jews. Things which are identical
with the same thing are identical with one another. But
if A, though identical with C, differs widely from B, it
is certain that B is not identical with C.

Such reasoning as this is perhaps too conclusive to be
convincing. So let us get to closer quarters with this
all-important problem. The God of the Jews, and
therefore à fortiori of the Pharisees, was first and foremost their Lawgiver. He was also their Ruler, but he
did not become their Ruler until they had accepted his
Law and promised to obey it. He was also their Judge,
but he did not become their Judge until they had begun
to regulate their lives by the Law. He was also their
Executioner, but he did not begin to execute judgment
on them until they had disobeyed the Law. It was
through the Law that he revealed his will to them. It
was through the Law that they knew him so far as
knowledge of him was possible. In their attitude towards
the Law we discern their attitude towards God. As
they conceived of the Law so they conceived of God.

How did the Jews conceive of the Mosaic law? As
a body of law which had been codified by God himself,
and all the rules of which were therefore binding on the
faithful. But here difficulties arose. No code of law,
however elaborate, can possibly foresee and provide for
the ever-changing conditions of man's existence. With
the gradual evolution and growing complexity of social
life, with the advance of knowledge—both scientific and
practical, with the acceptance and application of the
lessons of experience, with the consequent progress of
the race or of a people in what is called " civilisation,"

new cases of doubt and difficulty are ever presenting
themselves to the legalist, and his loyalty to the law
which he has inherited is more and more severely tried.

How did the Pharisees deal with such cases? The
Sadducees demanded strict adherence to the letter of
the Law. The Pharisees had the good sense to see that
this was impossible. What was to be done?

We shall best understand how the Pharisees attacked
this problem by contrasting their solution of it with that
which we owe to Jesus. This has been done for us by
the editors of *The Beginnings of Christianity*, and I cannot
do better than quote their words:

> Jesus . . . accepted the Law as the basis of righteousness.
> According to himself, he demanded a higher standard than
> the Scribes; according to the Scribes he was destroying the
> Law. The difference was one of interpretation, and can best
> be understood by his treatment of the law on the Sabbath
> and on divorce. The difficulty of a strict observance of the
> Sabbath was the cause of many discussions among the rabbis,
> and the Pharisees had introduced many rules intended to make
> it easier. But, as always happens with attempts to remedy
> oppressive legislation by amendment rather than abolition,
> these Pharisaic efforts resulted only in making the yoke of the
> Sabbath heavier. Jesus went to the heart of the matter by
> appealing from the letter of the Law to its purpose, and
> defined this as the advantage of man. " The Sabbath was
> for man's sake." . . . However difficult of application it may
> be, the verdict of Jesus remains unshaken in principle, not
> merely on the Sabbath but on all other laws. Their moral
> claim to allegiance is ultimately based on their advantage to
> men; and the supreme duty of legislators is to test the code
> entrusted to them by this standard. . . . Jesus' treatment
> of marriage and divorce illustrates the same principle, though
> its application in his hands led to different results. According
> to Mark he excluded divorce altogether on the ground that
> a man and his wife were created as one flesh and that the
> Mosaic permission to divorce was due to sin and not to the
> original plan of man's creation. . . . It may seem at first
> sight strange that Jesus relaxed the law of the Sabbath, and
> not that of divorce; but in each case he was appealing to
> their original meaning and relation to human life. . . . These

are the clearest examples of Jesus' treatment of the Law: it
was not an antinomian abrogation, such as the Jewish Christians attributed to Paul; nor was it a rigid adhesion to its
letter, such as the Sadducees advocated. It was similar to its
treatment by the Pharisees so far as it was " re-interpretation "; but it was of a wholly different type. The Pharisaic
re-interpretation, which is a phenomenon common in all
ages, endeavoured, consciously or unconsciously, to modify
the Law, while appearing to confirm it.   Their treatment
was based on two facts—they could not fulfil the letter of the
Law, but they desired to seem to do so. It therefore introduced a chain of subtle modifications and explanations, each
small in itself, which taken together sometimes reverses the
meaning of the Law *ex animo scriptoris*.   *The treatment of
Jesus, on the other hand, was based on the mind of the divine
author of the Law.*[1] When the letter of the Law interfered
with instead of furthering the purpose for which it was
written, it was the purpose, not the letter, which took precedence; and inasmuch as this purpose was the benefit
of mankind, a principle incontestably correct, though undoubtedly difficult, was laid down.

This is well put; but do the writers fully realise how
vast a revolution in religious thought and faith was
implicit in the simple words " The Sabbath was for
man's sake "? I cannot think that they do; for if they
did they could scarcely fail to realise that the God of
Jesus was *not* the God of the Jews. They tell us that
" Jesus' treatment of the Law " " was not an antinomian
abrogation of it." The Scribes, who devoted their lives
to the study of the Law, said that it was; and I am
inclined to think that they were right. The attitude of
Jesus towards the Law was no mere departure from the
orthodox attitude.   It carried with it an entirely new
conception of the " Knowledge " which leads " to life ";
and this, as we shall see, carried with it a new conception of God. " There is much," say the editors, " for
scholars to admire in the Rabbinical teaching of the
Law. At its best it is the recognition that Knowledge is

[1] The italics are mine.—E. H.

one of the roads to Life." I wish we had been given examples of rabbinical teaching of the Law "at its best." There may be much in that teaching for scholars to admire; but I doubt if there is much for ordinary men. Knowledge is indeed one of the roads that lead to life ; but not the knowledge which the Scribes exalted. Knowledge of reality, knowledge of the real meaning and purpose of life, the knowledge which delivers from bondage to illusory aims and false ideals, the knowledge which Buddha held to be necessary to salvation, the knowledge which was behind Jesus' own interpretation of the Law, does most assuredly lead to life. But knowledge of a code of law in all its meticulous complexity is more likely to lead in practice to hair-splitting and quibbling and casuistical evasion than to the right conduct which is the outward expression of a healthy inward life. Leaving it to the rabbis to delude themselves and their disciples with this sham and futile knowledge, Jesus based his own solution of the riddles of the Law on the tacit claim to possess the highest conceivable kind of knowledge—knowledge of the mind and will of God.

This tacit claim was pregnant with two momentous consequences—the abrogation of the Law as a law, and the transformation of the current conception of God. In his treatment of the problem of the Sabbath and the problem of divorce, Jesus resolved the Law into its own first principles. In taking upon himself to do this he claimed by implication the right to be a law unto himself. Such a claim, if allowed and pressed to its logical conclusion, involved nothing less than the ultimate supersession of the Law. St. Paul saw that the Jews had no monopoly of right doing and clean living. There were righteous men among the Gentiles, men who had never heard of the Law, and who yet obeyed its moral precepts. How was this to be accounted for? What had guided those Gentiles into the path of righteousness? Not the light of the Law, but an inward light, the light of conscience or moral intuition.

For when Gentiles which have no law do by nature the things of the law, these, having no law, are a law unto themselves; in that they show the work of the law written in their hearts, their conscience bearing witness therewith, and their thoughts one with another accusing or else excusing them.

It was as the champion of conscience against legal direction that Jesus confronted the Pharisees. It was also as the champion of a new conception of God. In resolving the Law into its own first principles, Jesus placed himself, as it were, by the side of God, undertook to read God's mind, to examine the Law from God's point of view, and to deal with it as God would have wished it to be dealt with. In dealing with the Sabbath he even went so far as to suggest to God (if I may so word it) a new point of view, for according to the Fourth Commandment, which was presumably given to Moses on Sinai, the Sabbath was instituted, not for the benefit of man but in order to commemorate the rest of God. What was it that emboldened Jesus to do all this? Was it not the conviction that he was guided by the Spirit of God, guided from within rather than from without, guided by a light which made the guidance of the Law unnecessary, and which therefore provided for the ultimate abrogation of the Law, *as a law*, for its resolution into the living principle which was at the heart of it, the principle which was embodied in the two great commandments, the principle of devotion to God and service to man. But the God who guides man from within, who guides the Gentile as well as the Jew, whose light lighteth every man, is a national God no longer, but the God of the whole wide world. Subconsciously, then, if not consciously, Jesus provided for the supersession of the Law by the inward light, and for the supersession of the God of Israel by the All-Father, the God of the universe, the God who is really, not nominally, cosmic, the God who does *not* make favourites, who does *not* take sides.

I will now briefly summarise the contents of this paper. The editors of *The Beginnings of Christianity* have told us, with an air of judicial authority, that the God of Jesus was the God of the Jews. I have given reasons for thinking that this judgment ought to be sent for revision to a higher Court. I have contended that when we are trying to determine the religious beliefs of a great teacher, the words which he used about God are not our only available source of evidence; that there are other sources at our service which have even more to tell us, and which it is for criticism, as distinguished from scholarship, to explore. In the case of Jesus an exhaustive study of those other sources of evidence would probably fill many volumes. I have contented myself with pointing out that in the attitude of Jesus towards the Jewish Law, as to which there seems to be no dispute, there was implicit a conception of God which was not merely unorthodox, but, in the fullest sense of the word, revolutionary.

As time goes on, we shall think less and less, when we are trying to read the heart of a prophet or a reformer, of what he actually said about God, and more and more of his general attitude towards the great problems that confronted him. "Men discover themselves," says Bacon, "in trust, in passion, *at unawares*." They believe what they do believe, not what they think they believe, still less what they say they believe. The New Psychology, of which we have heard so much of late, with its interest in and insight into the unconscious, is still in

its infancy, and some of its present pretensions are un-
tenable; but it has a great future to look forward to.
For one thing, it will open up new fields and new vistas
to critical thought.   Scholarship proper will continue
to occupy itself with the written and the spoken word,
and it is right that it should do so.   But criticism, in the
larger and deeper sense of the word, will turn more and
more to the study of the " buried life," the mysterious
underworld in which our beliefs originate and are gradually shaped, and from which they rise up into our
consciousness, their buried life being still their real
life, in that the very efforts which we make to become
conscious of them tend to stimulate them into fresh
activity, just as the pumping-up of water from a deep
well sets in motion all the waters in its subterranean
reservoirs.   The real faith of a great soul (if I may make
an abrupt change of simile) is like an iceberg, which
towers up grandly into the sunlight, and impresses us
with a sense of majesty and beauty, but which could not
do so if it were not that nine-tenths of it are submerged.

In the last sentence of their book the editors tell us
that they " have given unqualified statement to their
own opinions, chiefly in order to make easier a fuller
discussion of the questions involved."   If this is the
spirit in which they have written, they will, I am sure,
forgive me for having presumed to contribute my quota
to the " fuller discussion " of one of the questions on
which they " have given unqualified statement to their
opinions,"—a question on which, as it seems to me,
unqualified statement is inadmissible, in that of all the
questions discussed it is perhaps the most important
and the most difficult.

July 1921.

THE RECREATIONS OF THE SPITAL-
FIELDS WEAVERS

A PAPER READ AT THE NEW IDEALS IN EDUCATION
CONFERENCE AT STRATFORD-ON-AVON IN AUGUST 1921

I AM told that somewhere on this planet of ours there
is a fastidious professor who holds that the lower orders
(as we call them) ought to be kept in a state of semi-
serfdom, in order that the upper classes may have
leisure for culture. If this paradoxical theory were put
forward as a paradox there might be something to be
said for it; at any rate one might treat it as a joke and
pass it by with a smile; but I understand that it is put
forward in all seriousness; and, this being so, I propose
to subject it to serious criticism; and I do so the more
readily because in our fastidious professor I recognise
one of my own dead selves.

The first and most obvious objection to this thesis
is that the enslavement, or semi-enslavement, of the
lower orders is too high a price to pay for any end,
however intrinsically desirable.

A second and almost equally obvious objection is that
if culture demands for its advancement the permanent
degradation of seven-eighths of the human race, in the
very act of making this claim it proves that its estimate
of its own worth is unduly high. For if the effect of
culture on the cultured is to make them so callously
selfish that they will accept with complacence the sacrifice to their supposed interests of the well-being of the
masses—their comfort, their leisure and their economic

freedom—it is most emphatically *not* the humanising influence which it pretends to be.

A third objection to the theory is that it stultifies its own *raison d'être*. For what is the meaning, what is the value of culture? Is it a precious possession, the mere existence of which exalts and enriches the human race? Surely not. Surely it must be used and enjoyed, surely we must feed upon it in our hearts, if its potential value is to be converted into actual value. But if seven-eighths of the human race are to be forbidden to enjoy it, if they are to be denied the education and the leisure which might enable them to enjoy it, of what value will it be when produced? Of what value is culture if it is to be reserved exclusively for the delectation of a clique of connoisseurs and dilettantists, with a band of scholars and a few men of creative genius scattered among these, and is not to enlighten and elevate the mass of mankind?

A fourth objection, the most serious of all from our professor's point of view, is that the theory defeats its own avowed aim; that, if carried out, it would make for the degradation, not for the advancement, of culture. For culture, like a mountain, should be broad-based if it is to rise up to a lofty height; but, according to the theory which I am examining, it is of the essence of culture that it should have a narrow base, that it should be an Eiffel Tower or a sky-scraper, not a Mont Blanc. The great mountain, as Ruskin has well said, lifts the lowlands on to its sides. It is only by lifting the lowlands, by using them as the lower courses of its own structure, that it has been able to rise so high above them. The Eiffel Tower spurned the lowlands. It tried to take a short cut to heaven. But because it had made no attempt to identify itself with the lowlands or to incorporate them in its own structure, it failed ignominiously and had to be cut off, lest it should topple over, when it had reached the level of one of the humblest of Nature's hills. An eminent musician once told me that the folk songs, the songs of the people, are the lifted lowlands out of which the great creations of musical genius soar up to the sky. The ballads of a nation are the lifted lowlands of its poetry. When Gothic architecture was at the zenith of its achievement, it had behind it, not only the religious faith of the people but also their instinctive art, as expressed in their own handicrafts, and their practical skill.

I shall be reminded that the marvellous culture of ancient Athens rested on a basis of slave labour. This argument has been overworked by the advocates of an exclusively aristocratic culture. Athenian culture rested on a basis of slave labour in the sense in which the whole Athenian commonwealth rested on that basis. But to rest on a basis is one thing; to be rooted in it is another. Slaves in antiquity, especially in urban areas, played to a large extent the part which is played to-day by the mechanical contrivances which supply us with water, light, heat, power, drainage and transport, and which count for so much in our social life, that modern culture may almost be said to rest on a basis of applied science and organised machinery. That is why the number of slaves was so large in proportion to the number of enfranchised citizens. The slaves were not, as are our lower orders, an integral part of the social community. Athenian culture may have rested on a basis of slave labour, but it was rooted in the intelligence and good taste of the Athenian *demos*—a *demos* which could listen, with critical appreciation, to the tragedies of Æschylus, Sophocles and Euripides and gaze, with critical appreciation, on the works of Phidias and Praxiteles. "The whole Athenian nation," says Lewes in his *Life of Goethe*, " co-operated with its artists; and this is one cause why

Athenian art rose into unsurpassed splendour. Art was not the occupation of a few, ministering to the luxury of a few; it was the luxury of all. Its triumphs were not hidden in galleries and museums; they blazed in the noonday sun; they were admired and criticised by the whole people; and, as Aristotle expressly says, every free citizen was from youth upwards a critic of art." In other words, Athenian culture soared high because, within the limits of the social community, it was broad-based, as broad-based as it was possible for it to be.

When enjoyment of art is a pleasure which the connoisseur keeps to himself, the art in question, or at least that particular development of it, has begun to die, suffocated by its own technique. When the collector appears on the scene the art in question is dead. The intrusion of selfish exclusiveness into art is a sign of incipient decay. For its presence means that the artist has succumbed to the lure of finality and forgotten the call of the infinite, which was his inspiration when his art was young. What the connoisseur enjoys, what the collector prides himself on possessing, is something finished and finite, something which can be weighed and measured, and valued at last in terms of £ s. d. When an art is living and growing, when it is advancing towards its meridian, joy in it is " joy in widest commonalty spread." True art is an adventure into the infinite. As such it ministers to all, appeals to all, and calls for the devotion and service of all.

Our professor will tell us that the masses have no culture and care nothing for it. This may be so to-day. But was it always so? In the Middle Ages and in the earlier of the centuries which we call modern, the masses, though uneducated and ignorant, had a primitive culture of their own. They had their ballads, their folk songs, their village plays, their morris and other dances, their cottage architecture, their various handicrafts. They have lost most of these. Let this be fully admitted. But how did they lose them, and who is responsible for the loss? Not the losers themselves. They have been the victims of adverse fate. They have been forcibly decultured, if I may use such a word. But when was this tragedy enacted, and how did it come to pass?

In answer to this question I will tell the story of the Spitalfields weavers. When I have told it I shall be able to formulate a final objection to our professor's proposal to base the culture of his nation on the virtual enslavement of seven-eighths of its inhabitants. The professor is not alone in the low estimate of his fellow-men which is implicit in his cynical proposal. There is a widespread impression among the upper classes, especially among the persons who pride themselves on their culture, that the working classes have a congenital incapacity for making a profitable use of leisure, and that the shortened hours of work which are now the rule in most industries, will thus be disadvantageous to them as well as to their employers, and that therefore in their own interest as well as in the interest of the whole community they should revert to the longer hours which were usual before and during the war. There is no ground for this ultra-pessimistic assumption. Whippet-racing, pigeon-fancying, attending football matches, gambling and drinking are not ideal forms of recreation. But if the workers in this and other countries have lost the art of employing leisure, their loss is easily accounted for, and there is no reason why they should not recover what they have lost.

Let us go back a hundred years or so to the days before the poisonous harvest which the Industrial Revolution sowed had fully ripened. From A.D. 1769 to 1824 the wages of the Spitalfields silk weavers were fixed under an Act of Parliament by the Lord Mayor, Recorder and Aldermen of London, and masters who paid lower or higher wages were liable to a fine of £50. Taking one year with another the wages were high enough to enable the weavers to live in decent comfort and enjoy a reasonable amount of leisure. What use did they make of their leisure? What use were the leisured members of the upper classes at that time making of their superabundant leisure? For the most part they were engaged in gambling, duelling, dancing, swaggering about at fashionable resorts, hunting, shooting, horse-racing, cock-fighting, illicit love-making, and hard drinking. The recreative activities of the Spitalfields weavers were of a different order from these. An interesting picture of their varied interests was given in 1840 by Edward Church, solicitor, who had lived for thirty years among them in Spital Square. Of those thirty years, fourteen preceded and sixteen followed the repeal of the Wages Act. The Act applied to London only; and during the whole period from 1810 to 1840 the competition with the London silk industry of the labour-sweating, *rate-aided* silk industries in provincial towns was making itself increasingly felt. After the repeal of the Act the wages of the Spitalfields weavers fell so low that in order to live they had to work increasingly long hours. Hence the gradual decay of the various societies for mutual instruction and recreation which they had formed. Church describes these societies in the following words:

The *Spitalfields Mathematical Society* is second in time to the Royal Society and still exists. There was an *Historical Society* which was merged in the *Mathematical Society*. There was a *Floricultural Society*, very numerously attended, but now extinct. The weavers were almost the only botanists of their day in the metropolis. They passed their leisure hours, and generally the whole family dined on Sundays, at the little gardens in the environs of London, now mostly

built upon, in small rooms about the size of modern omnibuses
[1840] with a fireplace at the end. There was an *Entomological
Society*, and they were the first entomologists in the kingdom.
The Society is gone. They had a *Recitation Society* for Shake-
spearean readings, as well as reading other authors, which is
almost forgotten. They had a *Musical Society*, but this is
also gone. They had a *Columbarian Society*, which gave a
silver medal as a prize for the best pigeons of the fancy breed.
They were great bird-fanciers, and breeders of canaries, many
of whom now cheer their quiet hours while at the loom.
Their breed of spaniels called Splashers were of the best
sporting blood. . . . Many of the weavers were Freemasons,
but there are now very few left, and these old men. Many of
the houses in Spitalfields had porticos with seats at their doors,
where the weavers might be seen on summer evenings enjoying
their pipes. The porticos have given way to improvements
of the pavements.

An idyllic picture this, but as pathetic as it is idyllic.
The gradual decay of the once flourishing societies under
the inexorable pressure of falling wages and lengthening
hours of work, was a veritable tragedy. But the fight of
the weavers against adverse fate was not in vain. For
in the course of it they showed what the working-classes
were able to do in the way of recreation and self-education when they had decent wages *and leisure*. In the
pre-factory days, when weaving and other industries
were carried on in the homes of the workers, the combination of decent wages with leisure was by no means
rare. Those who have studied the social and economic
life of the eighteenth century tell us that in that age of
transition something of the primitive but genuine culture
which the lower orders had evolved in the Middle Ages
lingered on in the rural and the industrial villages. The
freeholders in the former and the homeworkers in the
latter, being to some extent their own masters and therefore able to regulate their working-hours, still had their
folk songs and their morris dances, and could do many
things with their hands which they cannot do now. It

was in the soil of that primitive culture that the splendid
initiative of the Spitalfields weavers may have had its
roots. Then came the Industrial Revolution, accompanied in the rural districts by the enclosure of the
common lands, and in the world of ideas by the rise
of political economy, which taught, or was understood
to teach, that labour was a commodity to be bought in
the cheapest and sold in the dearest market. The joint
action of these three movements reduced the working-
classes to a state of serfdom and semi-starvation. Wages
fell so low that in order to keep body and soul together
the labourers, both in town and country, *and their
children*, had to work from thirteen to fifteen hours a
day. Having no leisure they naturally lost the art of
making a profitable use of leisure. Then, to make matters
worse, came a wave of puritanical Evangelicalism which
swept over the country and carried with it the notion
(much favoured by the employers of labour) that all
recreation, at any rate on the part of the working-classes,
was " carnal," and that the harder the poor worked and
the less they enjoyed life, the more likely they were to
be " saved." At last things came to such a pass that
the public-house became the only place of recreation,
and drinking the only distraction from the monotony of
never-ending and ill-paid toil.

The workers now have reasonably high wages and a
fair amount of leisure. What use will they make of
the latter ? It is possible that at first they will go in
with redoubled energy for their favourite amusements—
whippet-racing, pigeon-fancying, football matches and
the rest. And they will probably give more time to
gardening, which has, I believe, always attracted them
whenever allotments were available. But the need for
a higher and wider range of activities will gradually
make itself felt. If the workers cannot at once rise to

the level of the Spitalfields weavers, the upper classes, who either robbed them of their leisure or acquiesced —with pious resignation—in the robbery, must bear the blame of this. The Spitalfields weavers have given a lead to the workers of to-day, which they will not fail to follow, especially if they have been allowed to have varied interests in their elementary schools, and encouraged to form societies for mutual improvement and amusement in their continuation schools.

For, be it carefully observed, whatever the weavers did in the way of self-education and rational recreation, they did for themselves. There was no one to help them. There was no Board of Education to provide them in their early years with schools and teachers. There were no earnest philanthropists to guide them, when they grew up, into the path of self-development. They sought and found that path for themselves, and they had travelled far along it when loss of leisure, enforced by the threat of starvation, compelled them to quit it. Perhaps one reason why they had travelled so far was that they had found the path and explored it for themselves. Their initiative had not been starved in childhood by a repressive education which left them no room for independent action. And what survived of it had not been extinguished in adult life by that well-meaning but fussy and over-officious philanthropy which postulates the helplessness of the lower orders and then does its best to make them helpless. There is a moral to all this which is so obvious that I will ask the members of this Conference to draw it for themselves.

I am perhaps looking far into the future when I say that the workers, when leisure has lost its novelty for them, the novelty which tempts them to misuse it, will follow the lead which the Spitalfields weavers gave a hundred years ago. But I am confident that the time of which I dream will come at last. For, above all, the weavers, now that the story of their doings has been given to the world, have killed the wicked superstition that the working-classes have a congenital disinclination and incapacity for self-improvement. They have killed this superstition by proving that it is a superstition, and nothing more. And there was need for it to be killed. When the " masters " in town and country—the mill-owners, the squires and the farmers—had done their best to debase and brutalise their labourers by persistently over-working and under-paying them, they and the rest of the upper classes—male and female, lay and clerical—had the effrontery to say that the social order, *as it existed then,* had been ordained by God, and in the strength of this self-flattering assumption they turned round upon the victims of their own rapacity and cruelty, and said (as some of them still say) that they were (and are) base-born brutes.

No, the lower strata of society are no more base-born than the higher. Their natural ability is as great. So is their latent capacity for self-sacrifice and disinterested devotion. I do not say that all men are born equal in these respects. I am very sure that they are all born unequal. But I do say most emphatically that we have no evidence that there is any natural inequality between class and class. Professor Cizek, the Viennese art master, the work of whose youthful pupils, now being exhibited in this country and in this town, has astonished and delighted all who have seen it, told one of his interviewers that his best pupils come from the " proletariat ": " I would rather have the proletariat child—I would much rather. He has more 'attack' and is less spoiled." In some of our schools original composition in prose and verse is now encouraged by the teachers; and the response which the children are making to this appeal to their creative impulse is on the whole surprisingly good. But the best compositions that I have yet seen come from a higher standard *elementary* school in York-shire. And this was not picked work. What was remark-able in that school, as in Professor Cizek's art class, was the extraordinary high level of attainment which the *average* child reached. In each case capacity had been liberated by the skill and sympathy of the teacher,— capacity, the existence of which would have remained unsuspected, had not the teacher, in Professor Cizek's words, taken the lid off instead of clapping it on.

This leads me to state the fifth and last objection to our professor's theory, an objection which is a corollary to and in some sort a restatement of the fourth. Our professor has taken for granted that the masses have a congenital distaste for culture. If I am not mistaken, he has also taken for granted that they have a congenital incapacity for it. Indeed, it is only by adding this assump-tion to the other that he can attempt to justify his theory. But the second assumption is as baseless as the first. There is reason to believe that the masses, in proportion to their numbers, are by nature as well able to enjoy and appreciate culture as are the more leisured classes, and also as well able to produce and diffuse it; in other words, that they are by nature as well endowed with taste, with talent and, above all, with creative genius. If I cannot prove this statement, I can at least defy its critics to disprove it. There is evidence in support of it. The results of the experiments of Professor Cizek and the gifted teacher of English — experiments which do not stand alone — raise a presumption in its favour. So does the long list of men in all lands and all ages who have risen to greatness in defiance of the many disadvantages of obscure and lowly birth. And the evidence that seems to tell against it is wholly inconclusive, comparison between social stratum and stratum, as regards capacity for culture, being impossible when the facilities for acquiring culture are glaringly unequal.

But if the natural capacity of the masses is equal, or even approximately equal, to that of the classes, the loss to culture, owing to its being to a large extent beyond the reach of the former, must be very great. And if our professor could have his way, the loss would be greater still. The masses are perhaps seven times as numerous as the classes. It follows that if all men, without distinction of class, from the hour of their birth, could have equal opportunities for self-development, we might have eight times as many poets, artists, men of letters, thinkers, historians, pioneers in science, etc., as we have now. And the broader this high plateau of culture, the higher, one might hope, would be the peaks that rose from it as their base.

It is in respect of their social, not of their protoplasmic heritage, of the circumstances of birth, not of birth itself, that the lower classes are less fortunate than the upper. They are born into an environment which is as a rule narrower, ruder, more cramping, more depressing, less stimulating, less inspiring, an environment which cuts them off, in no small measure, from the world's great tradition of art, of letters, of high thinking, of refined and gentle living; an environment which can scarcely fail to stamp its own defects, both positive and negative, on their impressionable hearts during childhood and adolescence. It is for education, first of the child and then of the adolescent, to redress this inequality by giving those who have been less fortunate in their start in life opportunities for all-round self-development. It is for education to lift the average level of the lower social strata, in respect of culture, to the average level of the higher. It is for education to do this, and then to do something more than this. The differences between stratum and stratum in respect of culture (in the true and deep sense of the word) are as nothing compared with the differences in this respect between man as he is and man as he might be. To lead the whole human race, without respect to class, in the direction of its own ideal, is the noblest task that education can set itself. And it is a task which education alone can undertake with any hope of success.

THE CONFESSIONS AND HOPES OF AN
EX-INSPECTOR OF SCHOOLS

SOMEWHERE in these islands there is a churchyard which contains a nameless grave; and on the headstone of that grave are inscribed the words, " Here lies a great but repentant sinner." When my life as a school inspector came to an end those words might well have been my epitaph. My life as a school inspector lasted nearly thirty-six years. During the first eighteen or twenty years I did as much mischief in the field of education as I possibly could. I spent the next ten or twelve years in realising, little by little, what mischief I had done. And I spent the last four or five years in making solemn vows of amendment and reparation, vows which since my official death I have been trying to keep.

I entered the service of " My Lords," as we called the Board of Education in those days, on 1st April, 1875, and was straightway initiated into the administration of the most fatuous and most pernicious educational system that the mind of man has yet devised. I bore the august title of Her Majesty's Inspector of Schools. In reality I was an examiner of little children and an examiner of the worst possible type. It was my duty to examine each individual child in each standard in each of the three R's, and to examine each standard, as a class, in what were known as " class subjects," viz.: geography, grammar, history and needlework. On the results of that examination depended the bread and butter of the teacher and the financial stability of the school. So many shillings were paid for each pass in the three R's, and so many shillings on each unit of average attendance, for each of two class subjects. A grant was also paid for singing. Where it was taught by ear, the children "sang a song for sixpence." Where it was taught by note the grant per head was a shilling.

A few years later a Commission was appointed to investigate the problems of elementary education in general, and of the payment of grant in particular. After many months of arduous labour the mountain of Whitehall gave birth to a ridiculous mouse. Instead of so many shillings per head being paid for each of three R's, the percentage of passes in the whole school was worked out, and a penny for each unit was paid on the number of children in average attendance. For example, if the percentage of passes in a school which had an average attendance of 200 was 90, the grant paid for the three R's was 90 pence, or 7s. 6d. × 200, which equalled £75. Separate grants were still paid for the class subjects and for singing, and a variable Special Merit Grant was introduced.

A few years later these various grants were abolished, and their place was taken by two block grants, a grant of 14s. (or 12s. 6d.) for instruction, and a grant of 1s. 6d. (or 1s.) for discipline. The idea of paying 1s. 6d. (or 1s.) a head for discipline will probably move my readers to derisive laughter; but it seemed quite right and reasonable in those days. Need I add that complete immobility on the part of the children was the feature of the discipline which entitled their school to the higher grant? Their strength was to sit still. About the same time, if my memory does not fail me, examination by sample in the three R's was introduced, and was supposed to be a great improvement on the examination of all the children in all the three subjects. In point of fact it left things pretty much as they were. For it was found that the fairest and most convenient way of examining by sample was to divide a class of (say) thirty children into three groups of ten each, and examine Group A in reading, Group B in writing, and Group C in arithmetic.

Such were the changes—none of them essential—which took place in the first twenty years of my official life. During the whole of that time the one essential feature of the education given in our elementary schools was that the teachers had to prepare their pupils for a yearly examination on a narrow and rigid syllabus, prescribed, and even formulated in the fullest detail, by the Education Department.

Let us consider what fruits such a system was likely to bear. I have said that on the results of the yearly examination depended, not only the financial stability of the school, but also the very bread and butter of the teacher. In far too many cases the teacher had a share of the grant, and in any case his value in the market tended to vary directly with his ability to secure a large grant for his school. It was therefore to his interest to work hard and to make his subordinates and his pupils work hard. The result was that the school in those days was a hive of industry.

But much of its industry was misdirected energy. The State, in formulating in the fullest detail a syllabus which had to be followed in all the subjects of instruction in all the schools in the country, did for the teacher what he ought to have tried to do for himself. It relieved him, in large measure, of the necessity for thinking, purposing, planning, contriving. It provided him with his educational ideals, or rather—for an ideal offers itself to those who are able to respond to its appeal—with his educational aims, larger and lesser; and, through the yearly examination on the official syllabus, it controlled his methods to an extent which was fatal to the true interests of education.

Let us ask ourselves what the preparation of young children, year after year, for a rigorous and inquisitorial examination would be likely to do to its victims. At its best, and even when applied to adult men and women, an examination is a very imperfect test of mental progress. In the examination game there are two principal players, the examiner and the teacher or crammer, each of whom is ever trying to outwit and outmanœuvre the other. The examinee, except when he is old enough and clever enough to be his own crammer, plays but a minor part. The function of the teacher is to pump into his pupils the kind and amount of information which the examiner is likely to demand, and to put them up to the tricks and dodges which will enable them, on the examination day, to use to advantage the information which they have accumulated. If the examination is to be passed with credit both the teacher and his pupils must use their wits. But the greater part of the thinking must be done by the teacher, whose superior age, wisdom, knowledge, and experience of the examination game make it necessary that the task of outwitting the examiner should in the main devolve upon him, and that his pupils should leave themselves, largely if not wholly, in his hands. The natural result of this is that the pupils, instead of learning to rely on themselves and to use their own powers and resources, become more and more helpless and resourceless, and gradually cease to take any interest in their work for its own sake, the results of the examination being the only things that matter in their eyes. The university student who has got up a certain book for a certain examination and had no question set from it, will tell you, without shame or hesitation, that the time which he gave to it was wasted.

If these are evils incidental to the examination of adult students, it stands to reason that they will be greatly aggravated when the examinees are young children. For, in the first place, the younger the child the more delusive is an external examination as a test of mental progress, the divergence between the outward and the inward results of education—between an examiner's marks and the actual development of the child's mind—being so great in the early years of life, that only by arresting mental growth can we make the outward results in any way commensurate with the inward. And, in the second place, the younger the child, the more ignorant he is, and the more helpless in matters which do not happen to interest him, and therefore the more ready to lean upon the teacher and to look to him for instruction and guidance.

It follows that to make a formal examination on a prescribed syllabus the test of a child's mental progress is to compel the teacher to look at education from a radically wrong point of view. And it follows further that the teacher who has been authoritatively deprived of freedom, initiative and responsibility, as the teachers of England were in the latter part of the nineteenth century, must, in self-defence, do to his pupils the wrong that has been done to him. For it is only by doing so that he can play his allotted part in the general scheme of education. If you turn a teacher into a marionette, he must turn his pupils into marionettes, or he will not be able to respond to the strings which control his movements. We can see, then, that in crushing the freedom and stifling the intelligence of its teachers, the State was taking effective measures, through all the dark years of payment by results, to arrest the mental growth of the boys and girls of England and to make their education as uneducational as possible.

When inspectors ceased to examine and began to inspect they realised what mischief had been done. The children in the lower standards had been drilled in the contents of their reading-books until they almost knew them by heart; but if you asked them to read or take down from dictation a simple passage which was new to them they too often failed ignominiously. Even in the highest standards there were many who had not the least idea how to tackle an unfamiliar word. As for enjoying or taking an interest in what they read, this was the last thing which they or their teachers thought of. In arithmetic they worked abstract sums in obedience to formal rules day after day and year after year, and were put up to various dodges which would, it was hoped, enable them to find out by what rules the questions on the arithmetic card were to be answered. But no attempt was made to train their arithmetical sense; and they were therefore liable to be floored by the simplest of problems, and to be upset by any change of procedure on the part of the inspector. If, for example, instead of saying " From 95 take 57 " the inspector said, for a change, " Take 57 from 95," the chances were that half the class would try to subtract the larger from the smaller number. They learned a few lines of poetry by heart—twenty lines were considered a year's work for Standard I. and forty for Standard II.—and committed all the " meanings and allusions " to memory, with the probable result that they hated poetry for the rest of their lives. In history, geography and English they were assiduously crammed with uninteresting and unprofitable information, which was kept, by periodical questioning, as near the surface of memory as possible, so that they might be able to disgorge it, to the inspector's satisfaction, on the examination day. And so on. No attempt was made, except in a small minority of the schools, to interest the children in what they were doing; and scarcely a thought was given to the thing that really mattered — the fostering of their mental, moral and spiritual growth. The dark shadow of the approaching examination lay on the school from the first day of the school year to the last. To secure a high percentage of passes and a large grant was the teacher's main concern. The distrust and suspicion on which was based the whole policy of the Board, were necessarily passed on from the teacher to the child. The child was not allowed to do anything for himself which his teacher could do for him. He had to do what he was told to do, to say what he was told to say, to think what he was told to think, to believe what he was told to believe, to feel what he was told to feel. And the directions given to him were as far as possible complete and minute. The less room he was allowed for free action the smaller was the chance of his going astray. It was the function of the skilful teacher to foresee possible aberrations and provide against them; and each of such acts of foresight and precaution was a fresh encroachment on the freedom of the child.

Such was the old régime—the régime of code despotism and payment by results. The aim of those who were responsible for it was, I believe, to remove the stain and reproach of illiteracy from this country. But the critic who studied it in itself and without regard to the circumstances of its inception, might be pardoned for thinking that it had been framed for the express purpose of deadening faculty and distorting growth. For he could not fail to see that, far from fostering the great expansive instincts which are latent in every child, it must have been ever tending to eradicate them, one and all, or, if that was impossible, at least to arrest their development. Its defenders will perhaps contend that it atoned, in part, for this work of wanton destruction, by making the child obedient, and industrious, and (within very narrow limits) accurate and thorough. But the answer to this argument is that enforced obedience and enforced industry are not virtues of a high order, and that accuracy and thoroughness, when divorced from intelligence, are the virtues of a machine.

I have brought grave charges against the old régime. But my indictment of it is not yet complete. Its crowning defect was that, deliberately and of set purpose, it repressed the outgrowth of that sense of well-being which is the surest indication of health—in the widest sense of the word—and which goes by the name of *happiness*. The children were not happy in their school life; and, what is more, it was not intended that they should be happy. They were working against the grain of their nature; and it was the purpose of those who educated them that they should so work. They were being treated as potential rebels and congenital blockheads; and it was being taken for granted that they would not exert themselves except in response to two base motives—competitive selfishness and fear. Their initiative, their spirit of adventure, their instinctive love of activity were being systematically repressed. And every care was being taken that the seeds of social life, which are dormant in every breast, should not germinate, that the spirit of comradeship should not awake in the school. Can we wonder that when the scholars were released at the end of the morning or the afternoon session, they rushed out into the road with wild war-whoops of exultant relief?

What was I doing during all those dreary years? Alas! I was a dutiful, industrious and almost ultra-conscientious official; and the pity of it is that when an official is administering a pernicious system, the more dutiful, industrious and conscientious he is, the more mischief he is fated to do. That is why I think of myself in those old, unhappy far-off days as one of the chief of sinners. So potent was the pressure of the system under which we all worked that it drove me deep into the deadly grooves in which it imprisoned the teachers and the children. I saw that the system had many defects, but I regarded these as inherent in any and every scheme of education for the masses; and I was well content to play my appointed part in that vast complex of machinery which had been elaborated by the wisdom and was controlled by the authority of Whitehall. It has been said that custom doth make dotards of us all; and it certainly came near to making a dotard of me.

But in the middle of the last decade of the past century a momentous change took place in the policy of the Education Department, a change which was carried out with but little previous warning. The annual Parade Day, as the more enlightened teachers derisively called it, was abolished, and the examination system was virtually scrapped. Inspectors ceased to be mere examiners, mere appraisers and tabulators of cut-and-dried results, and became, or were expected to become, inspectors, in the proper sense of the word—observers of ways and works, students of method, critics of the atmosphere, the moral and the spirit of a school, centres of sympathy and encouragement and friendly advice.

What effect did this dramatic change have on the teachers of England? What effect was it likely to have? If one who had long dwelt in darkness were taken out, without warning or preparation, into the light of noon-day, would he not be dazzled to the verge of blindness by this sudden exposure, and would he not be glad to creep back into the familiar gloom? If you treat a man as a machine, and do your best to turn him into a machine, it is unfair to expect him to act, at a moment's notice, as an intelligent and responsible being. The grooves into which thirty years of code despotism had driven the teacher had become too deep for him. The routine which had been forced upon him had too strong a hold upon him. Was it reasonable to expect men who had been authoritatively deprived of freedom and responsibility, to give any measure of freedom and responsibility to those who were under them? The teacher could indeed relax his own severe pressure on the child. And this he did, perhaps without intending to do it; for when the motive for exerting pressure is withdrawn, pressure tends automatically to relax itself. What happened in many schools was that the teaching remained as mechanical and routine-ridden as ever, but that the child gradually became slacker and less industrious. For the yearly examination had been his chief incentive to industry; and when this was abolished there was nothing to take its place. Had the teacher, when emancipated by the Board, been able to give his pupils a real interest in their work, they might have exerted themselves as they had never done before. But this would have involved a radical change in his attitude towards education; and to expect him to make such a change in a day or even in a year was unfair and unwise. What could the average teacher do but keep his pupils on the examination treadmill, which had for many years provided them with their chief mental exercise, and with the routine of which he and they were only too familiar? But the treadmill had ceased to be dangerous; and the pupils gradually discovered that they could take things easy on it without coming to grief. It might have been expected that the younger teachers would take advantage of the freedom which had been given them, and that a new spirit would gradually permeate the educational world. Unfortunately, the younger teachers had spent their own childhood and adolescence on the treadmill —for both the pupil-teacher centre and the training college were, as a rule, cramming establishments in those days—and when they took service under a head-master of the conventional type, they found no difficulty in falling in with his ways and carrying out his wishes. The rebels, if there were any, soon had " the nonsense knocked out of them " and were compelled to toe the line with the rest of the staff. It is true that even in the ranks of the older teachers there was a minority which had always been in secret revolt against the despotism of code and syllabus and schedule. These were now given their chance. The future of education was in the hands of them and their disciples. But the leaven of new ideas and new ideals works slowly; and it was long before these pioneers could make their influence felt.

What effect did the change from examination to inspection have on me as a typical inspector? I have briefly described the state of things which it revealed to me. I saw that things were bad—in some respects as bad as they could be—and I began to ask myself, gropingly and tentatively, how they could be made better. Like Goethe, in Matthew Arnold's poem, I could " strike my finger on the place " and say " thou ailest here—and here "; and I could even go so far as to suggest what seemed to me appropriate remedies. But that was not the way to reform education. Patching and mending and tinkering and filling up holes would not take me or the teachers very far. One thing, indeed, of paramount importance was borne in upon me—that far too much was being done for the children, that they were being treated as automata and reduced to a state of helpless dependence on their teachers. I fought against this tendency to the best of my knowledge and ability; and little by little I groped my way towards the vital truth that the child must in the main work out his salvation for himself.

But it took me many years to reach that goal. An emancipative leaven was at work in me, but it worked very slowly. The shadow of my impending retirement from official life had begun to fall on me when I was introduced by a friend and colleague to a certain school in his district. The day of my first visit to that school was the date of my conversion to what I have ever since regarded as the true gospel of education. But conversion has been happily defined as "the effective realisation of admitted truth"; and the saving truth that the child must be given freedom for self-development had long been familiar to me as a theory and a conclusion. What that day did for me was to change it into a *conviction*, and so give it the driving power which it had hitherto lacked.

The school to which I owe so much was a village school in the South of England. It was attended by about 120 children who were taught in three rooms. The older children, those above Standard II. — some fifty in all—were taught in the main room by the head-mistress, single-handed; and it was there that the real work of the school was done. I have described the school pretty fully in a book which I called *What Is and What Might Be*, and I will not now do more than call attention to two of its most salient features.

The first thing that struck me was that the children, one and all, were radiantly happy. The whole atmosphere of the school was electrical with the *joie de vivre* of the scholars. This experience was new to me, and it naturally set me thinking. In my indictment of the old régime, the crowning charge which I brought against it was that of making their school life repugnant to the children, and so giving them an unhappy childhood. But this is what education seems to have aimed at doing ever since it began. I must not let my readers think that the theory of education which I, as a school inspector, was compelled to put into practice, had its origin in the perverse ingenuity of " My Lords." There was nothing really novel about it. For thousands of years education had been dominated by the assumption that children are, by nature, naughty, stupid and helpless (except indeed for mischief), and therefore that their salvation must be worked out for them, dogmatically and dictatorially, with bit and bridle and spur, instead of their being encouraged and helped to work it out for themselves. Deliberately, therefore, and of set purpose the teacher in all ages has made it his business to give his pupils a bad time. The author of *Ecclesiasticus*, who gave excellent advice on many matters, can find nothing better to say about the bringing-up of children than this: " He that loveth his son causeth him oft to feel the rod, that he may have joy of him in the end. . . . Cocker thy child, and he shall make thee afraid; play with him, and he will bring thee to heaviness. Laugh not with him, lest thou have sorrow with him, and lest thou gnash thy teeth in the end. Give him no liberty in his youth, and wink not at his follies. Bow down his neck while he is young, and beat him on the sides, lest he wax stubborn, and be disobedient unto thee, and so bring sorrow to thine heart. Chastise thy son and hold him to labour, lest his lewd behaviour be an offence to thee." This advice has, I fear, been followed only too conscientiously by parents and teachers in all ages and in all parts of the world. What " My Lords " did was to apply the traditional theory and practice of education, without reflection and almost as a matter of course, to the children of the masses. Finding in the ignorance and illiteracy of the masses a *tabula rasa* ready to their hands, they were able to put the orthodox theory into practice with a ruthless thoroughness which is not often possible; and it was this and the greatness of the stage on which the drama was enacted that made the greatness of the tragedy.

Why were the children in Egeria's [1] school so happy? For many reasons, which may perhaps be summed up under two main heads. The first is that they lived in an atmosphere of good-will, sympathy and trust. Their teacher believed in them and expected the best from them. This made them feel that all was well with them; and feeling this they were happy. The second reason is that they were not only allowed but encouraged to energise freely and naturally, in many directions, under the inspiration and guidance of their teacher. Has not Aristotle said that ἀνεμπόδιστος ἐνέργεια is one of the chief elements in happiness? Unimpeded activity was certainly one of the most striking features of that school. I have described some of the activities of the children in *What Is and What Might Be*. Their programme of work was varied, elastic and well-balanced. The three arterial instincts, the sympathetic, the æsthetic, and the scientific—with their great sub-instincts, the literary and the dramatic, the artistic and the musical, the inquisitive and the constructive — instead of being ruthlessly repressed, were all skilfully and successfully fostered. The natural result of this was that the children were making vigorous and harmonious growth on all the planes of their being; and their consequent sense of well-being was realised by them as happiness. One might say

[1] "Egeria" is the name that I gave to the Head Mistress in *What Is and What Might Be*.

of them what Pestalozzi (that large-hearted lover of children) said of his pupils at Stanz: " They willed, they had power, they persevered, they succeeded, they were happy."

How happy they were and how well they loved their school will be gathered from the following incident. One afternoon, when school was over, I walked back towards my headquarters with a girl who had lived near the school and had recently moved to a village about three miles away; and she told me that she still attended school and would continue to do so till her school-days were over. I asked her what she would do if she lived six miles from her old home instead of three. She answered without a moment's hesitation, " I would come just the same." Shakespeare's

> Whining schoolboy, with his satchel
> And shining morning face, creeping like snail
> Unwillingly to school

would not have crept unwillingly if he had been one of Egeria's pupils. He would have been more likely to start off at a brisk trot so as to make sure of getting to the school before its doors were opened.

The happiness of the children was at once the proof and the cause of the success of their school. In education, as in other matters, there are " circles " which are the reverse of " vicious." Here is one of them. If you educate children in the right way you will make them happy, and if you make them happy you will be able to educate them in the right way. And the happier they become the greater will be their response to your appeal to them, and the richer will be the harvest which you, the sower of seed, will reap. A wise and gifted teacher—a woman also, let me say in passing—recently said to me, " I try to make my pupils happy, for I find that when they are happy I can get anything I like out of them." How the happiness of Egeria's pupils reacted on their mentality and their character I have told elsewhere. But there is one of its reactions to which I have never yet done justice, and of which I now propose to speak.

I have said that the first thing which impressed me when I visited the school was that the children were radiantly happy. The next thing that impressed me was that the wells of their happiness were ever overflowing into the channel of comradeship. Looking back to the days that I spent in the school, I can say without hesitation that, owing to the strength and unselfishness of its spirit of comradeship, it was a perfect social community. The ideal of " Each for All and All for Each " was fully realised in it. The co-operative spirit had killed the competitive. Though the children were all working at the top of their respective powers, competition among them was undreamed of. Prizes were as far beyond the horizon of their outlook as punishments. Places in class, merit marks, orders of merit and the like were unknown; and had they been introduced into the school, the first to resent their introduction would have been those who under a competitive régime would have been at the head of their respective classes. If any one was specially proficient at any subject, his reward was to be allowed to help others to rise towards his own level. Dramatic performances were a feature of the curriculum. The children decided among themselves who were to perform what parts; and this was done without any jealousy or heart-burning. Nowhere in the machinery of the school was there any of the heat which is generated by friction. All the bearings were lubricated by the oil of mutual good-will.

Why should happiness overflow into the channel of

comradeship? Wordsworth, in the opening lines of a beautiful sonnet, has answered this question:

Surprised by joy—impatient as the Wind
I turned to share the transport.

Is not this what each of us instinctively does when he is happy with the pure unselfish happiness of joy; when he is happy, not because Fortune has favoured him and his path is smooth before him, not because he has acquired this thing or achieved that, not because he has been able to gratify his vanity or his love of power or his love of pleasure—but because a sense of spiritual expansion has uplifted and transported him, and because under the stress of the vitalising forces which are at work in him, he feels that he must go out of himself into the lives of others? In the poet's case the sense of spiritual expansion was tempestuously sudden—so sudden that in a moment of forgetfulness he turned to share the transport with a dear dead friend. In the case of our village children the sense of spiritual expansion was generated by the steady, healthy, harmonious growth which they were making in mind and heart and soul. And they, too, had to share their happiness with others, and they naturally shared it with one another, and so became a band of brothers—and sisters.

For what is essential in the spontaneous overflow of good-will from the springs of happiness is that it is absolutely disinterested. There is no *arrière pensée* of self about it, no subconscious profit-and-loss calculation, no secret pride in performance or possession. In this it differs from all other forms of communal feeling —from *esprit de corps* (which you may find in a band of robbers), from family or tribal clannishness, from patriotism, from professional or party loyalty, from racial sentiment. In each of these devotion is given—in part at least—in return for what the community has done or may be expected to do for the giver. And in each case there is a latent sense of proprietorship, a feeling that the community is one's own, that one is the citizen of no mean city. But when the spirit of comradeship is in the ascendant, good-will to one's neighbour and devotion to the community to which oneself and one's neighbour happen to belong, are given freely, lavishly, uncalculatingly, given because one cannot help giving them, given because of the joy of giving.

It was for this reason, I think, that I never stayed long in Egeria's school without feeling that there was an element of religion, in the real sense of the word, in its atmosphere. It is true that the religious knowledge displayed by the children did not always satisfy the Diocesan Inspector; but that proved nothing except that they had not been crammed in preparation for a test which their teacher regarded as neither adequate nor fair. I have said nothing in my retrospect about the religious training of the young. I was supposed to know nothing about it. In point of fact I knew a good deal. I will say nothing about it now except that if we seriously believe we are making the masses religious by cramming them as children for a yearly examination in scripture and the rudiments of theology, we are deluding ourselves on a matter with regard to which delusion is fatal; and that if an examiner thinks he is testing religious knowledge when he asks such questions as " Was Absalom caught by his head or his hair? " he is the victim of a grotesque misconception of the meaning of the words " religious knowledge." Religious knowledge is knowledge of God, and knowledge of God is not to be won except through love of God. Now we know from experience that devotion to a community or a cause must always have at the heart of it devotion to a large community and a higher cause; for if not, there will be a germ of selfishness in it which will sooner or later eat the heart out of it. That being so, it is clear that the ultimate object of disinterested devotion, by whomsoever or to whomsoever it may be given, is God. For there is no community so large but we can dream of a larger, and no cause so high but we can dream of a higher; and therefore there is no rest for us, in our search for an adequate object of the heart's devotion, except in the infinitude of God. And so, whenever a man or a child gives good-will and affection and sympathy, freely, lavishly and uncalculatingly, he is laying an offering on the altar of God,

> the Receiver and the Lord
> Of every sacrifice.

Egeria's children were not consciously religious. They were too healthily natural for that. But in their spirit of comradeship, in their good-will to one another and their devotion to their school, and, above all, in their readiness to translate good-will and devotion into service, they

> worshipped at the Temple's inner shrine,
> God being with them, when we knew it not.

" For love is of God, and everyone that loveth is born of God and knoweth God."

So much for my confessions and my memories. Now for my hopes, which are still in the stage of dreams. It was Egeria's school that first set me dreaming; and I have been dreaming, on and off, ever since. I dream of a world in which the spirit of comradeship—comradeship between man and man, between class and class, between party and party, between nation and nation, between church and church—will have mastered and dispersed the fog of ambition and greed, of self-assertion and self-seeking, of envy, jealousy, hatred, suspicion and mistrust, which has long obscured our vision and paralysed our energies, and seems to-day to be denser and more poisonous than it has ever been. But if that dream is ever to be fulfilled, the spirit of true comradeship, the spirit of uncalculating devotion, of willing service, must be fostered in the young. We grown-ups are not past praying for—my own " conversion " took place when I was well on in the fifties—but most of us have grown hard in the moulds in which, first, a dogmatic and dictatorial education and then the prejudices which are engendered by environment—caste prejudice, class prejudice, political prejudice, national prejudice, racial prejudice, religious prejudice—have imprisoned us; and it is not easy for us to change our outlook on life. It took me ten or twelve years, from the time when my eyes were opened, to find salvation; and my conversion might never have been consummated had I never visited Egeria's school. The difference between youth and maturity, in respect of the capacity for vital change, is the difference between the tenderness and flexibility of the sapling and the hardness and stubbornness of the full-grown tree.

Our hope lies in the young. There is a strain of spiritual idealism, of altruism, there is a capacity for self-sacrifice in human nature, the seeds of which must have been implanted in nearly every human breast. If we could but cultivate these and bring them to maturity during the period in which growth is most rapid and most vigorous, all would be well. But how is this to be done? Is altruism, is unselfish love, is self-sacrifice to be taught as a subject in our schools? God forbid. For fifteen centuries, more or less, we have taught religion—the religion of Christ—to the child, the adolescent, and the adult, taught it by the most approved methods, dogmatically, dictatorially, with threat of punishment and promise of reward. And what has been the result? The horrors of the late war, and the miseries and iniquities of the so-called peace suggest to us that the teaching of religion in Christendom has been, to say the least, ineffective. Devout Christians tell us, with tears in their eyes, that the Western world is relapsing into paganism. Does not this amount to a confession that the experiment of making men religious by drilling religion into them has proved a disastrous failure?

But the idea that what is inward and spiritual can be forcibly imposed on the young is still widely prevalent. One meets it where one would least expect to find it. The late Benjamin Kidd, in his book, *The Science of Power*, promised us a new world at a comparatively early date if we would but give him the young. For my own part I would not have given him the young, for the reason that he had not studied the problems of education with sufficient care. As a writer he is still living, so I will speak of him in the present tense. He believes that there is a strain of altruism, of selfless devotion, latent in every child. There I go with him. And I go with him in the distinction which he draws between the social and the protoplasmic heritage of the individual, and in the predominance which he assigns to the former. But I cannot go with him when he proposes in all seriousness that " the emotion of the ideal," as he calls it, shall be cultivated by quasi-Prussian methods; that altruism shall be taught as a subject in our schools, just as patriotism was taught in the schools of Germany in pre-war days. The teaching of patriotism to the youth of Germany by the will and under the direction of the State our author seems to regard as an unqualified success. I am inclined to think that it was an unqualified failure. We are told that in thirty years it changed the character of the German people. Perhaps it did, but if so, it changed it, from all accounts, for the worse.

For this there are two reasons. The first is that education of the conventional type is ever tending to change character for the worse. One of the charges which I brought against the old régime was that it arrested growth. But to arrest growth is to distort it. For the forces which are at work in the growing child do not cease to work when they are checked and thwarted by education. The urge from within is too strong to allow them to do that. They continue to work; but they work in the dark and in wrong directions and within unduly narrow limits; and so, though the process of growth is not actually suspended, it is stunted and misdirected, just as the growth of a tree on the West Coast of Ireland is stunted and misdirected by the pressure of the Atlantic winds. We talk glibly and almost recklessly of forming character in school as if character was so much clay or putty in our hands. It would be well if we sometimes asked ourselves whether we were not deforming character in the very attempts that we make to form it. It is easy for education to deform character. The best way to form character—but this is far from easy—is to help it to form itself.

This is one reason why the teaching of patriotism in Germany changed the character of the people for the worse. The cramping pressure of dogmatic education on character was stronger in Germany, especially in Prussia, in the decades before the war than it had even been before. But this was not the only or the chief reason. There was one feature of the teaching of patriotism which Kidd seems to have overlooked. Apart from the call for self-sacrifice, there was no strain of idealism in it. On the contrary, it was a hard, narrow, jealous, exclusive, grasping, domineering, vain-glorious, self-centred type of patriotism which was officially taught; and it was to this feature of the teaching, not less than to the call for self-sacrifice, that the people seem to have responded. For we are all prone to indulge and assert and exalt self; and when this tendency receives the sanction of official recognition, when—to speak plainly—it is deliberately exploited by the State, it is but natural that its influence for evil should be raised to a high power.

Can we wonder, then, that the German people, with their traditional reverence for authority, should have responded, more or less readily, to the appeal which was made to their lower nature, during the impressionable years of childhood and adolescence, by the high authority of the State? Did they also respond to the call for self-sacrifice when the hour of their trial came? Undoubtedly they did; but so did all the belligerent nations. Kidd speaks in ecstatic terms of the " unparalleled sacrifices " which the Germans, as the result of the compulsory teachings of patriotism, made during the war. But all the belligerent nations made unparalleled sacrifices. We British made unparalleled sacrifices; and, owing to there being no conscription in our country, there was a voluntary element in our self-sacrifice which was wanting in Germany. In Kidd's own words, " The capacity for sacrifice in men . . . gave civilisation the example of millions of men enrolled by Great Britain and her peoples by voluntary enlistment with a cheerful and considered judgment on a scale which under such conditions is without any precedent in history." Yet there is no country in Europe in which the formal teaching of patriotism has counted for so little as in ours. Why have we neglected to teach it? Because we have felt instinctively that what is vital in patriotism, the element of love and self-sacrifice, cannot possibly be taught. "Le patriotisme," says a French writer, "c'est comme l'amour. Ça échappe au commandement." Love and self-sacrifice have secret springs of their own which do not flow at the word of command. If they are not there, you cannot produce them by turning on an official tap. If they are there, no tap can hold them back.

What, then, was the net gain to Germany of the great educational experiment which Kidd would have us imitate, *altruism* being substituted for *patriotism* as a subject on the time-tables of our schools? A *minus* quantity. The character of the people suffered, and their patriotic ardour was not strengthened. If anything, it was weakened. The spontaneous element in it was repressed by dogmatic direction, and the spiritual element was driven into the background by the authoritative appeal to base and selfish motives. Ludendorf tells us that the downfall of Germany was due to the patriotism of Germany having given way under the triple strain of privation at home, moral infection from Russia (after the Revolution), and incipient defeat in the field. The privations of the German people were no doubt much greater than ours. But they were not so great as the privations of the Serbians, the Belgians, or the inhabitants of the devastated parts of France. Yet the spirit of those peoples was never broken. They "bore it out even to the edge of doom." There were centres of moral infection in all the belligerent countries. And severe defeats on land as well as terrible losses at sea were endured without flinching by the nations which eventually won the war. That being so, it is surely a significant fact that the one country in which patriotism gave way at last under the prolonged strain of the war was the country in which it had been most assiduously and most systematically *taught*.

As a final comment on the teaching of patriotism in Germany in pre-war days I will quote the following words from a German writer: " By means of regulation, instruction and apologetical justification patriotism is to-day taught by zealots like a common school lesson with a merciless rigid catechism. Love to the Fatherland is made mechanical; it is drilled into pupils like a dead, disbelieved religion." Could patriotism be *taught* —taught as a school-lesson, taught as a subject which has a place of its own on the time-table—by any better method than this? I doubt it. The aim controls the means; and if you wish to mechanicalise a natural sentiment, you must mechanicalise the education which is to produce this result. But be that as it may. What is certain is that not by such methods as this is the emotion of the ideal, the spirit of unselfish devotion, to be kindled in the young.

Yet the broad fact remains that if we are ever to have the better and happier world of which we dream, the spirit of unselfish devotion must be kindled—or shall I say, *evoked*—in the young. How is this to be done? Let us go back to our village school. There the children were idealists without knowing it. They were idealists because they were happy in their school life, because their happiness was ever overflowing into the channel of comradeship, and because in comradeship, so far as it is spontaneous and uncalculating, there is a latent spirit of self-sacrifice which is capable of climbing to the loftiest height of spiritual achievement. Their happiness was the realisation in consciousness of wellbeing. Their well-being was due to the fact that they were making healthy, harmonious and many-sided growth. And the reasons why they were making such growth were these: they were being given freedom for self-development through self-activity, and, with freedom, help and guidance and inspiration; and they were living in the stimulating atmosphere of sympathy and trust.

The moral to be drawn from this is that if we are to reform the world we must first, or perhaps concurrently, reform education along some such lines as those which have just been sketched. How this is to be done is a problem which each educator who desires reform along those lines must solve for himself. The problem is complex and difficult, and demands much thought, much labour, and much patience. Yet the attempt is well worth making; for success in solving it, or even the approach to success, will be abundantly rewarded. I cannot promise a new world within the lifetime of the present generation. The mills of God grind very slowly; and the transformation of the ideals of a whole profession is not to be accomplished in a generation or even in a century. But that need not discourage us. The reward will always keep pace with the effort that deserves it. As the new educational ideas gradually diffuse themselves, a new spirit—new, and yet immemorially old—will gradually awake and accompany them in their movement, and help to vivify them and spread them—the spirit of generous comradeship, of unselfish devotion, a spirit which has thirst for the ideal at the heart of it, and which, on its way to the ideal of all ideals, to the highest and holiest of all altars, will gradually regenerate the world.

July 1922.

WHAT JOY DOES FOR THE YOUNG

I USED at one time to wonder why Pestalozzi was so highly esteemed by educationists. I could not see that he had made any notable contribution to the philosophy of education, or that he had been conspicuously successful as a practical teacher. But when I read his own account of his work in the orphan asylum at Stanz, I discovered the secret of his fame. For I saw that, following the dictates of his heart rather than his head, he had gone, directly and unerringly, to what is really the root of the whole matter in education. The orphans in the asylum were poor, ignorant and ill-cared for. He had not a single assistant. What could he do for them? " I was convinced," he says, " that my heart would change the condition of my children just as promptly as the sun of spring would reanimate the earth benumbed by the winter. . . . It was necessary that my children should observe, from dawn to evening, at every moment of the day, upon my brow and on my lips, that my affections were fixed on them, that their happiness was my happiness, and that their pleasures were my pleasures." Love and sympathy—he gave these freely and lavishly to his pupils, feeling sure that they were the most potent of all educative influences. That was his method. How did it work?

Without plan [says Compayré, in his *History of Pedagogy*], without apparent order; merely by the action and incessant communication of his ardent soul with children ignorant and perverted by misery; reduced to his own resources in a house where he was himself " steward, accountant, footman and almost servant all in one," Pestalozzi obtained surprising results.

And they were the best of all results. Pestalozzi himself has told us what they were.

I saw at Stanz the power of the human faculties. . . . My pupils developed rapidly; it was another race. . . . The children very soon felt that there existed in them forces which they did not know, and in particular they acquired a general sentiment of order and beauty. They were self-conscious, and the impression of weariness which habitually reigns in schools vanished like a shadow from my class-room. They willed, they had power, they persevered, they succeeded, and they were happy. They were not scholars who were learning, but children who felt unknown forces awakening in them, and who understood where those forces could and would lead them, and this feeling gave elevation to their mind and heart.

The results which Pestalozzi achieved, in spite of all discouragements and difficulties, were not of the kind which crammers aim at producing and which examiners measure and record. They were inward results, fruits of the spirit, changes for the better in mind and heart and soul. With the development of the latent powers of the children came that sense of general well-being which accompanies healthy and harmonious growth; and another name for the sense of general well-being is happiness.

We see, then, that Pestalozzi grasped—consciously or subconsciously, intelligently or instinctively—the vital truth that education is at its highest and its best when unselfish love on the part of the teacher evokes unselfish happiness in the child. Because he did this, if for no other reason, he deserves his fame.

Why does unselfish love on the part of the teacher evoke unselfish happiness in the child? Let me go back to the title of this paper. My theme is " What Joy does for the Young." Joy is another name for unselfish happiness. We must distinguish joy from pleasure. Pleasure is generated by the well-being, real or apparent, of a part of one, by the satisfaction of a particular sense, by the gratification of a particular desire. As such it has in it an element of selfishness which may easily corrupt the pleasure-seeking soul. For when a particular part of one regards its own well-being, real or apparent, as an end in itself, it will naturally seek to gratify itself, even at the expense of the well-being of other parts of one, and therefore of one's self as a whole. Then we have selfishness in what I may call the internal economy of the man who lives for pleasure. And we have also selfishness in his dealings with others. For he who pursues pleasure at the expense of his own health and true happiness will not hesitate to pursue it at the expense of his fellow-men. But joy is generated by the well-being of one's self as a whole. And if one's self as a whole is to achieve well-being, all the parts of it must work together, harmoniously and self-forgetfully, to produce this result. Selfishness in the internal economy of one's being is therefore incompatible with joy. So is selfishness in one's dealings with others. For in the first place, the self-seeking which makes a man heedless of the interests of others has its counterpart in a desire for pleasure, which tends to upset the internal harmony of the soul and therefore to mar its joy. And in the second place, the purer the joy and therefore the more perfect the spiritual health of a man, the more he will be willing and the better he will be able to serve his fellow-men. On the physical plane of one's being the equivalent of joy is " high spirits "; and we may perhaps define joy as the high spirits of the soul. If a man is what we call good-natured, as most men are, physical high spirits will move him to share his happiness with others; he must have an evil heart whose high spirits overflow, as in the case of Sir Ralph the Rover in Southey's poem, into the channel of mischief and spite. But the high spirits of the soul are always and of inner necessity unselfish, and the only channel into which they can overflow is, as we shall presently see, that of sympathy and good-will.

We have not yet traced the connection between the love which emanates from the teacher and the joy, or unselfish happiness, of the child. But Pestalozzi has done this for us. He felt sure that the love which he lavished on his pupils would act on them as the sun of spring acts on the frozen earth. What the sun of spring does to earth is to awake it to life and to growth. And that is what the sunshine of his love did to the orphans at Stanz: " My pupils developed rapidly; it was another race . . . they felt unknown forces awakening in them . . . they willed, they had power, they persevered, they succeeded, and they were happy." They were happy because, in the sunshine of their teacher's love, they awoke to newness of life and to vigour and luxuriance of growth. It is pleasant to feel that one is loved. But that is not the only reason why one who is loved is happy. In love, such love as a teacher might feel for a child, there are other elements than that of affection. There is the element of *sympathy*, which both pre-supposes and begets *understanding*, and there is the element of *trust*. To feel that he is understood and trusted is an incentive to a man to make the most of himself, to do and to be his best. It is an incentive to anyone, young or old. But on a child it acts like April sunshine on a growing plant. Under its influence the child discovers and develops his latent powers, and begins to find himself. In other words, he grows, and feels that he is growing, vigorously and healthily; and in the consequent sense of uplift and expansion he finds happiness, the high happiness of joy.

Thus the sunshine of love makes for happiness in the

child whom it warms and cheers, partly because the sensation of being warmed and cheered is pleasant, but chiefly because, through the medium of understanding and trust, it tends to foster the child's mental and spiritual growth. Can the teacher do anything to supplement this beneficent tendency? I think he can. He can give the child *freedom*—freedom for self-development, space to grow in, release from the pressure which arrests or distorts growth. This, if he has the heart of a Pestalozzi, he will find it easy to do. There is a close and vital connection between the giving of freedom and the giving of love. If the soul of the child is to expand in the sunshine of love, it must be allowed room for expansion; and if it is to be given the freedom which allows room for expansion, it must also be given the trust and the sympathetic understanding which, as we have just seen, are essential elements in love. That the denial of freedom to the young is as a rule accompanied by the denial of love, experience has amply proved. For thousands of years education has been dogmatic, dictatorial, coercive and repressive; and through all those years its systematic denial of freedom to the child has been accompanied, in the treatment of the child, by an attitude on the part of the teacher of distrust, suspicion, latent harshness, incipient disapproval; by reliance on brute force; by a constant appeal to fear; by an all-pervading atmosphere of depression and gloom.

For this attitude towards education, for this suppression of freedom at the expense of the happiness of the child, two familiar writers are partly responsible. " Chasten thy son," says the author of *Proverbs*, " while yet there is hope, and let not thy soul spare for his crying." " Foolishness is bound in the heart of a child, but the rod of correction shall drive it far from him." " He that spareth the rod hateth his son; but he that loveth him chasteneth him betimes." "Withhold not correction from the child; for if thou beatest him with the rod he shall not die. Thou shalt beat him with the rod and shalt deliver his soul from hell." The author of *Ecclesiasticus* speaks in the same strain: "He that loveth his son causeth him oft to feel the rod, that he may have joy of him in the end." "Cocker thy child, and he shall make thee afraid; play with him, and he will bring thee to heaviness. Laugh not with him, lest thou have sorrow with him, and lest thou gnash thy teeth in the end. Give him no liberty in his youth, and wink not at his follies. Bow down his neck while he is young, and beat him on the sides. . . ."

It was but natural and reasonable that the Jewish parent, and those who instructed and admonished him, should take this view of education. Under a legalistic conception of life, obedience is the first and last of virtues; and, as the child is father to the man, to enforce obedience, by whatever means, is the first and last duty of the parent and the teacher. We cannot wonder, then, that the glorification of the rod is the central feature of the pedagogy of the Jewish scriptures. The pity of it is that as those scriptures are supposed to have been divinely inspired, the "spare the rod and spoil the child" theory of education has been invested with a high authority which it is presumably impious to dispute. A friend of mine, an assistant in a grammar school, had the temerity to tell the head-master that he did not believe in punishments; to which the retort came promptly: "I suppose you think you know better than God."

The founder of Christianity was a revolutionary in his attitude towards children, as in other matters. Far from thinking that the rod alone could redeem them from perdition, he said to his disciples, "Except ye be converted and become as little children, ye shall not enter into the Kingdom of Heaven "; and when the disciples rebuked them that brought young children to him, " he was much displeased and said unto them, ' Suffer the little children to come unto me, and forbid them not; for of such is the Kingdom of God ' . . . and he took [the children] up in his arms, put his hands upon them, and blessed them."   There is a depth of meaning in the words, " Of such is the Kingdom of God," which has not yet been fathomed, but which, if we are to think aright about education and about life, we must at all costs try to fathom; for as they explain the little child in terms of the kingdom of God and the kingdom of God in terms of a little child, they hold, as it seems to me, the clue to the solution of the greatest of all our problems.   As they stand, they are a rebuke to the arrogant assumption which underlies our philosophy of education,—that the business of the teacher is to stamp himself, with all his defects and limitations, on the presumably plastic nature of the child.   For, in setting the kingdom of God before us as our ideal, and then telling us that if we are to enter into the kingdom we must become as little children, Christ has warned us, by implication, that in the undeveloped nature of the child there is a world of divine mystery, which for our own sakes we ought to explore, under the guidance of reverence and love.   This is what some of us are now beginning to do; but how much precious time has been wasted!   If only Christ's implicit warning had been heeded by Christendom, how different might have been the history of education—and of mankind!

But in the sphere of education it was the mantle of Judaism rather than of Christ that fell on the Christian Church.   The Church, believing itself to hold a commission direct from God, was, on principle, dogmatic and dictatorial; and it expected all who taught to defer to its authority and follow its example. Like Judaism, it regarded obedience as the first and last of virtues; but it added to obedience proper—obedience in the field of conduct—a new virtue which it called faith, by which it meant the obedient acceptance of defined doctrine.

It is to the joint influence of the Jewish scriptures and the Christian Church, each embodying in its own way the authority, and teaching in the name, of God, and to the lingering influence of the *patria potestas* of the Romans, that we owe the ascendancy, in all parts of Christendom and in all the centuries of the Christian era, of what I may call the orthodox type of education. The main features of that education are familiar to all of us. The child, as the future man, is to be " saved " by obedience, not by growth. This initial assumption determines the whole manner of his upbringing. His own instincts and inclinations count for nothing. His teachers know what is best for him, and his duty is to obey. As his instincts and inclinations are systematically disregarded, the chances are that many of the commands and precepts which he is expected to obey will be repugnant to him, and that his teachers will therefore have to work against the grain of his nature. How, then, is his obedience to be secured? By the methods prescribed in *Proverbs* and *Ecclesiasticus*; by the use of the rod (or its equivalent) and the appeal to fear. Promises of reward have indeed been mingled with the threats of punishment; but bribery is scarcely less demoralising than terrorism, and in any case it is on the latter that the teacher has chiefly relied. Under such a régime the happiness of the child is the last thing to be considered. Where dogmatic direction, enforced by severity, on the part of the teacher is answered by unwilling submission,

sometimes bordering on rebellion, on the part of the
child, the prevailing atmosphere must needs be one of
mutual antipathy and distrust. The sunshine of love
and sympathy and trust and understanding will be con-
spicuous by its absence. So will be the response of the
child to the stimulus of sunshine,—the response of
healthy growth, of the sense of well-being, of unselfish
happiness, in a word, of joy.

To lift from off the opening life of the child the dead
weight of an educational system, the first principles of
which were once, and in some quarters are still, believed
to have been laid down by God himself, is a formidable
task. But it is one which certain reformers have already
taken in hand. And, apart from the adventurous enterprises of individual pioneers, a general feeling that reform
is needed is to-day in the air. To this feeling many
influences are contributing. The foundations of the
orthodox education are being carefully examined and
adversely criticised by psychology; and the greater the
advance that is made in psychology, the more adverse
does its criticism become. The evils of repression—
the toxins which it causes the soul to secrete—are being
scientifically studied and exposed. The waste of energy
which is involved in systematically working against the
grain of the child's nature, is being gradually realised.
The immorality of the appeal which the teacher has to
make to such base motives as fear, cupidity and competitive selfishness, is being recognised and condemned.
And the belief is gaining ground that even in the average
child there are vast potentialities waiting to be realised,
potentialities which will never be realised until education
has been radically reformed. In these and in other ways
there is a movement—small in its beginnings, but gaining
strength from year to year—towards the conscious demand
for a new type of education, an education which shall be

based on trust in the child's nature and the desire to understand it and reckon with it, and which will provide for freedom being given, within reasonable limits, to the child, both for the sake of the teacher, that he may be the better able to study the laws and properties of the subject-matter of his craft, and for the sake of the child himself, that he may be free to grow.

I have already pointed out that there is an intimate connection between the giving of freedom and the giving of love. He who is by nature sympathetic and trustful will find it easy to give freedom. Indeed, he would have to work against the grain of his own nature if he were to try to withhold it. And he will give it more judiciously and therefore more effectively than one who believes in freedom as a principle, but is himself wanting in sympathy and trust. For with sympathy and trust come tact and insight; and these are indispensable qualities in the teacher who is to lead his pupils out of the house of bondage. Where tact and insight are wanting, theoretical devotion to freedom may easily lead the teacher astray and so cause his enterprises to miscarry; for no rules can tell him in what direction his emancipative work is likely to be most effective, or what safeguards and reservations may be necessary, or how far he can safely go.

But he who is ready to give freedom because he is by nature sympathetic and trustful, and is the more ready to give sympathy and trust because he believes in freedom, will find that his work as a teacher is " its own exceeding great reward." For the atmosphere of his school, besides being warm with the sunshine of his own trustful sympathy, will be electrical with the joy of his pupils; and in that atmosphere growth will be vigorous and healthy and many-sided, and all will be well.

Joy, as the final proof of well-being, is the most

significant of all symptoms. But it is more than a symptom. It is also an emancipative and transformative influence; and as such it has a magical power and a limitless field of action. Itself the sense of well-being which is generated by healthy growth, it is ever tending to react on and stimulate the processes of growth, and to evoke new powers in the soul. Joy in the doing of a task makes the task a pleasure instead of a burden, transforms drudgery into healthful exercise, sharpens the wits of the doer, clarifies his vision, widens his aims, raises his standard of excellence, and so leads him on from strength to strength.

This is one aspect of the beneficent action of joy. But there is another which is even more significant. The sense of spiritual uplift and expansion, which is of the essence of joy, is an overflow from the deep wells of the soul—an overflow, if it is free to choose its own channel, into the lives of others. No narrower channel will suffice to carry off its flood. He who is genuinely and unselfishly happy, happy because all is well with him, must needs share his happiness with others. So essentially unselfish is joy that, as an overflow from the wells of the soul, it will be content with no other channel than that of comradeship, disinterested devotion, desire to co-operate, desire to serve.

Joy, then, is at once the unfailing proof and the self-renewing source of inward and spiritual health. If it makes, as it surely does, for the welfare of the individual, it makes also, and in no less a degree, for the welfare of society, being indeed, as we have just seen, under one of its aspects, a spontaneous overflow from the individual into the communal life. It follows that the highest task which education can set itself is that of fostering the sentiment of joy. But if education is to accomplish this task, it must revolutionise its own aims and methods;

for hitherto, in its demand for blind obedience, and its consequent refusal to reckon with the central tendencies of human nature, it has enveloped the life of the child in a wet mist of disapproval and distrust, repressed his spontaneous activities, arrested the outgrowth of his latent powers, outraged his sense of justice and fair play, aroused mutinous or semi-mutinous feelings in his breast, and in general aimed, or seemed to aim, at the complete suppression of joy. But is it conceivable that education will ever revolutionise its aims and its methods? I cannot say. What I can say is that no less a price than this will have to be paid for the rebuilding of the world.

September 1922.